Desirable Literacies

Desirable Literacies

Approaches to Language and Literacy in the Early Years

Edited by

Jackie Marsh and Elaine Hallet

P·C·P

Paul Chapman
Publishing Ltd

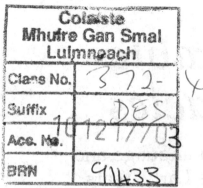
Selection and editorial material and Introduction © Copyright 1999 Jackie Marsh and Elaine Hallet
Chapter 1 © Copyright 1999 Jim McDonagh and Sue McDonagh
Chapter 2 © Copyright 1999 Eithne Dodwell
Chapter 3 © Copyright 1999 Suzi Clipson-Boyles
Chapter 4 © Copyright 1999 Elaine Hallet
Chapter 5 © Copyright 1999 Guy Merchant
Chapter 6 © Copyright 1999 Ann Browne
Chapter 7 © Copyright 1999 Nigel Hall
Chapter 8 © Copyright 1999 Jacki Rowley
Chapter 9 © Copyright 1999 Moira Monteith
Chapter 10 © Copyright 1999 Jackie Marsh
Chapter 11 © Copyright 1999 Carol Taylor
Chapter 12 © Copyright 1999 Mary Brailsford, Diane Hetherington and Evelyn Abram
Chapter 13 © Copyright 1999 Fran Paffard

First published 1999

 Paul Chapman Publishing Ltd
A SAGE Publications Company
6 Bonhill Street
London EC2A 4PU

SAGE Publications Inc
2455 Teller Road
Thousand Oaks, California 91320

SAGE Publications India Pvt Ltd
32, M-Block Market
Greater Kailash-I
New Delhi 110 948

British Library Cataloguing in Publication data

A catalogue record for this book is available from the British Library

ISBN 1 85396 446 8
ISBN 1 85396 447 6 (pbk)

Typeset by Anneset Ltd, Weston-super-Mare, Somerset
Printed and bound by Athenaeum Press, Tyne and Wear

A B C D E F   4 3 2 1 0 9

Contents

Acknowledgements

With warm thanks to all the contributors to this volume – it has been a real pleasure to work with you. We are also indebted to Marianne Lagrange at Paul Chapman for making the process so smooth. Jackie would also like to thank Julie for her amazing resilience throughout this process and Guy for his encouragement and excellent advice. Finally, Elaine would like to thank her friends for all their support and patience.

Notes on Contributors

Evelyn Abram worked for many years in the nursery at Sharrow Nursery Infant School in Sheffield before being appointed joint Head of Nursery two years ago. She lectures on the PGCE 3–8 and BA/BA (Hons) Early Childhood Studies at Sheffield Hallam University. She is currently working towards a Masters in Education and is interested in the relationship between language and literacy and the arts in the early years.

Mary Brailsford is Deputy Headteacher at a large nursery school in Sheffield. She has been interested in language and literacy in the early years for many years and has delivered INSET on the subject to other under-5s workers. She has been an active member of the Sheffield Early Years Association (SEYLA) since its foundation and has contributed to a number of its publications.

Ann Browne is a Lecturer in Education at the University of East Anglia where she works with intending and practising teachers on language, literacy and early years courses. She trained as an early years teacher and spent many years working with young children before entering higher education. She has written a number of articles and books about language and literacy.

Suzi Clipson-Boyles is a Senior Lecturer in Language and Education at Oxford Brookes University where she directs The Catch Up Project. She is the author of many publications including *Supporting Language and Literacy* and *Drama in Primary English Teaching*.

Eithne Dodwell was born in Ireland. She did her initial degree in French Studies and has lived, worked and taught bilingually in France, Switzerland and Israel. She is currently teaching in a Bradford primary school where she ran the nursery for some years. Before that, she worked in a combined services Family Centre for Bradford Social

Services and ran a PPA playgroup as well as working in various other educational contexts with children and adults. She is a member of Bradford's SACRE and Race Equality Commision. Eithne has published articles about her research into children's emergent bilingualism.

Nigel Hall is Reader in Literacy Education at the Didsbury School of Education, Manchester Metropolitan University. He has authored or edited a large number of books in the field of language and literacy, has authored many chapters in other books, and lectures extensively throughout the UK and the rest of the world. He is the Co-director of The Punctuation Project.

Elaine Hallet has a wide experience working in the early years field. She has worked in a range of early years settings as a teacher and an advisory teacher. Presently, she is Lecturer in Child Care and Education at West Nottinghamshire College, teaching on a range of initial and post-qualifying programmes in the area of early years education and early childhood development. She teaches on the part-time BA/BA (Hons) Early Childhood Studies at Sheffield Hallam University. Elaine has a particular interest in early literacy development and has been involved in working with early years professionals through school-based literacy projects and in-service courses. She established the Sheffield Early Years Literacy Association (SEYLA) as a means of enabling professionals to share their research and practice in literacy provision.

Diane Hetherington is a Deputy Headteacher at a nursery school in Sheffield, where one of her roles as curriculum co-ordinator has been to develop planning. She has been involved in staff development in her own nursery and has delivered in-service training in other early years settings, most recently on planning for under-5s. Diane is also a project teacher on the joint Sheffield University/Sheffield LEA 'Raising Early Achievement in Literacy' (REAL) Project. Diane is currently undertaking work towards a PhD.

Jackie Marsh is a Principal Lecturer in the Centre for English in Education at Sheffield Hallam University. She teaches on a range of graduate and undergraduate ITE courses and is Course Leader for the BA/BA (Hons) Early Childhood Studies. She has worked on a number of early years language and literacy projects and is currently involved in research relating to popular culture and media education with nurseries and primary schools.

Jim McDonagh is a Senior Lecturer in the Centre for English in Education at Sheffield Hallam University. He teaches on the undergraduate ITE programme and is currently undertaking research for his PhD on teacher knowledge about teaching English as an additional language.

Sue McDonagh has worked for many years in nursery classes and primary schools and is currently teaching in Rotherham. She has recently completed a Masters degree on the reading strategies used by bilingual children.

Guy Merchant is a Principal Lecturer in the Centre for English in Education at Sheffield Hallam University. As Head of Centre, he co-ordinates the work of colleagues involved in initial and in-service teacher education. He is involved in a number of major language and literacy evaluation projects with LEAs and is currently involved in research into reading comprehension. He has published a number of articles and chapters and is co-editor with Jackie Marsh of *Co-Ordinating Primary Language and Literacy: The Subject Leader's Handbook.*

Moira Monteith is a Principal Lecturer in ICT at Sheffield Hallam University. She has published widely on ICT and language and has edited two books: *Computers and Language* and *ICT for Learning Enhancement.* She is a member of the NCET Literacy focus group and of their closed conference on literacy.

Jacki Rowley works as a Reception teacher in Sheffield and is currently seconded part-time to the post of Education Officer at the Crucible Theatre in Sheffield. She has delivered drama INSET to a wide range of groups including teachers and youth workers.

Fran Paffard is a Bilingual Support Teacher for the under-5s in the London Borough of Southwark. She has taught for many years in nurseries and infant schools and has had extensive experience of delivering INSET to early years practitioners. She has an MA in Early Years from Goldsmith's College. She is a Distance Learning Tutor on the Early Childhood Programme at the University of North London and has written a number of articles on early years education.

Carol Taylor is the Director of the Read On – Write Away! Project in Derbyshire and Derby City. She originally trained as a primary teacher and then worked in secondary and FE before going into community education in Derbyshire. Carol has also worked in the advisory service.

Introduction

Jackie Marsh and Elaine Hallet

This book aims to introduce readers to different aspects of the teaching and learning of language and literacy and provides a range of suggestions for practical activities which can be carried out in early years settings and schools. It is recognised that there is already much valuable material in this field and so a secondary aim is to guide readers towards other texts which they may find of value. Given the 'books about language industry' (Whitehead, 1997, p. ix), what contribution can this particular text make? Some of the chapters provide an overview of developments in particular areas. They pull together a number of threads in order to help the reader, who may be new to the field, make sense of what can be a bewildering array of material. Other chapters introduce areas that have received scant attention in books of this nature and suggest a number of ways in which the ideas presented can be incorporated into early years settings and classrooms. The primary audiences for this book are students on a range of early years courses and newly qualified practitioners, although there may be aspects of the book which will be of interest to more experienced early years educators.

There is an expectation that readers will adapt the material and broad guidelines presented here for use in their own situations, whether that is working in early years settings or infant schools. Inevitably, there will be differences in the provision offered by childminders, playgroups, nursery schools, nursery classes, family centres, combined nursery centres, day nurseries, private nurseries, reception classes and Y1 and Y2 classes. Staff in these various settings will have had a wide variety of types of training; the settings will be resourced differently; there will be specific curriculum frameworks to work to, or none at all. In addition, different contexts affect what we can do. If we are part of a multi-disciplinary team in a Young Children's Centre for example, then we have a range of possibilities for working with families and the wider community on early language and

xiv *Desirable Literacies*

literacy development. These possibilities can also be exploited if we are in a small team in a nursery class, but we have to work hard to make effective links and maintain communication when the wider context in which we work may impose specific limitations. Similarly, if we are working with children in a refuge playgroup and rely on voluntary contributions gained through tireless fund-raising activities, then the resources available to support language and literacy activities will be limited. This book offers examples from nursery classes, nursery schools and primary schools but this is not to suggest that the activities outlined here cannot be adapted where possible to suit the needs of other early years settings.

One of the concerns of *Desirable Literacies* is to emphasise the importance of a broad-based conception of literacy. The rich variety of literacy practices we see interwoven into the fabric of our daily lives are as varied as our communities and early years educators need to recognise and cherish this diversity. It is clear that the nature of literacy practices within society is changing (Street, 1997; Kress, 1997). Children are engaged with a wider range of texts, both printed and tele-visual, outside of educational establishments than they are within (Millard, 1997). There is more environmental print surrounding us than ever before; children have access to a wider range of comics and magazines; the nature of the reading process is changing as we interact with text on screens and follow hyperlinks, switching from one type of text to another with relative ease. It is essential that early years educators recognise this 'changing landscape of communication' (Kress, 1997, p. 160) which affects many children's literacy practices in the home and respond to it appropriately. In addition, educators need to acknowledge the social and cultural influences on children's lives and recognise the various threads which are woven into the tapestry of their literacy experience. This is the case whether a child is monolingual or bilingual; the literacy repertoire of all children is multi-stranded. Street (1997) suggests that these different experiences do not constitute different *literacies* but instead can be recognised as a variety of *literacy practices*. All of these literacy roads lead to the same place, that is the development of the individual as an active meaning maker within his or her environment[1], for as Yetta Goodman remind us: 'There is no single road to becoming literate' (1997, p. 56). Thus early years settings and schools need to avoid closure on the concept of literacy and provide a myriad of opportunities for children to celebrate each facet of their language and literacy experiences.

In addition, we would want to consider the relationship between children's literacy development and their overall experiences in the early years. Given the holistic nature of children's learning, what relationship does language and literacy as a distinct 'subject' have to the early years curriculum? This is not a straightforward question. Children's experiences of language and literacy in the early years are embedded in explorations of, and responses to, the world around them, experiences which also lead to the development of skills, knowledge and understanding in a wide range of areas of learning. It is widely acknowledged that young children do not learn 'subjects' but rather gain skills, knowledge and understanding across the complex web of experiences and activities they encounter. What sense can we make of studying language and literacy separately from children's development in other areas? It is, perhaps, the wrong question. Rather, we need to acknowledge the place of language and literacy development within the larger framework and ask, 'How can oracy and litereracy be stimulated in ways which encourage children to integrate different aspects of their experience?' Whilst we would not wish to deny that children learn in an holistic way and make links between different areas of learning, we would want to support Wood and Attfield's assertion (1996) that this standpoint:

> . . . gives only a partial view. Teachers need to know what these links are, how they occur spontaneously as part of children's 'everyday common-sense knowledge and learning', how they can be planned intentionally, and how they can be presented in ways which are compatible with children's understanding.
>
> (Wood and Attfield, 1996, p. 83)

It is necessary, therefore, to consider the nature of language and litereracy as a distinct area of learning and develop our own subject knowledge accordingly. At the same time, we need to explore the degree of synthesis with other areas of learning in order to plan these meaningful links. This opening out of the discourse will also enable us to embrace a broad and encompassing view of language and litereracy. As Whitehead (1997) points out:

> . . . literacy itself will suffer if it is not established on a broad and deep foundation of worthwhile experiences of symbolizing and representing meanings through nonverbal communication skills, gesture, movement, dance, music, listening, talking, drawing, painting, modelling, building, storytelling, poetry sharing, scientific and mathematical investigations, rituals and religious celebrations. Literacy in the written forms of a culture is only one form of literacy: the long list above represents the other 'literacies' and many symbolic languages (Edward, Gandini and Foreman, 1996) that early educators must establish and build on.
>
> (Whitehead, 1997, pp. 177-8)

Thus literacy becomes a living, fluid concept that takes its shape in the daily experiences of young children. This book is concerned with both the contours and further shaping of those desirable literacy practices.

In the first chapter, Jim McDonagh and Sue McDonagh guide the reader through the complex field of theories on language acquisition. The chapter reviews key concepts in early linguistic development and provides a range of suggestions for developing oracy in early years settings. In Chapter 2, Eithne Dodwell considers the needs of bilingual children and suggests ways in which we can value and build successfully upon children's linguistic repertoire. Suzi Clipson-Boyles includes work on multilingual rhymes in her chapter on using rhymes and poetry in the early years curriculum, Chapter 3. This chapter contains a range of stimulating ideas that early years workers and teachers can use in their quest for promoting and extending children's language and literacy skills.

In Chapter 4, we move on to consider key principles in early reading development. Elaine Hallet considers the role that environmental print has to play in children's reading development and analyses the role of the adult in this process. The adult role is not specifically defined as there is a recognition that *all* of the adults a child encounters in the early years have a crucial role to play and are all, in their different ways, educators and collaborators in the process of acquiring reading skills, knowledge and understanding. In Chapter 5, Guy Merchant presents a useful overview of the wide-ranging research into early reading development and brings us up to date with recent initiatives. His chapter provides an introduction to ways of developing children as readers in the early years and stresses the need to provide children with rich and stimulating literacy environments.

Children's reading and writing skills are inextricably linked and, in Chapter 6, Ann Browne provides a comprehensive overview of the nature of writing in the early years. She outlines a range of ideas for stimulating children's writing development in early years settings, nurseries and classrooms and suggests ways in which we can support children's emergence as successful writers.

Role play areas have a central role to play in developing children's understanding of the real-life uses of reading, writing, speaking and listening. In Chapter 7, Nigel Hall considers what we have learned over the years about the ways in which children use literacy resources when involved in role play. He provides a useful framework for planning literacy in role play and uses examples of teachers' work in order to demonstrate how role play can extend children's understanding of contextualised uses of literacy. Role play and drama are part of a continuum and, in Chapter 8, Jacki Rowley demonstrates how we can use a range of strategies to develop children's experience of drama in the early years.

We are living in an increasingly sophisticated technological age in which the use of computers can inform many aspects of our work on language and literacy in the early years. In Chapter 9, Moira Monteith reviews some of the possibilities and suggests how teachers can harness the available technology to extend children's reading, writing, speaking and listening skills. Children are now interacting with a range of media technology and, in Chapter 10, Jackie Marsh examines how we can utilise the intrinsic interest many children have in the media and popular culture in order to engage them in stimulating oracy and literacy practices.

The recognition of the role of families in children's language and literacy development is crucial if we are to forge genuine partnerships and value the different strengths that each party brings to the task of facilitating children's oracy and literacy development. Partnerships with parents have been strengthened through some of the exciting work which has been carried out in family literacy projects. Chapter 11 outlines some key principles which should underpin such projects and Carol Taylor provides the reader with an overview of work in the field.

Mary Brailsford, Diane Hetherington and Evelyn Abram have much succesful experience of planning the early years language and literacy curriculum in nurseries and, in Chapter 12, they provide some practical guidance on ensuring that this planning is coherent and comprehensive. This chapter relates specifically to planning in nurseries which operate the standard academic year (with three terms), but the authors do discuss underlying principles which should underpin all planning in the early years. Planning is inextricably linked to assessment and the final chapter examines how we can ensure that what we observe of young children's learning informs our future work with them. In Chapter 13, Fran Paffard offers us a vision of assessment which is based on some fundamental beliefs about how children learn and she provides some useful guidance on harnessing our thoughts and observations in order to build a holistic picture of a child's attainment.

All the authors in this volume acknowledge explicitly or implicitly the need to keep the vision of the child as a motivated individual, engaged in purposeful literacy practices, at the heart of our teaching. Recent years have seen a shift in educational policies and practices in England and although many of us have welcomed a number of the initiatives, there is a danger that a vision of literacy which is based on the need to have 'goals for learning' towards which children should make 'maximum progress' (QCA, 1998) will fail to take account of the complex ways in which children become . . . 'truly rich, strong and powerful' (David, 1998, p. 64) in relation to language and literacy. There is an implicit assumption in these pages that the language and literacy experiences and activities offered to, negotiated with and initiated by children need to be guided by educators who have a clear understanding of the very nature of oracy and literacy in current cultural landscapes, educators who recognise and respond to the fact that 'we are living in a period of intense change in the way in which we communicate with one another' (Dombey, 1998 p. 40). In the face of increasing prescription and a 'one size fits all' approach to the language and literacy curriculum, early years educators need to continue to be reflective about this process of change and development in order to ensure that they are offering children an appropriate and enticing array of 'desirable literacies' with which to engage.

Note

[1] Throughout the rest of the book, the pronouns 'him' and 'her' will be used interchangeably and at random.

References

David,T. (1998) Learning properly? Young children and desirable outcomes, *Early Years*, Vol. 18, no. 2, pp. 61–64.

Dombey, H. (1998) A Totalitarian Approach to Literacy Education? *Forum*, Vol. 20, no. 2, pp. 36–41.

Goodman, Y. (1997) Multiple Roads to Literacy in Taylor, D. (ed) *Many Families, Many Literacies*, New Hampshire: Heinemann Trade.

Kress, G. (1997) *Before Writing*, London: Routledge.

Millard, E. (1997) *Differently Literate: Boys, Girls and the Schooling of Literacy*, London: The Falmer Press.

QCA (1998) *Desirable Outcomes for Children's Learning on Entering Compulsory Education*, London: HMSO.

Street, B. (1997) The Implications of the New Literacy Studies for Education, *English in Education*, Vol. 31, 3, pp. 45–59.

Whitehead, M. (1997) *Language and Literacy in the Early Years*, 2nd Edition, London: Paul Chapman.

Wood, E. and Attfield, J. (1996) *Play, Learning and the Early Childhood Curriculum*, London: Paul Chapman.

1

Learning to Talk, Talking to Learn

Jim McDonagh and Sue McDonagh

We can take it for granted that by the time a child enters nursery she will have acquired much of the grammatical system of her native language, much of the sound system and a substantial vocabulary. Although there will be individual differences between children, all will have used language to express meanings, to communicate with others and to make sense of the world in which they are growing up. In using language they also learn about language – their own and the language of others. This chapter focuses on the important role speaking and listening activities have in the life of the young child. It begins with an overview of the child's early language acquisition and the different perspectives offered by those researching language, and goes on to discuss the role of the adult in developing a child's spoken language. The complexity of the acquisition process can only be lightly sketched here, the emphasis being on the importance of interaction in learning and learning to talk. This is followed by suggestions for classroom or home-based activities.

Language acquisition – differing perspectives

Until the late 1950s, the prevailing views on language acquisition were largely influenced by behaviourism until the work of Noam Chomsky marked a turning point in theories about the nature of language and the nature of language acquisition. The behaviourists' claim that language is learned through the acquisition of linguistic habits and that imitation of adults' speech plays an important role in learning is strongly countered by Chomsky's assertion that language is 'creative', i.e. human beings produce novel utterances when they speak, rather than imitations of what they have heard before:

> The normal use of language is innovative in the sense that much of what we say in the course of normal language use is entirely new, not a repetition of anything that we have heard before, and

1

not even similar in pattern – in any useful sense of the terms 'similar' and 'pattern' – to sentences or discourse that we have heard
in the past.

(Chomsky, 1972, p. 12)

To account for this ability to produce and understand novel utterances, Chomsky claims that human beings possess an innate capacity to acquire language through the language acquisition device
(LAD), a mental mechanism specifically concerned with language.
According to Chomsky, the adult utterances a child is exposed to are
often too ill-formed and incomplete to serve as a suitable model to
imitate. A child learning his first language will abstract *rules* from this
rather shapeless language he encounters and incorporate these into
his production/understanding of language, and will do so in a relatively short space of time.

It appears that we recognise a new utterance as a sentence not
because it matches some familiar pattern in any simple way, but
because it is generated by the grammar that each individual has somehow and in some form internalised. Chomsky asserts that natural languages are governed by complex rules that are not apparent in
'surface structure', the actual utterances of a language. If a child
acquiring a language had to rely solely on the snatches of language
heard in her environment she would not be able to abstract, and so
acquire, the rules. Evidence that children do not acquire language
through imitation of adults can be seen from the 'overgeneralisations'
evident in their speech: 'It got broked', 'She putted it on the carpet'.
In one experiment, McNeill (1966) effectively demonstrated that if a
child is not ready, she will not be able to imitate an adult's utterance:

Child: Nobody don't like me.
Mother: No, say 'Nobody likes me.'
Child: Nobody don't like me.
           (Eight repetitions of this exchange)
Mother: No, now listen carefully: say 'Nobody likes me.'
Child: Oh! Nobody don't likes me.

If anything, an adult will imitate a child's utterance, although few
sober adults would ever say 'All-gone milk' or 'I sawed two mouses'.

Chomsky's ideas on language led to important studies of children's
acquisition of language in the 1960s. Evidence was provided that a
child's language develops through hypothesis-testing, that the child
is actively involved in acquiring the mother tongue, and not just a
passive recipient, as some behaviourists would claim. Through testing out hypotheses the child's language develops 'by successive

approximations passing through several steps that are not yet English' (McNeill, 1966, p. 61). The aim of first language acquisition studies was to describe these successive approximations or interim grammars.

Research such as that of Brown (1973) and de Villiers and de Villiers (1973) demonstrates that children follow a natural sequence of development in their acquisition of language. Although the rate of development might vary between children, the order in which language is acquired remains invariant. If we look at just one area that has been extensively studied – that of sentence structure – we can see that by the age of 3 or $3\frac{1}{2}$ the child is acquiring complex sentence structure with the use of co-ordinating conjunctions such as 'but' and 'and' as well as subordinating conjunctions like 'because'. Comparative forms emerge ('this is *bigger*'; 'this is *more better*') and we see the beginnings of relative clauses: 'This is one *what* Mummy got'. Over the next year or so the child will acquire many of the irregular forms of verbs and nouns and make fewer overgeneralisations in his speech. However, many overgeneralisations will persist until much later in a child's development. It is not uncommon for eight-year-olds to say ' I hurted my knee', for instance. Pronouns are largely acquired during this stage, auxiliary verbs such as 'can', 'will' and so on, and the beginnings of passive forms of the verb: 'I got smacked'. The creativity Chomsky mentioned as characteristic of human language is very much in evidence during this period with children producing unique utterances.

Communicative competence

In his writings Chomsky is concerned with discovering the mental reality behind actual behaviour, in arriving at an understanding of a native speaker's *competence*. In Chomsky's view a grammar of a language is a model of the linguistic abilities of a native speaker of that language, which allow him to speak/understand that particular language. This is the speaker-hearer's competence: 'the speaker-hearer's knowledge of his language' (Chomsky, 1965, p. 4), which is distinguished from Chomsky's notion of *performance*: 'the actual use of language in concrete situations' (*ibid*.). For Chomsky, the actual use of language in concrete situations is rather untidy and not deemed worthy of serious study. Others have argued, however, that language is dependent on the social context and that interaction plays an important role in language acquisition. Michael Halliday has proposed a 'functional' view of children's language development and contends that:

Learning language is learning the uses of language and the meaning potential associated with them; the structures, the words and
the sounds are the realization of this meaning potential. Learning
language is learning to mean.

(in Kress, 1976, p. 8)

Halliday's 'meaning potential' is akin to Hymes' (1972) notion of 'communicative competence', but differs from Hymes' in that Halliday is
not interested in 'the artificial concept' of competence, that is what the
speaker-hearer *knows*. His concern is with what the speaker-hearer *does*
with language in sociolinguistic or functional terms.

Hymes (1972) and Campbell and Wales (1970) both recognise the
limitations of Chomsky's definition of 'competence', and propose the
notion of *communicative competence* as encompassing a range of ability broader than just grammatical knowledge. Campbell and Wales
(1970), in a discussion of developments in language acquisition theory, define competence as:

the ability to produce or understand utterances which are not so
much *grammatical* but, more important, *appropriate to the context
in which they are made*.

(Their emphasis. Campbell and Wales, 1970, p. 247)

'Competence' then is extended beyond exclusive grammatical knowledge to include contextual or sociolingual competence, knowledge of
the rules of language use.

The importance of interaction

Chomsky's claim that the linguistic input children received from
adults was 'degenerate' and not worthy of analysis and that the only
interface between input and output was located in the child's mind
has been challenged by those researchers who have examined the
interactions children have with their 'caretakers'. Those who have
studied first language acquisition from an 'interactionist' perspective,
like Jean Berko-Gleason, emphasise the contribution of external as
well as internal factors to language acquisition. She argues that children do not acquire language all by themselves:

They are not simply miniature grammarians working on a corpus composed of snatches and fragments of adult discourse.

(Berko-Gleason, 1977, p. 199)

By examining interactions between children and their mothers (or
other 'caretakers') researchers have established the existence of

'motherese', speech that is produced by an adult (or older child) in interaction with a child whose linguistic competence and cognitive development are perceived as limited. Mothers' or caretakers' speech to children is: simple and redundant; contains many questions, many imperatives, few past tenses, few co- or sub-ordinations, few disfluencies; and is pitched higher with an exaggerated intonation (Snow and Ferguson, 1977).

'Motherese' varies according to the communicative demands of the situation, and even experienced caretakers cannot produce adequate 'motherese' if the child is not present to cue him or her. Landes (1975) points out that parents and other caretakers modify their speech in various ways until the child is at least ten years old. From the research into 'motherese' we find claims that the best input for a child is one step beyond the stage the child is at (Gleitman, Newport and Gleitman, 1984).

In addition to the presence of the LAD (language acquisition device) proposed by Chomsky, Jerome Bruner (1983) suggests that there is also a LASS (language acquisition support system). According to Bruner, adults provide a framework of 'scaffolding' which enables the child to learn. In contexts that are familiar and routinised the adult, one step ahead of the child, cues the child's responses. By providing ritualised dialogue and constraints through questioning and feedback to the child, the adult prepares the cognitive base on which language is acquired. Cazden (1983) also uses the term 'scaffolding' to refer to the adult's role but makes a distinction between vertical and sequential scaffolding. Vertical scaffolding involves the adult extending the child's language by, for instance, asking further questions. Sequential scaffolding occurs in the routinised activities adults and children share – games, bath time, meals and so on. The predictability of the language used in routinised situations provides a framework for language to develop. Cazden also claims that adults support children through providing language models, often in response to children's utterances. If a child, for instance, says, 'She taked my crayon,' the adult's response might be: 'She *took* your crayon, did she?' To these two aspects of the adult's role, Cazden adds a third, direct instruction. This is mostly seen in contexts where the rules of social convention apply and the child is expected to repeat a word or phrase, for example, 'Say bye bye'.

Evelyn Hatch takes the view that the need to converse precedes the acquisition of specific language features. She writes:

One learns how to do conversation, one learns how to act verbally, and out of this interaction syntactic structures are developed.

(Hatch, 1978a, p. 404)

There are a number of stages in this process, beginning with attention-getting, either verbally or non-verbally. Once attention has been gained, the next task is to nominate a topic. Hatch provides an example of the two stages from the conversation of a 5-year-old Taiwanese boy, Paul, with an adult:

Paul: Oh-oh!
A: What?
Paul: This (points to ant)

A: It's an ant
Paul: Ant

Paul: This
A: A pencil
Paul: Pencil

(Hatch, 1978b)

Once a topic has been nominated, the conversational partner is constrained by the rules of conversation to make an appropriate response. Conversations are then built up ('vertical structures') which serve as the prototypes for the syntactic structures ('horizontal structures') which develop from them (Scollon, 1976). It would appear, though, that these structures evident in the exchange between an adult and child above are not typical of child–child speech. One notable difference between adult–child conversation and child–child discourse is in the use of 'functions' (Ochs Keenan, 1983) by children. According to Ochs Keenan, 'functions' are ways of making a relevant response in conversation through repeating, modifying or recombining elements of what the other child has said. In her study of 2–3-year-old children she found that the children made great use of sound play, songs and nursery rhymes. For instance, a child might repeat the whole of a previous turn:

Child 1:   You know why?
Child 2:   You know why?

or substitute a part of the other's utterance:

Child 1:   You know why?
Child 2:   You know what?

By the late 1970s the prevailing model of the language development process was seen as a combination of *social* and *cognitive* characteristics which recognises, but goes beyond, the Chomskyan perspective on language. In the early stages, caretaker and child are involved in interactions that provide a framework on which language is built. We now turn our attention briefly to some further social issues.

Deficit or difference?

In the English-speaking world there has been a tradition of negative views towards other languages and dialects, and amongst teachers there still persist prejudices against working class, non-standard speakers of English. In a study of reception teachers and headteachers, Hughes and Cousins (1990) found that the vast majority held 'deficit' views of their pupils' language. These teachers made assumptions about the language spoken in the home and felt that children were arriving at school suffering from linguistic deprivation. In the 1970s language deficit views, through the work of Basil Bernstein (e.g. 1960) and Joan Tough (e.g. 1977) amongst others, were extremely influential and lent academic weight to language enrichment programmes such 'Headstart' in the USA. It is in the USA that language deficit models came under attack from linguists such as Labov (1972) who argued that the language of the black working class children he studied was not deficient but 'different' from that used by their middle class peers. Unlike the work of Bernstein and Tough, which did not collect evidence of children's language in the home, research which actually examined language in the homes of children tended to support Labov's views. In a longitudinal study which charted children's language development in the home and at school, Gordon Wells (1986) concludes that

> there is no justification for continuing to hold the stereotyped belief that there are strongly class-associated differences in the ways in which parents talk with their children. Nor is there justification for forming expectations about children's oral language abilities on entry to school that are based solely on their parents' membership in a certain social class.
>
> (Wells, 1986, p. 140)

Where there was a difference it was not in relation to their experience in oral language, but in literacy practices that did not match those of school. Wells goes on to argue that schools may perpetuate the disadvantage experienced by assessment procedures which emphasise literacy skills rather than speaking and listening. In their study of four-year-olds at home and at nursery Tizard and Hughes (1984) lend weight to the argument that children receive rich linguistic experiences regardless of their social background. In their research they found that:

> the conversations in the working class homes were just as prolific as those in the middle class homes. There was no question of these children 'not being talked to at home', and few signs of the language deprivation that has so often been described . . . the working class children were clearly growing up in a rich linguistic environment.
>
> (p. 8)

Tizard and Hughes also found that children had few encounters with adults in the nursery school and staff had different expectations from the children's mothers. In the USA, Shirley Brice-Heath's (1983) intensive study of three communities also found that there was a mismatch between the language of the home and that of school and that what was valued in the community was not readily valued by teachers. Brice-Heath was interested in how children acquire language and literacy as part of their socialisation into the norms and values of their community. Differing ways of using language based on the different world views of social groups meant that continuity in children's socialisation was broken once they entered school.

Talk in the early years

The ability to participate as a speaker and listener is essential to a child's linguistic, social, emotional and cognitive development in their early years at nursery and school. Vygotsky (1962) suggests that talk plays an important part in laying the foundations for a child's intellectual ability in later life. The practice of speaking enables a child to become an active learner and to be able to explore her experiences and relationships. Talking is also a means by which learning across the curriculum can be developed into understanding. The current emphasis on the raising of standards in literacy has meant that there is a danger that the role of speaking and listening has become marginalised. There is little official emphasis on the value of talk in the nursery or classroom at the present time. How then are we to maintain the status of talk? The teacher's role in finding ways of planning for and valuing talk is essential if children are to grow confidently as learners and thinkers.

The National Oracy Project (Norman, 1990, 1992) outlined three important aspects of speaking and listening:

- social – how we use language to interact with others
- communicative – how we transfer meaning
- cognitive – how we learn through talk.

Children need to have opportunities to talk in a variety of settings in order to support their language developments in these three dimensions. These opportunities for talk need to be planned for and resourced by schools and nurseries and the adult's role in valuing talk is essential if it is not to be sidelined.

Role of the adult

If we are to enable young children to develop as speakers and listeners we need to consider our role in the process and how we act as speakers and listeners ourselves. We model the forms and functions of language in our dealings with children, their parents and other adults. If we expect children to listen to others with respect we need to model this behaviour also. This means listening to what children have to say and responding to what interests them, without interrupting or hurrying them on. An important aspect of the adult's role is to 'scaffold' what children offer, to extend and expand on their utterances. When we question children we need to include 'open' questions which invite children to think: 'What do you think about . . . ?' 'How do you feel about . . . ?' in addition to 'closed' questions which enable us to check children's knowledge and understanding: 'Which of these is blue?'

At times we need to be participants, not just supervisors, in activities, taking on a role, for instance, in the café or home corner. We need to provide children with appropriate vocabulary in the different contexts in which they talk and we need to develop their metalinguistic awareness (knowledge of the language we use to talk about language) through talking about talk and drawing their attention to how we use language.

We need to plan speaking and listening activities to make the most of the opportunities for meaningful talk and we need to monitor and assess the talk that takes place. In assessing children's speaking and listening, the purposes, contexts and audiences for talk have to be considered. Because talk is transient (unless we record it) it is useful to keep notes of children's talk based on our observations. For this purpose, a notebook or talk diary, in which observations are recorded, should be close at hand. In addition, occasional planned observations using a format such as The Primary Language Record (Barrs *et al.*, 1992) or a 'talk audit' (Godwin and Perkins, 1998) which specifies the purpose, context and audience, will supplement incidental observations.

Although adults need to begin with children's contributions and be responsive to the topics they introduce, curriculum planning needs to include a range of opportunities for speaking and listening. Early years workers can use a wide range of activities which stimulate talk. They need to ensure that they are planning a range of purposes for talk and enabling children to use talk in a variety of situations and for different audiences. Figure 1.1 includes a list of possibilities for purposes and audiences in relation to talk.

Activities which promote joint collaboration on tasks across all areas of learning will facilitate the use of talk. In addition, early years workers can plan specific activities which develop speaking and listening skills. The following section outlines a range of practical activities for promoting talk in early years settings.

Some purposes for talk in the early years	Possible audiences for children's talk in the early years
Communicating thoughts, feelings, ideas Making friends Negotiating roles Asking for help/clarification/information Speculating and hypothesising Relating Reflecting Reporting Narrating Arguing Presenting ideas Persuading Explaining Instructing	Peers Inanimate objects, e.g. dolls/puppets Adults: parents/carers, teachers, early years workers Older children Younger children Visitors Members of local community Unknown (e.g. when taping)

Figure 1.1. Purposes and audiences for talk

Promoting talk in the early years setting

Story as a focus for talk
Children discuss, retell, describe and give opinions on events and characters. Children use the language structures in well-known stories as a foundation for their own use of language. Children's comments on books can be recorded and displayed in the book corner.

Story sacks

Sacks containing a story book and objects and props are retelling the story. These can be used by adults to encourage children's language development around the story. For example, a story sack based on Eric Carle's *The Very Hungry Caterpillar* might contain, in addition to the book itself:

* a toy caterpillar
* a selection of plastic fruit that the caterpillar eats
* a big green felt leaf with holes in it
* a butterfly; the other food eaten – cake, pickle, ice cream and so on (scanned and laminated so children can handle them)
* a non-fiction book on the life-cycle of a butterfly
* a board game based on the foods that the caterpillar eats.

Language/story packs

Cut-out pictures from well-known stories can be used to put on a story board or white board. Children are invited to use these props to retell the story or make comments on characters. For example, from *Rosie's Walk* (Hutchins, 1968) children can make Rosie walk across the yard, around the pond, over the haystack, past the mill, through the fence and under the beehives, talking through each step as they go. From *Brown Bear, Brown Bear, What do You See?* (Martin, 1983) figures of all the animals can be put on the board and the children ask each animal, 'What do you see?', deciding which animal comes next in the book.

Show and tell/news time

Children are asked to talk about something they have brought to show the rest of the group, or something that has happened to them. The other children are invited to ask questions and make comments. Spoken news can be recorded in a 'news book' as a way of valuing the child's talk. News and comments can also be recorded into a tape recorder and played back.

As a variation on this theme a 'talking TV' can be made from a box large enough to fit over a child's head. When it is 'switched on' the person on TV can tell the news.

Songs and rhymes

Songs and rhymes regularly practised can encourage children's language development and their understanding of rhythm and rhyme. This is particularly useful for those children whose first language is not English. Songs and rhymes can be used with props such as pictures and puppets to encourage understanding and discussion. For instance, from *Litttle Mousie Brown* ('Up the tall white candlestick crept Little Mousie Brown') a finger puppet of Mousie can be made to go up the candlestick and children can talk to him, asking how he felt when he could not get down. Teachers can model questions the children might ask.

Games and play

Games such as snakes and ladders and other board games can encourage interaction and turn-taking. These games quite often need adult support initially so that the language can be modelled. Imaginative play with 'small world' toys, construction equipment and natural materials such as sand and water can stimulate a great deal of talk and interaction between children This play is particularly useful when supported by an adult who can provide a model of language for the children. For example, if using wild animals in a jungle setting with logs, trees and sand, talk can centre on finding the young animals and matching them to their parents, on discussing which is the biggest or smallest animal, what animals like to eat and so on.

Picture/object as stimulus

Children are invited to give their comments on a picture, photo or object. They are asked to discuss what they can see, how it makes them feel, why something is happening, what something looks like, what it reminds them of and so on. For example, using a shell, questions might include: What is it? Where can you find it? Can you tell us about when you saw one? What does it feel like?

Magic microphone

Children sit in a circle and an object – for example, a stone or a microphone – is passed around. The person who has the microphone or object can speak; the others must listen without interrupting. The adult might provide the topic for discussion or the children might talk about things that have happened to them.

Shared story writing/telling

Children contribute to telling a story. This is recorded in their words by an adult and made into a book which can be kept in the book corner. Children can also tell a story by speaking into a tape recorder. At the end of the story it is played back and children are invited to make comments. Tapes of stories told by other adults, including other languages if the children are bilingual, can be made and used in the classroom.

Storytelling picnic
Children can be taken on a picnic on a fine day. After food and drinks, children take turns to add a sentence to a story or tell stories to each other in pairs. Parents and carers can be invited to come along and tell stories also.

Making photograph books
Children make books based on photographs taken of their activities as a stimulus for talk.

Speaker's chair
Like the 'author's chair' or 'storyteller's chair' in many classrooms, the speaker's chair allows a child to address the rest of the group about some work – a story, an opinion, news and so on.

Hot seating
Children take turns to adopt the role of a character from a book or song/rhyme and face questioning from their classmates. (See Jacki Rowley's chapter on drama for further information on hot seating.)

Role play
Imaginative (for example, a dark cave) or realistic settings (for example, a café or post office) provide a stimulus for a lot of child–child talk. Children learn to re-enact situations they have seen adults in, and add their own contributions. Use of pairs of telephones can encourage conversations between children. Adult models of language within the role play area can be important at the outset for a short time. For instance, a doctor's surgery might include talk about appointments, times, illnesses, medicine, etc. A 'talk corner' with a telephone box, a sofa with a table containing stimuli, and so on, serves a similar function.

Curriculum talk
These are talk sessions around a theme or a piece of work done by the children; for example, a painting or science experiment. Children's comments can be recorded and discussed by the adult. They can be displayed on a 'talk board' or 'talk wall' in speech bubbles or brightly coloured cards.

Props for talk
Hats, jewellery, a cloak and so on can allow imaginative talk as children take on the role of other characters. A crown, for example, might encourage talk around the questions, 'Who would wear this?' 'How

would she speak?' Puppets also provide a lot of stimulation for talk for even very shy children.

Other people speaking
Visitors and parent can be invited in to speak to the children or tell them stories. The use of other voices, dialects and languages can enrich the language environment in the early years classroom.

Listening centre
Taped stories and rhymes can be used in a listening centre where several children can listen in at the same time.

Art talk
Children can be presented with stimulating pieces of art work in a variety of media in order to stimulate discussion. Visits to art galleries can be a valuable means of stimulating such talk, particularly if the pictures are hung at the children's level. Early years settings could, if space allows, have their own gallery section which contains pieces of artwork which are changed regularly. Some museums and art galleries offer a loan service to schools. Similarly, pieces of music can be used to stimulate discussion.

The activities listed above cover a range of purposes, contexts and audiences for children's talk. We need to ensure that children are provided with opportunities to engage in this range and to join in these oracy activities in pairs, small groups and large groups.

Children can also be encouraged to reflect on their own developing oracy skills. Self-assessment can be a crucial element in children's progression. Children can be asked:

- Who do you like talking to?
- When do you like talking?
- When don't you like talking? Why?
- When are you good at talking?
- What do you find hard about talking?
- What do you remember about learning to talk?
- What helps you to learn new words?

Talking about talk can, as stated earlier, develop children's metalinguistic awareness, but it can also enable them to become aware of themselves as active learners. This may, in time, improve their ability to identify areas of weakness and set themselves targets for improvement. Very young children may not be able to discuss their own linguistic competence in any depth but by beginning to talk with them about their talk, we are setting strong foundations for future development in oracy.

Conclusion

We cannot assume that because children like talking and appear to us to be competent speakers that this aspect of their education can be left to develop without support. Speaking and listening skills underpin children's ability to understand the whole curriculum. As Browne (1996) suggests:

> Perhaps the most important reason for developing children's oral language is that all learning depends on the ability to question, reason, formulate ideas, pose hypotheses and exchange ideas with others. These are not just oral language skills, they are thinking skills.
>
> (Browne, 1996, p. 7)

As early years educators we need to ensure that all children have opportunities to develop this essential tool for learning.

Suggestions for further reading

Garton, A. and Pratt, C. (1989) *Learning to be Literate: The Development of Spoken and Written Language*, Oxford: Blackwell.
Wells, G. (1986) *The Meaning Makers*, London: Hodder & Stoughton.
Whitehead, M. (1997) *Language and Literacy in the Early Years*, 2nd edition, London: Paul Chapman.

References

Barrs, M. *et al.* (1992) *The Primary Language Record*, London: CLPE.
Bernstein, B. (1960) Language and social class, *British Journal of Sociology*, Vol. 11, pp. 271–6.
Berko-Gleason, J. (1977) Talking to children: some notes on feedback, in C. E. Snow and C. A. Ferguson, *Talking to Children: Language Input and Acquisition*, Cambridge University Press.
Brice-Heath, S. (1983) *Ways with Words: Language, Life and Work in Communities and Classrooms*, Cambridge University Press.
Brown, R. (1973) *A First Language*, London: Allen and Unwin.
Browne, A. (1996) *Developing Language and Literacy 3–8*, London: Paul Chapman.
Bruner, J. (1983) *Child's Talk: Learning to Use Language*, New York: Norton.
Campbell, R. and Wales, R. (1970) The study of language acquisition, in J. Lyon (ed.) *New Horizons in Linguistics*, Harmondsworth: Penguin.
Cazden, C. B. (1983) Contexts for literacy: in the mind and in the classroom,

Journal of Reading Behaviours, Vol. 14, no. 4, pp. 413–27.

Chomsky, N. (1965) *Aspects of the Theory of Syntax*, Cambridge, Mass.: MIT Press.

Chomsky, N. (1972) *Language and Mind*, New York: Harcourt Brace Jovanovich.

Gleitman, L. R., Newport, E. L. and Gleitman, H. (1984) The current status of the motherese hypothesis, *Journal of Child Language*, Vol. 11, pp. 43–79.

Godwin, D. and Perkins, M. (1998) *Teaching Language and Literacy in the Early Years*, London: David Fulton.

Hatch, E. M. (ed.) (1978a) *Second Language Acquisition*, Rowley, Mass.: Newbury House.

Hatch, E. M. 1978b. Discourse analysis and second language acquisition, in Hatch (1978a) *op. cit.*

Hughes, M. and Cousins, J. (1990) Teachers' perceptions of children's language, in D. Wray, (ed.) *Emerging Partnerships: Current Research in Language and Literacy*, Clevedon: Multilingual Matters.

Hymes, D. (1972) On communicative competence, in J. B. Pride and J. Holmes (eds.) *Sociolinguistics*, Harmondsworth: Penguin.

Kress, G. R. (ed.) (1976) *Halliday: System and Function in Language*, London: Oxford University Press.

Labov, W. (1972) *Language in the Inner City*, Philadelphia: University of Pennsylvania Press.

Landes, J. (1975) Speech addressed to children: issues and characteristics of parental input, *Language Learning*, Vol. 25, pp. 355–79.

McNeill, D. (1966) Developmental psycholinguistics, in F. Smith and G. A. Millar (eds.) *The Genesis of Language*, Cambridge, Mass.: MIT Press.

Norman, K. (1990) *Teaching Talking and Learning in Key Stage One*, London: National Curriculum Council/National Oracy Project.

Norman, K. (1992) *Thinking Voices*, London: Hodder & Stoughton.

Ochs Keenan, E. (1983) Conversational competence in children, in E. Ochs and B. B. Schieffelin (eds.) *Acquiring Conversational Competence*, London: Routledge and Kegan Paul.

Scollon, R. (1976) *Conversations with a One Year Old*, Honolulu: University of Hawaii.

Snow, C. E. and Ferguson, C. A. (eds.) (1977) *Talking to Children: Language Input and Acquisition*, Cambridge University Press.

Tizard, B. and Hughes, M. (1984) *Young Children Learning: Talking and Thinking at Home and at School*, London: Fontana.

Tough, J. (1977) *The Development of Meaning*, London: Allen and Unwin.

de Villiers, J. and de Villiers, P. (1973) A cross-sectional study of the acquisition of grammatical morphemes in child speech, *Journal of Psycholinguistic Research*, Vol. 2, pp. 267–78.

Vygotsky, L. (1962) *Thought and Language*, Cambridge, Mass.: MIT Press.

Wells, G. (1986) *The Meaning Makers*, London: Hodder & Stoughton.

2

'I Can Tell Lots of Punjabi': Developing Language and Literacy with Bilingual Children

Eithne Dodwell

This chapter outlines approaches that can be taken to foster the development of language and literacy with children who speak English as an additional language. As with monolingual children, bilingual children's literacy learning needs to be based in a rich, active experience of oral language, in concrete situations, and developed through rhyme and story. Little has been written specifically about the early years education of children in the first stages of learning English. Their educators often find themselves re-inventing the wheel as they adapt ideas from the traditional early years curriculum, with its stress on discussion and negotiation, to meet the challenges of teaching children with whom they do not share a language. At the same time they have to adapt ideas about bilingual education to the needs of children in the early years. This can be unexpectedly challenging for experienced educators, whatever their pedagogical style. This chapter outlines some of the ways in which this may be done. It begins by considering the ways in which bilingual children develop language and the implications this has for playgroups, nurseries and classrooms. It is important to learn as much as we can about our pupils' home languages and cultures so that we can support the development of their entire language repertoire. The chapter discusses ways in which adults who work with children can use approaches which value the linguistic repertoire children bring with them to nursery and school and build upon it in meaningful ways. It offers practical suggestions as well as challenging some of the assumptions we may make about bilingual children's experiences.

Terminology

'Bilingual' is a common label for children who speak a different language at home from the one used in nursery or school. However, it must not be assumed that 'bilingual' refers to an equal facility in two languages. In the early stages of acquiring an additional language, children may not be fluent in both, or all, of their languages but are developing skills and be achieving at different stages in their first and additional languages. In these instances, it is perhaps more appropriate to refer to 'emergent bilingualism' (Skutnabb-Kangas, 1981). Some children can use more than two languages effectively in a wide range of contexts and are therefore not bilingual, but multilingual. However, for the purpose of clarity, throughout this chapter the term 'bilingual' will be used to refer to children who are learning more than one language.

The language children have learned at home is variously referred to as their 'first' or 'home' language, their 'mother tongue' or 'heritage language'. However, more than one language is spoken in many homes, and the home language may be a dialect of the heritage language. A child may have contact with yet another language, possibly with another script, often in religious contexts. Members of a family with such a wide experience of language may find it hard to apply labels such as 'first' or 'home' to any one language. Our preferred language varies according to where we are, who we are with and what we are talking about. It changes not only between topics and social contexts, but often over time. For those of us who are geographically or socially mobile, the language with which we identify most strongly may not be the one which we use the most often, or in the widest range of contexts. It may not be the one spoken at home, or during our formal education. Throughout the chapter the language first learned by the child, used predominantly in the home and community, will be referred to as her 'first language'.

The development of English as an additional language

We know that the vast majority of young children entering nursery and school are accomplished constructors of meaning. They know that spoken language has regular patterns relating to objects, actions and their relationships, as well as to conventions of verbal interaction. They have learned how to use the patterns and conventions of their first language to achieve at least some of their physical, emotional and social needs. These conventions and patterns may be very different from those they will meet in the nursery or school. However, children's expectation that the nursery/school culture and language have patterns and conventions, as well as the knowledge and experience of the world they have gained whilst learning their first language, form an effective basis for learning across the whole curriculum.

Language is an important tool for thinking and learning inside and outside nursery and school, and for making links between different domains of human life. In a truly bilingual educational situation, educators are bilingual and both languages are used across the whole curriculum, and accorded equal status. References to bilingual education in England can therefore be misleading, since emergent bilingual children are often taught exclusively in English by teachers with little or no knowledge of their pupils' home languages, although the employment of nursery nurses and teachers who can speak at least one community language is slowly increasing. The presence of staff who share the same language as a child can be very reassuring for young children who enter nursery or school. The experience of facing peers and adults with whom they cannot communicate can be very stressful for children so that nurseries and playgroups often have difficult settling-in periods. Staff need to ensure that family members are given every encouragement to stay as long as necessary; if they feel at home in the nursery, they may offer to stay to help to settle other children in. So it is clear that bilingual staff are crucial to the effectiveness of both the induction and education of bilingual children. However, although there is a broadening consensus (Baker, 1993) that all children should have the right to be educated in their preferred language, this does not appear to be a practical proposition in England in the foreseeable future.

Whatever the language repertoire of teaching staff, it is important that children of all ages should be encouraged to use their preferred language to support and extend their thinking in small group tasks and other social situations. As they become more competent, or work in groups which include monolingual English speakers, their preferred language is often English. This is very similar to the language development of monolingual children who speak a local dialect at home whilst moving towards the use of standard English in formal situations. It is now generally accepted that whatever children's linguistic repertoire, their skills should be valued and built upon, not ridiculed, ignored or suppressed. It is therefore vital that teachers encourage children's use of their first or home language in nursery or school.

Research suggests that children acquire a second language in much the same way as they develop their first; through supported scaffolding from peers and adults and the development of language in meaningful contexts (Edwards, 1996; Gregory, 1997). As Bruner (1983) and Vygotsky (1978) stressed, we learn language in order to communicate with others; the social interaction we engage in is crucial to our development of spoken language. This is no different whether we are learning a first or additional language. We cannot do it in isolation; the language we are learning becomes more meaningful when we are using it in concrete situations. Thus, whatever language they speak at home, young children in the early stages of acquiring English have the same needs and learning processes as other children. They need meaningful interactions with supportive adults. They need success and praise. They need a curriculum firmly based in concrete experiences with a balance of security and stimulus. They have to tackle the same curriculum as monolingual children and they need a flexible English language repertoire to do it with, though their overall language repertoire and language awareness has the potential to be much greater than that of their monolingual peers.

The cognitive sophistication of children learning English as an additional language is often greater than they can express in English. Like many monolingual English speakers trying to use GCSE foreign languages on continental holidays, they may be frustrated by the simplicity of the meanings they can convey, whilst listeners may seriously underestimate their abilities. Failure to distinguish language difficulties from learning difficulties has probably been one of the chief causes of the well-documented underachievement of many children from ethnic minorities (Gillborn and Gipps, 1996).

It is particularly important that children in the early stages of learning English are offered a carefully structured, stimulating curriculum soundly based in direct, unmediated concrete experiences. Extra care and attention needs to be given to ensuring that spoken language is contextually supported by visual aids, eye contact, facial expression, gesture and tone of voice, and that it is based as far as possible on previous shared experience. The adult will have to contribute a far larger share of talk than is generally considered acceptable, but should be careful to allow supportive pauses which are long enough to allow children to contribute should they so wish. Children who are reluctant to contribute individually or in a small group may be quite happy to join in a chorus, answering questions or joining in key phrases and rhymes. Children acquiring an additional language sometimes have long periods where they do not speak in that language. They understand far more than they can communicate. At this stage, the adult working with the child should be undeterred by lack of verbal response and continue to talk to the child using gestures and physical props where appropriate to support their meaning.

Even the simplest speech act can be a serious compositional challenge in a new language. Quite apart from the fact that young children's attention is usually fully occupied with meaning, the short-term memory of anyone speaking in a new language is at least partially absorbed by managing the structures of that language. Handsley (1997) offers the metaphor of language as a vehicle which takes experienced drivers wherever they want to go, but which offers the novice such mechanical challenges that navigation is out of the question, let alone discussion of the scenery. Because of this, children in the early stages of acquiring English may appear to have a very short attention span. Independent tasks may be much more problematic for them; by the time they have identified their materials, they may have forgotten the task. They are even more likely than other young children to run out of steam by the end of the session, with all the normal consequences. Failure to take this into account can lead to a vicious cycle of low expectations, behavioural problems and/or underachievement.

The skills of children who speak English as an additional language have often been underestimated and neglected because teachers have tended to focus on things that they cannot do, rather than what they can do. Many educators have felt that bilingual children must face constant confusion and difficulties and that the first language 'interferes' with the acquisition of the second. This is not at all the case. The fact that the children are already aware of the nature of language and have an understanding of syntactic structure means that they have a secure basis on which to build. As Browne (1996) states:

> Not only is the learning of a second language more straightforward than some people believe but it can also be advantageous to the learner. It has been suggested that speakers who are proficient in more than one language have a greater linguistic awareness than monolingual speakers. Through gaining control over two language systems learners may gain an analytic awareness of language which contributes to a more conscious understanding of linguistic patterns, since a first language is acquired unconsciously but a second language is acquired with 'conscious realization and control' (Vygotsky, 1962).
>
> (Browne, 1996, p. 149)

Children's first language, rather than being ignored, needs to be acknowledged and encouraged in order to develop children's linguistic confidence and expertise.

It is enormously encouraging for the child if teachers can develop the confidence to use words from a child's first language to support their work with bilingual children. It is often wise to use the English and the community language words together, with a brief explanation of their different connotations, if possible. It is also important to use a wide range of descriptive language alongside the simple forms: once children understand 'big', we can use 'great, big' then 'huge, big, enormous', asking children for equivalents in their home language. Similarly once children can use 'go' and 'get' to convey basic meanings, they can move on to 'walk', 'run', 'drive', 'creep', 'hurry' and so on, again matching them with the corresponding terms in their first language. It is also useful for us to find out about the way in which the children's home languages work, and to identify any particular features of a language which may inform our work with children. In our discussions with children about language, children should be introduced to the terms used when talking about language: 'language', 'word', 'meaning' and so on. We can also begin to draw children's attention to word boundaries, so that they know, for instance, that 'itsa' is composed of three words: 'it', 'is' and 'a'. This work will develop children's metalinguistic awareness; that is, the ability to think and talk about language itself. This in itself has a positive effect on cognitive development and, as Browne suggested earlier, research has highlighted the fact that bilingual children's metalinguistic skills are often more highly developed than those of monolingual children.

Children's early attempts in communicating in an additional language should be accepted as the courageous communicative gestures they are, our response confirming and extending their meaning whilst offering a model:

Khawar: (confident, articulate rising-five commenting on teacher's failure to communicate with much younger child): She no ... English

Teacher: No, she can't speak very much English yet. She only came to nursery last week.

Khawar: I can ... English

Teacher: Yes, you can, you speak English very well. And you can speak Punjabi. I can't – I can only ... You speak a lot of Punjabi and a little English, I speak ... (getting in a muddle)

Khawar: (rescues Teacher with interruption) I can tell lots of Punjabi

Teacher: (too grateful for the rescue to tackle modelling 'speak' versus 'tell') Yes, you can, you're very clever.

The teacher in this example is extending Khawar's knowledge about language as well as his ability to speak English. She is also, in her own time, learning some key words and phrases in Punjabi. She routinely, but briefly, discusses the children's and her own developing bilingualism with them. She makes a point of teaching them the English names of their different languages so that languages become a topic in their own right. This teacher's attempts to learn Punjabi are a practical way of showing respect for, and supporting, her pupils' first language development, and of modelling language learning processes. They also give her invaluable insight into bilingual language learning processes and experiences. She is, for example, still regularly taken aback by how hard it is to correctly repeat even a simple correction of a common language error; it is particularly hard if we have been repeating this error for some time, if it conveys our meaning effectively and if it is based on language structures which are correct in our first language. Equally, the teacher is regularly unable to manage both correct verb form and correct suffix or comparative form in even the most common sentence. Her efforts encourage the less confident children to take risks and support discussion of language forms and word meanings. The benefits of such talk about language are discussed further by Dodson (1985) who suggests that it need not happen very often to have a positive impact on children's success in additional language learning.

Planning

Planning for bilingual learning is important. The language associated with each activity needs to be carefully thought out and a list made of concepts and related target words that need to be introduced to the children in the session. Target words are those words which the teacher feels the child is developmentally ready to acquire, words which fit into a specific topic or are key words in a child's linguistic repertoire. This is not to suggest that the introduction of such vocabulary should become a mechanistic drumming in of such words; rather they are introduced within context, in a naturalistic way. It is also helpful if the adult can reinforce learning by introducing related terms in the child's first language. There are a number of bilingual dictionaries, with phonetic transcription of words to aid the teacher, which can be used for this purpose. Space can be provided on planning sheets for recording target words used in the session in as many as possible of the relevant languages. Children new to English may not be familiar with technical or mathematical language in their first language; use of the latter will not necessarily clarify misunderstandings, although it might. This should not prevent us teaching it if we can, we just need to be aware that it may be new and thus need further work . Carefully chosen stimulus experiences or objects, however simple, can be invaluable in supporting children's understanding, enabling them to link their experiences in and out of nursery or school. Educators, whatever their language repertoire, can help children make these links by encouraging them to talk about their experiences in whatever language they choose and by showing a genuine interest in whatever aspects of it are new to them.

Where possible, it is best to introduce new concepts in familiar language, and introduce new language in relation to familiar experiences or concepts. This can be harder than it sounds when we have only very limited linguistic means of exploring the child's experience out of nursery or school. Equally, even universal experiences such as family life, eating, cooking, shopping or celebrating can vary enormously across cultures, at least from the point of view of a child. The teacher must be sensitive to these cultural differences and not assume that all the children will have the same experience.

Thus if activities are planned to build upon children's previous experiences, to encourage their use of their first language and to introduce new concepts and terms in a focused yet meaningful way, children will have a careful structure on which to build new learning. New concepts and related target words should be introduced in a variety of different ways and approached from different angles in order to reinforce learning. If, for example, a child is being introduced to the English word for the colour 'blue', he could be provided with blue paints in the art area, blue crayons in the graphic area, blue lego bricks in the construction area and blue 3D shapes when working with shape and space. The corresponding word in the child's first language could be introduced alongside the English version. The words can be introduced in context and the adult refer to the blue properties of the range of artefacts in a naturalistic way.

The role of the adult in providing this type of support and scaffolding, and offering a model of language, is vital in all stages of children's learning, whether children are monolingual or bilingual. However, it is particularly important for adults working with emergent bilinguals to be absolutely clear about the nature of the scaffolding to be provided and the specific language to be introduced and extended. The structure is needed in order to ensure, for example, that a wide and potentially confusing range of terms are not used to introduce a new concept.

The importance of play

Language is learned in active use. Imaginative role play is an ideal medium for bilingual children to explore language use. Wood and Attfield (1996) outline how essential play is to children's cognitive development:

> learning and development depend on cognitive structures which are both complex in their origins and subsequent evolution. Processes such as exploration, practice, repetition, mastery and revision are important in forming, extending and connecting cognitive structures. Play can be seen as a means whereby children try to impose some structure or organization on a task and make sense of their world, and as a continuous rehearsal of these cognitive processes.
>
> (Wood and Attfield, 1996, p. 76)

It would seem important, therefore, to provide children who are in the early stages of acquiring English as an additional language opportunities to take part in play activities which allow them to explore, make and test hypotheses, cement understanding and practise skills without fear of failure or censure. Bilingual children who have been introduced to concepts using English vocabulary and encouraged to engage in play which allows them to explore these concepts have been observed practising the new terminology and trying to apply it to new situations. Play is thus extending their development of English and developing confidence.

Gregory (1997) outlines how bilingual children often learn chunks of the target language which they use in conversations with others, either appropriately or inappropriately. They are playing with language rather than using it to communicate a specific meaning. She suggests that play can provide opportunities for this element of language learning to occur:

> In his study of a child's language between the ages of one and two, Ron Scullen (1979) describes how much is learned in the form of 'pre-packaged' routines, language which is incorporated from adults' speech without being internally analysed. This type of approach in second language learning appears to take place only during early childhood, since older children and adults are constrained by the fear of having to make a relevant reply in conversations. Play, then, provides an ideal opportunity for young children to learn formulae which can be used as 'chunks' of appropriate language. The language during play is predictable, repetitious and well-contextualised which contrasts

sharply with the 'Wh...' questions children are likely to meet from an adult.

(Gregory, 1997, p. 106)

The use of structured role play areas is a valuable means of extending language and literacy practices, as Nigel Hall outlines in Chapter 7. Again, bilingual children have much to gain from engaging in such play. Careful provision of appropriate opportunities for role play which promotes literacy activities can give children a safe space to explore the differences between their two cultures and to experiment with speech and script. This is more likely to happen if children's different cultures are generally visible and acknowledged in meaningful contexts throughout the nursery and school. In role play areas, care should be taken to include artefacts and examples of literacy from children's home communities. This will enable children to feel more comfortable in the role play situation and also support their use of their first language. Examples of artefacts which could be used are:

- dressing-up clothes which reflect children's own dress, e.g. shalwar chemise
- small versions of cooking implements and tableware which are used in children's homes
- calendars and pictures which are found in children's homes
- leaflets, newspapers and magazines which are written in children's first languages.

When choosing such artefacts, we need to consult adults from the local community or draw upon our own recent experience of home visiting. The contents of professionally produced catalogues or other literature may not reflect the reality of children's everyday lives. Structured role play areas can be set up which will reflect children's home experiences and encourage interaction and engagement. Fabric shops, grocery stores and restaurants may be familiar to the particular community of children you work with and so would be a good focus for a role play area. One nursery which served a mainly Turkish community set up a Turkish take-away in its role play area and children enthusiastically made and sold kebabs, engaging in activities which stimulated a range of language and literacy events. Role play areas which are transformed into airports or travel agents can enable children to engage in imaginative play relating to their family's original country of origin, where they may still have family or friends.

Approaches to literacy

In the past, it has been suggested that for children learning literacy in an additional language, literacy learning should not begin until they have a firm basis in spoken English. However, as Elaine Hallet points out in Chapter 4, it is clear that children interact with literacy from the very early stages through their awareness of the print which surrounds them. Literacy is an integral part of life and therefore children cannot help but become familiar and interested in it. This interest should be encouraged and developed in nursery whatever, the child's linguistic repertoire. However, this approach should be informal, rooted in the child's experience and based on a solid foundation of oracy. Mills and Mills (1998) describe how in many European areas with large bilingual populations (for example, Hungary, German Switzerland and Flemish Belgium), children do not tackle formal reading or writing activities until they are six or seven years old. In the early years, they are provided with a range of structured activities which develop speaking and listening skills, the focus on oracy being paramount. We need to ensure that our nurseries and early years settings embrace, celebrate and extensively develop oracy, as Jim McDonagh and Sue McDonagh stress in Chapter 1.

The use of rhyme and song is invaluable in a multilingual playgroup, nursery and classroom. Songs and rhymes introduce children to particular patterns of language which facilitate development of English. Songs and rhymes in children's first languages can be learned and enjoyed by the whole class. Parents and other family members can be encouraged to join in and teach favourite rhymes and songs in their home language and the enterprising teacher can ask permission to tape these for future use! Counting rhymes are particularly useful for developing oracy as they often contain highly structured and repetitive patterns which can be illustrated through the use of props.

Bruner (1986) and others have argued that story appears to be a universal human vehicle for both learning and pleasure. This in certainly so in a multilingual classroom. Children learning English as an additional language can understand and respond to far more complex language structures in a good story than in almost any other context. The most fruitful stories to use are ones which use patterned language with repeated phrases. There are many modern and traditional tales which children can join in with. As children chant, 'Run, run as fast as you can, you can't catch me I'm the Gingerbread Man!' they are also learning about the use of intonation and expression when reading. Books which provide a range of semantic and pictorial cues can also enable children to join in easily. However, it is only too easy to get so focused on clarity and meaning in the acquisition of a new language that bilingual children are not introduced to a wealth of rhymes, songs and poetry in language that is technically beyond them. This is selling them short: they are as susceptible as anyone else to the pleasures of word music. Ellis and Barrs (1996) provide a useful list of books which are appropriate for any multilingual early years setting.

Nurseries and classrooms need to contain books which reflect the lives and cultures of children who enter them. There are many delightful texts which are rooted in the experiences of a range of children. However, it is important not to forget to introduce stories from cultures not represented in the class. Quite apart from their intrinsic delightfulness, *Eat Up, Gemma* and *Handa's Surprise* go down just as well with children with cultural origins in Asia as in the West Indies or Africa. Books about animals can be cross-cultural, although we must be careful not to assume this. Often the human-like environment in which the animals live is based very much on the writer's own cultural background! Teachers need to be sensitive to the fact that, for some children, pigs are distasteful creatures and not a fitting character to be introduced in stories. This is the case for Jewish and Muslim children, for example. *The Three Billy Goats Gruff* may be a better choice than *The Three Little Pigs*. There are interesting parallels between them, since goats play the same role in some Eastern cultures as pigs used to in Western Europe. Modern retellings of Old Testament stories such as Lucy Cousins' *Noah's Ark* can be truly multicultural with their inter-linked Jewish, Christian and Muslim histories, a fact which often interests older children.

Bilingual children's oracy and literacy development can also be extended by the use of puppets and artefacts related to familiar stories. Listening corners which contain recorded versions of well-known stories in children's first languages, with accompanying puppets or magnet board figures, are invaluable. Parents and other family members can be involved in developing a set of stories on tape. It is also useful to extend children's experiences of stories into other areas. For example, role play areas can be turned into a setting based on a favourite book. *The Three Bears' Cottage* is a favourite example, but equally powerful have been the cave featured in *Can't You Sleep, Little Bear?* and the train in *Oi! Get Off My Train!* (complete with stuffed animals). Tables or trays can contain scenarios modelled on books, with appropriate props and small figures. These experiences enable children to retell stories, to practise chunks of language learned and to play with remembered words. This can also be developed by the provision of multiple copies of texts which have been introduced to children at story times. Children can gather to engage in a shared discussion on a text with a group of children who share the same language. Sometimes it is much more fun to do this when you each have your own copy rather than having to share! Big books are also very useful for this purpose and adults can use them to engage a group of children in talk about the book or focused work on print. Increasingly, there are dual-text books appearing in big book format.

Reading material for children with English as an additional language needs to be carefully chosen to be both accessible and stimulating, moving gradually from the known to the new. The starting point is environmental print, particularly the child's name. Other visible print in the nursery or classroom needs to have a clear purpose, so that children's attention is naturally drawn to it. Labels for equipment can be accompanied by pictures or outlines of the material stored. The list is endless, and familiar. We may have to draw print to the attention of bilingual children, using it as an opportunity for work on the alphabet, word boundaries or syntax. Extra care is needed with the use of alphabet friezes, posters and so on. A Pushto speaking five-year-old – the only one in a predominantly Punjabi speaking class – was putting a lot of effort into learning to read and write, copying every bit of print in sight but mystifying his teacher by his efforts to decode and compose. Eventually, when she gently refused to accept his 'n' is for 'doctor', he dragged her to the alphabet frieze on the classroom wall and showed her how 'n' is indeed for doctor (nurse), just as 'p' is for black bear (panda) and 'd' is bird (duck). The poor child had been blocking out the waves of English and Punjabi washing over his head during carpet sessions by trying to teach himself literacy from the alphabet frieze, interrupted only by the teacher's increasingly exasperated attempts to keep him part of the group. His teacher lent the mini version of the frieze to his mother, who was only too glad to spend time teaching it to him at home.

The nursery and school environment should model as many literacy functions as possible, in meaningful contexts. Scripts from the first language should be used wherever possible. However, a plethora of expensive multicultural posters and labels to which no one refers may have less positive impact than a genuine interest shown in a letter, greetings card or food package from the country of origin. Great sensitivity is needed when approaching adults from different communities for help with reading or writing in the first language: whether they were educated in England or in the country of origin, they may well not be literate in their home language. Not all community languages have written scripts. For example, written Punjabi is based on the Sikh religious script, Gurmakhi, and is not normally used to represent the Punjabi spoken by Muslim Punjabi speakers whose families originate from Pakistan. The latter is generally not written, apart from rare occasions when it is transcribed in Arabic script. The national language, Urdu, is used in formal situations. It is wise to ask not: 'Can you read/translate this for me?' but rather: 'I can't read/translate this, do you know anyone who could do it for me?' Equally, if sending home dual-language books, we need to be careful that we are doing this because the child has chosen it or as a goodwill message and not in the blithe assumption that someone at home will be delighted to read it to the child. They may, or they may be embarrassed about not being able to. If the script they read is normally written from right to left, they may be disconcerted by the page order of a book printed and bound according to left to right conventions; either way, the language will not flow since the pages will be experienced as back to front. This could easily be avoided if pages were bound at the top, as in *Send for Sohail* (1993). Where it can be achieved, with the help of bilingual colleagues, of their friends and relations, or of older members of children's families, home-made dual-language books (big and small) or cards containing favourite songs or poems will be constantly read. In order to ensure a copy is preserved, it may well be worth photocopying original pages before colouring them or incorporating them into books. If practical, it is also worth transcribing the community language into the Roman script, as well as the first language, for the benefit of monoliterate adults.

Children with experience of scripts with different conventions from the Roman alphabet may need extra support in learning to read and write from left to right. They will profit from clear explanations that conventions such as script running from left to right, or hanging from rather than sitting on the line, are simply conventions which differ from script to script: neither is right or wrong in itself. They need to be given the vocabulary with which to discuss both the content and the form of what they read, as well as strategies for tackling it. However, it must be stressed that having print around the walls which originates from the child's first language does not confuse children. Children are very quick to learn to distinguish one script from another. Rather, it enriches their experience and sends them the message that their linguistic experience is valued; for monolingual children, such experience of scripts does much to broaden their understanding of language. Children also enjoy writing which is based on the script of their first language. They often experiment with letters in their first script in the same way that children whose first language

Figure 2.1. Asia's writing

is English do with the Roman script, demonstrating the range of principles outlined by Ann Browne in Chapter 6. In Figure 2.1, we can see that Asia's mark-making is based on the Urdu script.

Writing, particularly composition, makes even more demands than does reading on the short-term memory of children learning English as an additional language. Many bilingual children will progress towards independent writing in the same way as their monolingual peers, experimenting with letter shapes from both English and first language scripts and gradually learning letter–sound correspondence to aid independent spelling. Graphic areas should contain examples of the range of scripts familiar to children and their early attempts at mark-making encouraged and discussed. Adults modelling writing in the playgroup, nursery or classroom could include family and community members. Writing is inextricably linked to oracy and reading and, for bilingual children, these links need to be carefully planned into the curriculum. Writing activities based on familiar texts or writing which introduces particular patterns of familiar language are important. In later stages of development, key words and topic words need explicit introduction and practice, in meaningful contexts. Some children may find maths, science or technology, with their precise vocabulary and scope for labelling, describing and simple retelling, less intimidating contexts than writing stories. Children may need models of different sentence structures, e.g. ways of asking questions, in order to help them break away from the safety of the first effective ways they have learnt to convey meanings in the new language. Topics relating to food or to 'our street' offer plenty of scope for simple recording of direct experience, whilst retelling stories such as *Handa's Surprise* or *On the Way Home* can extend children's descriptive and imaginative vocabulary.

Shared writing sessions can be a valuable means of introducing bilingual children to the conventions of English script. Bilingual staff can work with monolingual staff to model dual-text writing sessions, differently coloured felt pens for the different scripts making the task even clearer to children.

Conclusion

Children's additional language learning builds on the understanding of verbal communication that they have gained whilst learning to use the language(s) of their primary care-givers. The more we know about the home languages of children new to English, the more easily we can understand their language learning processes. Our literacy curriculum is more likely to be effective if it is based on a wide, meaningful experience of spoken language and takes into account the conceptions of literacy and literacy learning that children experience at home (Brice-Heath, 1983). We need to constantly widen and update our awareness of these conceptions and the effects they have on children's literacy development. This chapter has outlined some of the ways in which early years settings, nurseries and schools can address the literacy development of bilingual children. However, one of the most crucial approaches is to enter into a meaningful dialogue with children's families and communities in order to engage in a joint venture into literacy. Shared understandings will lead to shared goals and achievements.

Suggestions for further reading

Gibbons, P. (1991) *Learning to Learn in a Second Language*, Australia: Primary English Teaching Association.
Gregory, E. (1996) *Making Sense of a New World*, London: Paul Chapman.
McWilliam, N. (1998) *What's in a Word?* London: Trentham.

References

Baker, C. (1993) *Foundations of Bilingual Education and Bilingualism*, Clevedon, Avon: Multilingual Matters.

Browne, A. (1996) *Developing Language and Literacy 3–8*, London: Paul Chapman.

Bruner, J. (1983) *Child's Talk: Learning to Use Language*, Oxford University Press.

Bruner, J. (1986) *Actual Minds, Possible Worlds*, Cambridge, Mass.: Harvard University Press.

Dodson, C. J. (1985) Schools' Council Bilingual Education Project (Primary Schools) 1968–1977: an independent evaluation, in C. J. Dodson (ed.) *Bilingual Education: Evaluation, Assessment and Methodology*, Cardiff: University of Wales Press.

Edwards, V. (1996) *The Other Languages: A Guide to Multilingual Classroom Readings*, Reading: Reading and Language Information Centre.

Ellis, S. and Barrs, M. (eds.) (1996) *The Core Book: A Structured Approach to Using Books within the Reading Curriculum*, London: CLPE.

Gillborn, D. and Gipps, C. (1996) *Recent Research on the Achievements of Ethnic Minority Pupils*, London: HMSO.

Gregory, E. (1997) *Making Sense of a New World*, London: Paul Chapman.

Handsley, M. (1997) Extract from Conference Speech, T. F. Davies Professional Development Centre, Bradford (7 November).

Mills, C. and Mills, D.(1998) *Dispatches: The Early Years*, London: Channel 4 Television.

Skutnabb-Kangas (1981) *Bilingualism or Not: The Education of Minorities*, Clevedon: Multilingual Matters.

Wood, E. and Attfield, J. (1996) *Play, Learning and the Early Childhood Curriculum*, London: Paul Chapman.

Vygotsky, L. V. (1978) *Mind in Society: The Development of Higher Psychological Processes*, Cambridge, Mass: Harvard University Press.

Children's books referred to in the text

Browne, E. (1994) *Handa's Surprise*, London: Walker Books.

Cousins, L. (1993) *Noah's Ark*, London: Walker Books.

Grange Road First School, Bradford (1993) *Send for Sohail*, Bradford and Ilkley Community College: Partnership Publishing.

Martin, L., Crawley, S. and Fry, E. (1993) *The Gingerbread Man*, Jamestown: Heritage Readers.

Ormerod, J. (1989) *Eat Up, Gemma*, London: Walker Books.

3

The Literacies and Language of Poetry and Rhyme

Suzi Clipson-Boyles

Poetry and society

When asked, many adults will tell you that they don't like poetry! The reasons they give can offer a fascinating reflection of our society, and, in particular, the curriculum, pedagogy and philosophy of the education which they have experienced. Some people make the mistake of believing that poetry is exclusively academic, written in difficult language, on remote, often historical subjects, with secret codes to meaning which only 'clever people' can understand. Others associate poetry with social structure, perceiving it to be the domain of the middle classes – an esoteric luxury.

There are two distinct ironies in all this. Firstly, poetry touches the lives of everyone in our society each day without them necessarily recognising it. And secondly, very young children demonstrate a natural instinct towards poetry, which is all too often stunted and prevented from developing because of this very lack of awareness on the part of adults of the power and presence of poetry around them. In this chapter we shall be exploring ways in which we can support and extend the language and literacy development of young children through poetry and rhyme, by providing enjoyable activities which integrate appropriately into a high quality early years curriculum. But before we do that, let us begin by considering just what is meant here by 'poetry'.

What is poetry?

The negative attitudes towards poetry described above are acquired, in part, because of restrictive definitions. Using art as an analogy, it would be ludicrous to define 'art work' as nothing less than Da Vinci's *Mona Lisa*! Think of the different styles of painting through the ages, think of contemporary art, think of sketches, comic strips, advertise-

34

ments, collages, cartoons, wallpaper, fabrics, greetings cards, photographs, doodles and so on – all visual expressions of different styles, sizes, quality, media and values because they are produced for different purposes. In the same way, it is divisive to consider poetry as nothing other than the classic literary works of great poets. A broader and more creative consideration of what we mean by poetry can encompass a rich variety of genres and contexts.

Of course, there is no denying the wonderful literary verse which has been crafted to perfection by those who will always be remembered – poetry which has been written within established forms, is studied, dissected, debated, and also read for pleasure. (And yet, even the wealth of such literature covers a spectrum of styles from Chaucer to Betjeman, the changes of which have often been the subject of outrage by academics through the ages!) Arguably, the considered professional crafting of poetry is at the heart of the discipline. However, in addition we have a wealth of less formal contributions, equally rich in social tradition, and arguably more accessible to everyone because of their detachment from academic curricula – puns, limericks, songs and proverbs from the past are regular currency in pubs and clubs! Indeed, they are arguably so embedded within our culture that we take them for granted, and in doing so we fail to acknowledge the literary colours of everyday communication.

Not only do we inherit a wealth of language from the past, we also have a rich oral tradition of playing with language in the present. The wide communication net of the media has made a significant contribution towards establishing new vocabulary, constructs and language play into the collective repertoire. If you have ever heard Terry Wogan on Radio 2 in the morning reading letters from people like Tyrone Shulays, Betty Dlyke-One, and Juan Bjorn Evryminit, you will know how appealing it is to many people to have a bit of fun with language during the otherwise tedious journey to work – indeed, much of the correspondence to Terry is actually written in verse! Likewise, listening to the sheer emotion of the rhythmic chanting by a (happy) football crowd can be a powerful experience, and poetic structures such as alliteration, pun and *double entendre* are used widely in newspapers and magazines. The extract in Figure 3.1 includes alliteration ('My Most Memorable Morsel' and 'fresh look at a favourite fish'), pun ('Cannes'), and a mixture of the two ('nicer than Niçoise').

Other examples of playing with language include:

- radio jingles
- pun and *double entendre* in news headlines
- limericks

MY MOST MEMORABLE MORSEL

tuna
in Cannes

Rosemarie Ford, the roving reporter on *Rolf's Amazing World Of Animals*, thinks there's nothing nicer than Niçoise. Antony Worrall Thompson takes a fresh look at a favourite fish

Figure 3.1. Reproduced by kind permission of *The Express on Sunday Magazine*

- pop songs
- TV and radio advertisement slogans
- rap
- proverbs
- jokes
- spoonerisms.

This extension of boundaries to encompass a more inclusive approach to what we mean by poetry is not intended to redefine the status or dilute the quality of classical and contemporary literature, as some might protest. Rather, it is intended to raise awareness and appreciation of the rich and complex ways in which we all use and play with language in our lives. This heightened awareness can increase the pleasure in such language, and empower more people to feel ownership of a breadth of literacies.

Having liberated our ideas of what we expect poetry to be, we can devise activities for young children which can enable them to feel confident about exploring and experimenting with language. Giving children a head-start during their early years can contribute to a more confident approach to the creation and appreciation of other literature later in life. So let us now take a closer look at the benefits of including poetry and rhyme in the early years curriculum.

Poetry in the early years curriculum

Many traditional rhymes can be traced back through history, 'A Ring a Ring o' Roses' being perhaps the most commonly documented example of a song about the plague. However, most of these originated from adult activities, during times when entertainment was a much more socially interactive process than it is today.

> Very few of the rhymes still in circulation were originally intended for young children. Indeed the rhymes continue to reverberate with faint echoes of their sources in ballads, folk songs, rituals, street-cries, drinking-songs, mummers' plays, wars, rebellions, prayers, satires and romantic lyrics.
>
> (Whitehead, 1993, p. 46)

Nevertheless, poetry and rhyme in early years settings are not new or revolutionary. Indeed, the very fact that some have long been referred to as 'nursery' rhymes is an indicator of their place in children's lives and learning. It would be interesting (though impossible) to track the extent to which adult rhymes have been adapted through the ages *for* children, compared with the extent to which they were adapted *by* children, for as we know, children of all ages love to mimic, imitate and generally fool around with adult language. Rude poems are particularly appealing! This natural instinct to play with language is easily observable in young children, and should be used as a springboard for developing their language and learning.

There are eight main learning links to be made directly from poetry and rhyme:

- language development
- enjoyment of literature
- social skills
- multi-cultural understanding
- physical development
- critical thinking
- music
- transmission of knowledge.

It is important to remember that, in practice, these areas are integrated and therefore have a mutually beneficial relationship with each other. However, it is helpful to separate these out for the purposes of discussion.

Language development

Playing with the sounds, rhythms and meanings of poetry can help children to become confident users of language. New words will extend their vocabulary, new constructions of meaning will add to their own creative language crafts, and speaking and listening skills can be taught, practised and enjoyed through oral activities. Likewise, early reading and writing skills can be assisted greatly by poetry, and there is much evidence now to show that the early development of rhyming awareness is linked to reading and spelling competencies further on in the educational process. This will be discussed in more detail later in the chapter.

Enjoyment of literature

There is sometimes a danger that in the scrupulous search for teaching and learning objectives, sheer pleasure and enjoyment are lost or forgotten. In the past, enjoyment has not always been synonymous with education! And yet if we are preparing children for life ahead, the enjoyment of literature is surely something which we must foster from the earliest opportunity. Reading poems, chanting poems, performing poems, playing poems, changing poems, making poems and so on can all have a vital role to play in helping children to develop a sense of ownership of literature. It is there for them, and can be created by them. Such pleasure and ownership provide a sound foundation upon which others should build as the child continues along the education route, so that they continue to enjoy literature into adulthood.

Social skills

Poems and rhymes in early years settings are usually shared and explored in a group setting. They involve turn-taking, listening, sharing, responding, and sometimes associated actions and activities. Chanting in unison can have a tremendous bonding effect upon a group and requires co-operative skills. Poems can also be used to express emotions, face fears, or seek comfort, and in a one-to-one between adult and child, poems can offer a supportive and interactive way of communicating and engaging with each other.

Multi-cultural understanding

The inclusion of poetry and rhyme from a variety of cultures is vitally important in early years settings. The pleasure which these can bring supports the development of new learning, respect and understanding for all children. This, in turn, brings a sense of positive mutual acknowledgement and integration to all which contributes to self-esteem and confidence. It also brings cross-cultural links into learning, where shared meanings and values are encountered, bringing a bond of unity within the diversity. For example, the following traditional Punjabi street-cry has wonderful rhythms and sounds, but also describes a common denominator for all cultures – food!

Rayri Wallah Geet

Gurum unday gurum unday,
gurum unday, gurum unday.
Ke-le Ke-le Ke-le Ke-le.
Cholay masahlay, cholay masahlay,
Cholay masahlay, cholay masahlay
Cha cha cha cha cha
Cha cha cha cha cha.

gurum unday = hot eggs
ke-le = bananas
cholay masahlay = chick peas and herbs
cha = tea

Physical development

Poetry and rhyme in early years settings often involve physical actions, small and large. These can range from the finger actions of 'Incey Wincey Spider' to trooping under 'London Bridge'. Young children are learning most effectively when they are involved in engaged activity. Concepts can be acquired, for example, the use of prepositions through the physical enactment of 'up and down', 'round' and 'through', syllabic awareness through clapping the rhythms of words, sequencing and memory can be assisted through enactment and so on.

Critical thinking

Nursery rhymes and poems can be used, like children's picture books, as a starting point for inquiry and critical thinking activities. The development of these skills arises from the children asking and answering their own questions, rather than those of adults. Such interrogation of texts, written or spoken, can extend their analytical approach to other areas of learning. Modelling the questioning process first ('I am really puzzled about why Jack fell down the hill – what a strange thing to happen! How many different reasons can we think of for that happening?') is an important part of helping the children to generate open rather than closed questions. It is also a good way of establishing that there is often more than one answer to a question. Even more generally, asking what else they would like to know about a poem can generate interesting extensions of thoughts leading into problem-solving activities.

Music

The rhythms and sounds of nursery rhymes and poetry have important direct links with music, whether or not they are sung. Chanting or singing in unison is primarily an enjoyable activity for children to share. The choral nature plus the simultaneous joining in of an adult provides important scaffolding for children's learning, and assists their memory. Other dynamics such as speed, volume and pitch can also be explored and developed.

Transmission of knowledge

Many teaching styles and media are used to help with the transmission of knowledge in early years settings. Poetry and rhyme offer a good context for making links between areas of the curriculum and imparting language and concepts about these subject areas. For example, the following poem could make a good introduction to activities on health:

I Can

I can tie my shoelace
I can comb my hair
I can wash my hands and face
And dry myself with care.

I can brush my teeth, too, And button up my frocks;
I can say 'How do you do?'
And put on both my socks.

(Anonymous)

Desirable outcomes for children's learning

Each of these eight learning links relate directly to the learning goals for children by the time they enter compulsory education (QCA, 1998). In other words, poetry and rhyme have an important part to play, not only in the ongoing development of children during their early years education, but also in the preparation of basic skills, concepts and knowledge upon which future learning can build. In doing so, the links also demonstrate that poetry and rhyme have many educational benefits for young children beyond the more obvious relationship with language and literacy.

Children's own literacies

It is sometimes very apparent that we adults are so busy imposing our own agendas on to children that we ignore the fact that they also have their own literacies. Solo talk and experimentation with language, fantasy talk during play, talk with their peers, the language of their favourite films and TV programmes, the language of their homes, communities and religions all contribute towards the total language experience of every child.

Children's own language can be used as a useful starting point for creating poetry and rhyme. Likewise, the multi-faceted world of popular culture and the media offer tremendous potential for creating language activities which have the additional benefits of using children's own literacy worlds. Such benefits include high motivation and interest levels. An increased sense of partnership between child and adult can also be engendered when the implicit message that the child's literacies are valued is an integral part of the work. Here are some examples of the types of activities which might start from children's literacies:

- copying the language of TV characters
- creating poems and songs for characters
- creating new lyrics to popular songs
- bringing in rhymes from home
- prayers and songs from religions
- community songs and slogans
- collecting family rhymes, poems and proverbs, especially from grandparents

In Chapter 10, Jackie Marsh discusses the possibilities of including popular culture and the media within the literacy curriculum more widely.

Rhyme and learning to read

During the past few years, much attention has been paid to the links between phonological awareness in pre-school children and their levels of achievements in learning to read and spell later on (Bradley and Bryant, 1985; Goswami, 1986, 1991). The way in which this awareness develops is usually attributed to their experience of nursery rhymes. In hearing, chanting and experimenting playfully with such rhymes, children start to recognise similarities in sound between words which have different meanings. It has been demonstrated that this prepares them well for learning about orthographic links between words once they begin the formal construction of linking phonemes to graphemes (Maclean, Bryant and Bradley, 1987).

Despite this crucial contribution which nursery rhymes can make to the development of literacy, the role of nursery rhymes and rhyming games has been regarded by many adults working in early years settings as social rather than linguistic. The majority of nursery teachers in a study at Birmingham University said that they included nursery rhymes in their curriculum to help children with participation and group skills (rather than to teach literacy). 'Preparation for reading in these classes was primarily concerned with visual skills such as left-to-right tracking and the discrimination of fine detail' (Layton and Upton, 1992, p. 34). In other words, poetry and rhyme were not being planned systematically into the nursery curriculum for the specific purpose of 'phonological training'. More recently, a strong oral tradition of playing with rhyme, onset and rime, and later making analogies from known sight words has flooded pre-school and primary education and become an established part of good practice in teaching language from 3 to 11.

There are two particularly important implications of the work of the so-called Rhyme Researchers:

1. Firstly, all children should be provided with oral and rhyming activities in order to secure an appropriate developmental framework for subsequent literacy learning.
2. Secondly, assessing children's phonological awareness through rhyme and alliteration on entry to nursery or reception classes, and periodically throughout the pre-school phase, can help teachers to identify children who need additional input. Indeed, a *resistance to developing rhyming skills* has been said to be an effective early indicator of later learning difficulties (Bradley and Bryant, 1985), which can help teachers to target children appropriately with early intervention.

However, it is also important to beware of the dangers of using such research evidence to justify de-contextualised rhyme activities, which have no apparent purpose or pleasure for the children. Indeed, in studies where early phonological interventions have *failed* to have an impact upon the later writing skills of children with earlier rhyming resistance (e.g. Layton and Upton, 1998) we perhaps need to consider the nature of intervention in relation to child development. Nursery rhymes have long been a natural part of early years curricula, and it is important to retain and develop best practice rather than imposing a 'potential take-over of the traditional nursery rhyme corpus by word-and-letter identification driven reading instruction' (Whitehead, 1993, p. 42). Similarly, merely chanting nursery rhymes is not enough to ensure secure foundations. Rather, it is the opportunities to explore, experiment, reflect upon and talk about the linguistic features which are developing an intellectual awareness and understanding (Lundberg, Frost and Peterson, 1988).

The resurgence of interest in traditional rhymes is, nevertheless, a positive change, in particular the return to a strong emphasis on the value and importance of oracy. However, we need to beware of allowing nursery rhymes to be reduced to cold linguistic tools at the expense of their rich contribution towards children's literature. The findings of the Rhyme Researchers should certainly be informing the practice of those who work with pre-school children, but they should not dominate the agenda. Playing with language is at the heart of what all poetry is about. As with most issues in education, a healthy balance should be struck! So let us turn now to looking at some of the fun which we can share with young children in relation to poetry and rhyme.

Playing with language

If children are to maintain contact with literature when they become adults it will only be because they enjoy it. Therefore, actively catering for children's enjoyment has to be one of our primary objectives when planning poetry activities. Sharing poetry with children does not always have to be teacher reading while children listen. It can be done in many different ways which maintain the fun whilst also providing appropriate teaching opportunities. The roles can be varied so that it is not always the teacher who is taking the lead, and there is much scope for changing other dynamics. Figure 3.2 gives some practical examples of how the roles might vary.

Of course this list isn't definitive, but it is intended to draw attention to the fact that sharing poetry with children can take many forms, and variety is the spice of life...

Sharing approach	Example
Teacher reads/recites. Children listen.	When introducing a new poem.
Teacher reads using a big book to focus on text.	When counting words (concepts of print).
Teacher reads/recites, accompanied by children.	When enjoying an old favourite.
Teacher reads, children fill in certain words or lines.	When focusing on certain characters' speech.
Teacher reads and deliberately misreads certain words for the children to correct.	When encouraging them to listen for rhyming sounds.
Individual child recites.	When focusing on dynamics (e.g. volume).
Children recite together, teacher listens	To foster a sense of control and ownership over the form.
Children reciting into a tape recorder.	To provide a focus for 'performance' and an audience. Putting the tape into the listening area gives a good message that their oral work is valued.
Visiting poet reads to the children.	During a Bookweek event.
Puppets to act out the poem, controlled by the children as the teacher reads/recites. (See Chapter 8 for more details on drama activities.)	To focus listening skills.
Poems with finger actions.	To assist concentration and understanding.

Figure 3.2. Different ways of sharing poetry with young children

Teaching points can be fun too!

If children are to become empowered users of language and literature, they need to develop an awareness of the potential and possibilities of playing with words. Such play is broadening their vocabulary and extending their language experiences which might then be transported into their own independent play. Here are some examples of some teaching points which can be planned into enjoyable activities.

- **The sounds of words:** making silly rhymes, adding sound effects to pictures (e.g. making sound effects of the sea).
- **The descriptive power of words:** young children are perfectly capa-

ble of exploring adjectives, simile and metaphor, although they need not learn the labels for these at this stage.

- **Rhythm:** exaggerating, or clapping the rhythms of poems, moving around the room in rhythms! This can also provide useful introductory work on syllables, helping to foster an early awareness of word construction.
- **Alliteration:** listening out for pairs or strings of words which begin with the same sound, then adding to the list.
- **Volume:** experimenting with the volume as you read or recite and drawing the children's attention to the effects of this – they will always want to try it for themselves!
- **Speed:** playing with the speed at which words are said can be hilarious for little children, and provides good experience of early segmentation skills and the awareness of the phonetic components of words.
- **Characterisation:** performing the 'voices' of different characters in different ways is great fun and helps to extend children's understanding of character whilst at the same time enabling them to explore the dynamics of voice.

Developing listening skills

Good listening is not just about sitting still and quietly. Indeed, some children can actually be miles away in a dream as they sit with such perceived perfection! Good listening results in:

- understanding
- memory
- response.

In early years poetry activities the first two are fairly self-explanatory. The third can include different things; for example, response might mean enjoyment or it might equally mean the expression of not enjoying something and explaining why. Equally, it could mean following an instruction, giving an opinion, solving a problem and so on. The observation of such responses can be a good way to assess the child's understanding, and, if there is a time lapse, memory. Understanding and memory can also be assessed through skilful questioning, and this is another important area for consideration when planning poetry and rhyme activities.

Questioning techniques

It is important to strike a fruitful balance between enjoying the poetry and learning about and from the poetry. Most readers will be famil- iar with the painful approaches to studying poetry which can turn learners off poetry, and prejudice them against it forever onwards. Such approaches turn poetry into a chore, where the questioning allows no time for reflection, creativity or pleasure. Very often, the problem is caused by the style and nature of the questioning Here are five simple guidelines to bear in mind when asking young children questions about poetry.

1. Be clear about why you are asking a question. For example, a closed question might test understanding, whereas a more open question might be encouraging problem-solving skills.
2. Don't interrupt the flow at first reading (this can interfere with the understanding of the whole); go back and read again with ques- tions interspersed.
3. Sometimes, ask the questions before you start the poem in order to focus the children's listening. These might be about word level fea- tures (e.g. 'Try to listen out for two words which sound like the wind'), or they might be about the meaning (e.g. 'At the end I want you to tell me which animal ate the most food at the picnic').
4. Make space for the children to ask questions.
5. Remember that sometimes you needn't ask questions at all!

Resources

It is important to provide many genres for the children, helping them to learn that poetry includes many forms. (Children who only ever hear rhyming couplets are likely to develop a limited awareness of poetry and the power of words.) There is a rich and varied range of anthologies available for early years teachers. Shape poems, theme poems, action poems, themed anthologies, humorous poems and col- lections of poetry from different cultures are all available in addition to the traditional collections of nursery rhymes. A list of particularly appealing anthologies is included at the end of this chapter. It is also important not to forget the embedded rhymes and rhythms within other examples of children's literature such as *Each Peach Pear Plum* (Ahlberg, 1989) and *Are You There, Bear?* (Maris, 1986).

Young children should have access to poetry books, even if they are not established independent readers. They are usually very keen to look again at a poem which has been read to them and enjoy the accompanying pictures. It has been widely argued that the illustrations in children's books have an important part to play in developing reading and response (e.g. Beard, 1987; Graham, 1990), and it has been shown that four-year-olds can make useful critical judgements about the styles of different artists in relation to the same nursery rhymes (Marriott, 1992).

Resources also come in the form of people, and visiting poets[1] can be a tremendous way to provide enjoyable poetry-in-action events for young children; for example, poets who dress as clowns, puppet show poets, and robot poets who perform to the children's command. Such visits not only offer the sheer entertainment and learning through the experience of poetry, but they also provide exciting writing role models for children. Poets talking about their work, showing their drafts, pointing to their own names on the covers of books, etc. are assisting in the wider process of developing concepts about literature and print.

Writing poetry

Poetry and rhyme can offer exciting and creative opportunities for the development of children's early writing skills. Fun, play and experimentation should again be the driving force of such activities, combined with the skilled structuring of explicit teaching. For example, whilst children are creating alliterative words and associated art work to describe rain and puddles ('splish', 'splosh', 'splash', etc.) they can be encouraged to repeat and chant the words, asked to say the beginning sounds, asked to say the ending sounds, shown the words in written form and asked to point to the letters which are the same and so on.

Here are some examples of early years poetry forms which can be fun to use with young children.

- **Word collage:** creating a visual collection of shapes, pictures and words on a theme. The aim should be to promote descriptive language orally, and then model the writing process by incorporating the language into a visual form, combining it with art work. These can be created in a variety of ways such as painting a background, cutting certain colours or pictures from magazines, writing or painting words, cutting out words, teacher scribing words for children to cut and stick. Popular themes might include such topics as fire, water, seasons, colours, weather and so on. They can be created in groups or by individuals.
- **Word pictures:** sometimes called Concrete Poetry, these are produced by creating a shape with the letters which links with the theme of the poem. There are good models around to show children. The genre can be quite sophisticated and complex, but with

younger children it can be a good way of getting them to experiment with the shapes of letters.

- **Class poems:** prioritising oral work and discussion, then scribing for the children, either on a flip chart, white board or monitor, can give status to their ideas, and again provides a good opportunity to model the writing process.
- **List poems:** these provide a tight structure for descriptive writing. They might be simply describing thematic objects (e.g. fruit) as follows:

An apple is shiny
A banana is . . .
A strawberry is . . .

It is easy to see how even this simple structure might be differentiated: for example, the list might just be about colour, or it could include two adjectives per fruit to describe the inner texture. The lists can be created in many different ways. For example, On Monday I . . ., On Tuesday I . . .

- **Songs and prayers:** children know songs well and love to make their own alternative lyrics by providing either single rhyming words or total verses.
- **Parody:** imitating other poems which they know well can be great fun.
- **Writing walls:** providing a display board covered with white paper and a variety of felt tip pens can offer a wonderfully tempting opportunity for children to write and experiment with making marks freely. Linking it with poetry might mean taking a theme (e.g. The Sea) and explaining that this is for ideas. Modelling by the teacher, plus stimulating pictures and artefacts will provide an additional aid. Referring to the board each day can be another way of endorsing the children's attempts and further modelling, ('"Sssssssss" lots of people have written the sound of the sea! Here and here and here . . .').
- **Writing area:** Of course, all good early years settings will have a writing area, with a tempting range of materials, computer, typewriter and so on. Modelling the poetry process will mean that children can use their time in the writing area to experiment. It can help this process to supply different sized paper, different coloured paper, different shaped paper, shapes drawn on the paper and so on. It is also important to provide audiences for children's work by reading it in the public domain, and to publish children's work (for example, anthologies).

A more detailed discussion on writing in the early years can be found in Chapter 6.

Poetry across and beyond the curriculum

Good early years education makes meaningful connections between subject areas through themes, rather than segmenting learning out into disjointed areas of content which, from the child's perspective, have no apparent context. This mirrors the way in which children learn most effectively, as we can see when we observe any young child exploring and learning independently. Poetry can play a part in this in three key ways:

- as an introductory stimulus to generate discussion or material for further work
- as an additional information resource during the work
- as an outcome or record of the work.

Figure 3.3 gives some examples of how poetry might be used in different curriculum areas.

Maths
Counting rhymes such as 'One, two, buckle my shoe' can be used as an introduction to counting and number recognition activities.

Science
'If you're happy and you know it clap your hands' can be used as a model for inventing new verses and actions about different parts of the body (e.g. scratch your nose, kiss your thumb, pull your hair, etc.)

Technology
Building and testing the strength of different sorts of walls for Humpty Dumpty.

Art
Relating colours to moods, painting patterns, and adding adjectives (e.g. experimenting with shades of red to show anger, teacher writes words suggested by the children to describe how they feel when they are angry).

Music
Playing accompanying percussion to a favourite nursery rhyme.

Geography
Making sand-tray models of the hill and home in Jack and Jill, then re-enacting the journey.

Social and moral development
Finding ways of helping a character in a poem who has a problem, e.g. the mouse in Hickory Dickory Dock who can't get enough sleep!

Dance
There is enormous potential for movement in many poems, particularly from more abstract themes (i.e. expressing the movement of the North Wind is more challenging than merely enacting a character walking).

Figure 3.3. Poetry across the curriculum

Conclusions

Poetry is embedded within many everyday traditions of our society. This spreads from and beyond the literary forms which are traditionally and academically regarded as 'poetry'. Acknowledging these multi-faceted forms and taking joy in their richness can help us as adults to generate enthusiasm for word play and crafting with young children. Rhyme activities also have an important part to play in the developing literacy skills of young children. Likewise, poetry can enhance social skills, physical development, critical thinking, musical skills and multi-cultural awareness, and can be used as an effective vehicle for the transmission of knowledge.

Such a useful and important part of early years education should be planned carefully and systematically into the continuous patterns of young children's learning, whilst at the same time appearing spontaneously or unexpectedly on appropriate occasions. Indeed, poetry and rhyme should be part of the very fabric of quality early years provision, in ways which complement children's interests and natural tendencies to play with, imitate and explore language. In enabling this to happen, we are assisting a process whereby more children will grow up to become adults who feel pleasure in, ownership of, and control over the power of language and literature.

Notes

1. For more information about how you can arrange a poet to visit your nursery or class, write to:

   The Poetry Society
   22 Betterton Street
   LONDON
   WC2H 9BU

   They can also provide a wealth of information about books, publishers, arts associations and events around the country.

Suggestions for further reading

Balaam, J. and Merrick, B. (1987) *Exploring Poetry 3–8*, Sheffield: NATE.
Ellis, S. (ed.) (1995) *Hands on Poetry: Using Poetry in the Classroom*, London: CLPE.

References

Ahlberg, A. (1989) *Each Peach Pear Plum*, London: Oliver & Boyd.
Beard, R. (1987) *Developing Reading 3–13*, London: Hodder & Stoughton.

Bradley, L. and Bryant, P. E (1985) *Children's Reading Problems*, Oxford: Blackwells.

Goswami, U. (1986) Children's use of analogy in learning to read: a developmental study, *Journal of Experimental Child Psychology*, Vol. 42, pp. 73–83.

Goswami, U. (1991) Learning about spelling sequences: the role of onsets and rimes in analogies in reading, *Child Development*, Vol. 62, pp. 1110–23.

Goswami, U. (1995) Phonological development and reading by analogy: what is analogy, and what is it not? *Journal of Research in Reading*, Vol. 18, no. 2, pp. 139–45.

Graham, J. (1990) *Pictures on the Page*, Chester: NATE.

Layton, L. and Upton, G. (1992) Phonological training and the pre-school child, *Education 3–13*, March, pp. 34–6.

Layton, L. and Upton, G. (1998) A pre-school training programme for children with poor phonological awareness: effects on reading and spelling, *Journal of Research in Reading*, Vol. 2, no. 1, pp. 36–52.

Lundberg, I., Frost, J. and Peterson, O. P. (1988) Effects of an intensive programme for stimulating phonological awareness in pre-school children, *Reading Research Quarterly*, Vol. 23, no. 3 pp. 262–82.

Maclean, M., Bryant, P. E. and Bradley, L. (1987) Rhymes, nursery rhymes and reading in early childhood, *Merrill-Palmer Quarterly*, Vol. 3, no, 3, pp. 255–81.

Maris, R. (1986) *Are You There, Bear?* London: Puffin.

Marriott, S. (1992) Reading pictures: children's responses to nursery rhymes, *Education 3–13*, October, pp. 39–44.

QCA (1998) *Desirable Outcomes for Children's Learning on Entering Compulsory Education*, London: HMSO.

Whitehead, M. (1993) Born again phonics and the nursery rhyme revival, *English in Education*, Vol. 27, no. 3, pp. 42–51.

Useful Poetry Books for Young Children

Agard, J. (1983) *I Din Do Nuttin*, Red Fox.

Agard, J. and Nichols, G. (1994) *A Caribbean Dozen*, Walker Books.

Benjamin, F. and Moxley, S. (1998) *Skip Across the Ocean*, Frances Lincoln.

Bennett, J. (1987) *Noisy Poems*, Oxford University Press.

Bennett, J. (ed.) (1993) *Early Years Poems and Rhymes*, Scholastic.

Bennett, J. (1995) *A Jumble of Clothes*, Corgi.

Cope, W. (1988) *Twiddle Your Thumbs – Hand Rhymes*, Faber and Faber.

Foster, J. (1991) *Snow Poems*, Oxford University Press.

Foster, J. (1991) *Dragon Poems*, Oxford University Press.

Foster, J. (1993) *Night Poems*, Oxford University Press.

Gardner, S. (1996) *Playtime Rhymes*, Orion.

Magee, W. (ed.) (1989) *Madtail, Miniwhale and Other Shape Poems*, Puffin.

Matterson, E. (ed.) (1991) *This Little Puffin*, Puffin.

Pace, D. (1996) *Shouting Sharon*, Frances Lincoln.

Rosen, M. (ed.) (1993) *Mini Beasts*, Puffin.

4

Signs and Symbols: Environmental Print

Elaine Hallet

Defining Literacy

Literacy is the ability and willingness to exercise mastery over
the processes used in contemporary society to encode, decode
and evaluate meanings conveyed by printed symbols.

(Wray, Bloom and Hall, 1989, p. 169)

This definition of literacy became particularly relevant during a study
visit to Japan. I was spending time in and around the Tokyo area visiting schools in order to observe their teaching of literacy. As a monolingual speaker, reader and writer of English, I was surrounded by
the printed symbols of a language I could not derive any meaning
from. I needed to make sense of the patterns, signs and symbols
around me in order to live (or even survive!) within the Japanese society in which I was a temporary resident.

My research involved visiting four schools in order to investigate
the teaching of literacy to primary aged children. I was travelling to
the schools by public transport. I had arranged for an interpreter to
meet me at each school to assist me during my visit. However, my
first task was to arrive at the school. At the simplest level, it was
important for me to read the train timetable in order to catch an
appropriate train to begin my journey to the school. I had to be able
to read the station sign at the end of my journey. I managed to complete several successful journeys to and from the schools in order to
carry out my research. How did I do this? I developed my own strategies to 'decode and evaluate meaning' from the print in the environment which surrounded me. One strategy I developed in order to
reach the final destination of my journey on the Tokyo underground
was to count the number of stations the train stopped at: one, two,
three, four, five . . . . I knew that I had to get off the train at the tenth

station which was Rippongi, my destination. I counted the stations repeatedly during several journeys until I was able to remember visually the pattern of black marks which comprised the station's name, so arriving safely.

This experience enabled me to develop an awareness of a young child's perception and understanding of her world. I had been placed in a similar position to that of a young child or an adult with limited literacy skills. They develop individual strategies for decoding the print around them in order to understand and live within their society, just as I had done. A baby is born into an environment in which she is surrounded by patterns, shapes, logos and symbols, all of which represent some aspect of the world in which she lives. Each child's understanding of her society develops as she grows and interacts with the environment and the adults and children within it. This 'social experience' enables a child to live in a 'literate society' (Wray, Bloom and Hall, 1989, p. 1) in which literacy is valued as an essential life skill. For children to become part of this literate culture, it is important for them to talk, read and write using the languages of the society in which they live. For some children, this may involve acquiring the language and literacy skills of more than one communication system. As Eithne Dodwell pointed out in Chapter 2, many children are competent in developing literacy skills in their community language as well as the predominant language of the society in which they reside.

Environmental print, then, is often the first contextualised and meaningful print which a child encounters. In the early stages, children recognise whole words which they see as a pattern or shape, not necessarily attending to the individual letters. This is known as the 'logographic phase' (Frith, 1985). There are a myriad of opportunities for developing children's logographic skills in the home, the outdoor environment and the early years setting. The next section considers the nature and range of environmental print.

Environmental print inside and outside the home

The environment which surrounds us comprises many forms and types of texts. Print is visible on everyday objects, signs we see, information we read. We see print on paper and on screen (through the use of Teletext and computers). This print helps us to function in everyday life. Through reading the print around us we are able to eat the correct food, travel on the accurate road to our destination, be aware of potential danger, turn the television on for our favourite programme, set the video to record a programme at the right time, read instructions in order to play a computer game, go to an appropriate shop for our shopping and pay the required price for our cinema, bus or train ticket. In the outside environment, it is possible to see advertisments, road signs, street names, forms, packaging, shop signs, car logos, bus, train and tram timetables, tickets, greeting cards, theatre and cinema information sheets, football programmes, fast food packaging – the list is endless! In a multilingual city, many of these signs will be in scripts other than English.

Thus environmental print is integral to our daily lives and plays a strong functional role within it. If we are confident in our literacy skills, we take for granted the countless transactions that enable us to complete our daily tasks.

There are many more everyday situations that provide opportunities for interaction with print such as a visit to: the baby clinic, the park, a relative or neighbour's home, a toy shop, a playground, a café, a bank, a post office, a cinema, a theatre, a museum, the seaside or the countryside. These encounters are crucial to children's developing awareness of the forms and purposes of print.

Moving from the outside environment to the inside, a child's home is a rich source of print for babies, toddlers and young children. As Leitcher (1984, in Hall, 1987) points out: 'Print does not merely reside in a household but rather flows through it' (Leitcher, 1984, p. 16). The home is a child's first exposure to the printed word and there are many potential sources for encounters with texts. Take a look around your own home and make a list of the printed matter, signs and symbols you can see. Figure 4.1 gives some examples of print which can be found in the home. You may like to add to the room lists.

This is not to suggest that all homes will contain this range of print. Inevitably, the types and amount of print will vary from family to family. However, all homes will contain some of these or similar items, however small a number, and so the commonly held deficit model of a home that is 'print-free' is simply not feasible in today's society.

A child is surrounded by this richness of print and absorbs it as her literacy development is beginning. Children need to be given a daily diet of environmental print experiences and opportunities to engage in. We underestimate the potential the environment provides for such literacy learning experiences. In order to gain an understanding of what the possibilities are, take a look at a fictional child, Claire, and her 'environmental print day'. The outline has been devised in order to demonstrate the potential for encountering print within and outside the home. Imagine that Claire is four years old and attends nursery.

Claire's environmental print day

Claire gets up and draws her curtains which have letters of the alphabet on. As she looks out of her window, she notices the paperboy walking down the street carrying a bright orange bag with the word 'News' written on it. She wonders if her older brother Craig will be reading the newspaper already. Claire goes downstairs to have her breakfast. Yes, Craig is reading the newspaper. There are some big black letters on the front page and a picture: 'Princess Diana'. It must say this as there is a picture of Princess Diana next to it. On her plate, there is a postcard from her Granny. Her mum reads the word 'Blackpool' on the front. She then reads the message on the postcard. Evidently it is raining in Blackpool, but her Grandad has managed to paddle in the sea. 'What cereal do you want, Claire? Come and choose,' her Mum says.

Claire looks at the four packets on the breakfast table. She recognises the bright yellow cereal packet with a blue 'W' for 'Weetabix' and chooses this. As she puts one Weetabix into her bowl, she notices a red token on the side of the packet and asks her Mum to cut it out as she is collecting them for a 'Weetabix Monster'. She needs three more in order to send for the monster. She drinks her milk from her favourite cup that has a 'C' for Claire printed on the side. Claire can see other things in the kitchen that begin with the 'c' in her name: carrots, candle, a can of beans and Candy their cat.

After finishing her drink, she goes upstairs to get ready for her morning at the nursery. Claire brushes her teeth using a new tube of 'Colgate' toothpaste. It's got a 'c' in it, just like her name. 'What shall I wear today?' she asks herself. Claire looks in her wardrobe and sees her blue jumper which her granny knitted for her. It has a picture and the name of 'Tinky Winky', her favourite Teletubby, on it. Granny had sewn her name into the back collar so she could read it and know which way to put it on. Claire puts on her new shoes. They have a bright white 'tick' on them which shines in the dark and they leave a pattern and the word 'Nike' in wet sand. Claire picks up her book bag containing the book *Spot's Birthday Party* (which she shared with her Mum last night) safely tucked inside. She will be able to borrow another one from the nursery library today. Her book bag has a house drawn on it with children playing around it and the words 'Nursery House' written on the door. It is just like the nursery where she is going for the morning.

The short journey to nursery on the bus is quite busy. Claire knows she is going the right way as she recognises some shop, street and road signs along the way: 'Daniel's the Hairdresser' (where she has

The kitchen

Recipe books
Calendar
Symbols and logos on kitchen appliances
Written and pictorial labels on food packages
Sticky labels on fruit
Written and pictorial labels on washing powder packages
Cooking instructions on food cans and packages
Numbers, letters and symbols on the dials on the cooker, microwave, fridge, washing machine
Note to the milkman
Written shopping list
Till receipt from the supermarket
Advertising leaflets
Bills
Family noticeboard with items pinned to it, e.g. dentist and doctor appointment cards, letters from school, takeaway menus, advertisement leaflets
Words on storage jars – 'Tea' 'Sugar' 'Coffee'
Children's pictures and writing stuck onto the fridge
Words and messages on mugs
Magnetic letters and fridge magnets (words and logos) on the fridge
Plastic carrier bags, advertising shops
Money
Cheque book

The sitting room or lounge

Television
Newspapers
Magazines
Books
Comics
Catalogues
Radio and TV Times
Telephone directory
Address book
Message pad and pencil by the telephone
Birthday cards
Letters
Forms
Knitting pattern
DIY leaflet
Written words, symbols and numbers on the electric or gas fire

The bathroom

Words on soap and toiletries
Words on towels, flannel and bath mat
Foam letters for bath play
Waterproof book for bath play
Words, symbols and numbers on taps and shower

Figure 4.1. Print around the home

A child's bedroom

Comics
Books
Magazines
Catalogues
Postcards
Posters
Story tapes
Words and symbols on bedding (quilt and pillow case) and curtains
Toys and game packages and their contents
Clothing
Footwear
Computer
Television
Tape recorder

Figure 4.1. Cont.

her hair cut), the letters 'BP' in bright yellow shows her the petrol station where cars are filled up with petrol, the sign 'Time and Plaice' with the smiling fish is where her Mum buys fish and chips for tea and 'Sally's Sweet Shop' is where Claire goes to spend her pocket money on sweets. The black, white and red sign showing a parent and a child tells her that she is near 'Nursery House' and the sign tells drivers to drive carefully as there are children around. As Claire walks up the drive she can read the sign on the front door: 'Welcome'.

Claire and her Mum go inside. She finds her coat peg to hang her coat. It has got a picture of a brown and white dog and the word 'Claire' underneath. Claire shows her Mum her painting on the wall. Claire had told Tracey (the nursery nurse) about it and she had written underneath 'Claire with her cat Candy'. Claire now reads this to her Mum. There are many messages and words for Claire to read in the nursery. These tell her where things belong and tell her what to do. In the toilets, a sign reminds her to 'Wash your hands'; in the painting area a sign tells her to 'Hang your apron up here'; above the Book Corner a big sign invites her to 'Come and read a book'; her name written on a label stuck onto a milk bottle shows Claire which is her bottle to drink at Snack Time. The menu by the door tells her that her snack today is an apple. In the Home Corner, there is lots to read (comics, newspapers, catalogues, recipe books) and lots to write on (a pad by the telephone, a calendar, a diary, paper and envelopes to write letters on). Claire joins in all the activities during the morning. She enjoys going outside with Tracey to look at the cars in the car park and examine the number plates on them. Tracey points out that some of the black marks are numbers and some are letters. Inside the nursery, Tracey reads her group the story of *Mrs Wishy Washy* from a big book. Claire is able to read the story and she joins in with the noises: 'wishy, washy, wishy, washy', when the animals are washed. Claire chooses the story of *The Gingerbread Man* to take home from the nursery library as it has farm animals in like those in *Mrs Wishy Washy*.

The morning session is soon over and Mum comes to take her home. On the journey home, they stop at the newsagents. Mum buys a magazine for herself and a 'Postman Pat' comic for Claire. Claire asks for a tube of 'Smarties' as she likes to find the hidden letter inside the lid. What letter will it be? A look on the lid reveals the letter 'r'.

Claire's afternoon is spent doing several activities. She reads her comic, plays with words, numbers, shapes and colours on her 'Talking Computer' and sings along to the songs on her 'Nursery Rhyme Time' video. On children's television, she enjoys watching the story of *Kipper* who goes with his friend Tiger camping. At tea time, Claire has great fun playing with the spaghetti letters on her plate. She finds a 'c' for cat and 'm' for Mum. At bath time, Claire makes her name on the side of the bath by throwing the wet sponge letters onto the bath side. Once dry, she snuggles down under her quilt which is covered with letters and numbers. She remembers the activity at nursery and looks for some numbers in and amongst the alphabet letters on her quilt, finding a '5', '3' and '7'. Her Mum comes in to read her a story. Claire chooses *The Gingerbread Man* which she borrowed from her nursery library. Before she drops off to sleep, she has joined in the rhyme, 'Run, run as fast as you can, you can't catch me, I'm the Gingerbread Man!' several times.

Claire has had a busy day and has been surrounded by letters, words, logos, signs and pictures. She has listened, watched and played with them, learning about her world and the part literacy plays in communicating meaning to her. It must be stressed that children would not normally have access to all of these experiences. The picture presented here is deliberately extreme in order to demonstrate the potential that the environment has for surrounding children with print and texts. However, all children will have some opportunity to interact with print in their everyday life.

Environmental print within an early years setting

Bruce (1997) points out that the child, the knowledge and the environment are key elements within an early childhood curriculum. Every child consolidates his or her skills, knowledge and understanding through the interaction of these three elements. In recent years, there has been much more of a focus on the kind of environment needed for literacy learning within an early years setting. In the last fifteen years, the work of Hall (1987), Hannon (1995), Goodman (1980) and others has helped us to recognise the knowledge and skills that children bring with them to nursery and school. As we have seen, the acquisition of literacy is developmental and begins early in life. The early years setting needs to build on the experiences children have before coming to school and provide an environment which stimulates further meaningful interactions with print. Barratt-Pugh (1997) describes the environment in a family day care centre:

> In the Day Care Centre, we see children learning about literacy through their use of print around the building. They are learning that print can be used to give and organise information, give instructions, denote ownership, send messages, depict a song, tell a story and recount an event. They are learning that print is meaningful and that it serves many different purposes; they are beginning to recognise the functions of print. Much of the environmental print in the family centre is contextualised in that meaning can be derived from the surrounding context. For example, photographs of each child's family members, accompanied by a written caption and each person's name, helps the children to make connections between the pictures and the writing.
>
> (Barratt-Pugh, 1997, p. 62)

As this example suggests, having print around the early years setting is not enough; such print needs to be contextualised. Hall (1988) describes three conditions necessary for the creation of a curriculum which supports emergent literacy in the nursery school:

- Children must have access to a literate environment
- Children must have access to literate adults
- Children must have opportunities to practise literacy

(Hall, 1988, p. 16)

Research suggests that children begin to make meaning from the print through the context in which the text occurs and that they initially read using environmental clues and visual patterns, not attending to the actual structures of words (Frith, 1985). Thus the context in which literacy activities are provided within an early years curriculum is important. As Nigel Hall points out in Chapter 8, role play can be an excellent means of providing meaningful contexts for print. Structured play situations such as a dentist, hospital, café, home, shop, post office and so on, in which socio-dramatic play takes place as children take on different roles, enable children to take part in literacy activities which mirror the functional uses of print in society. Language from the outside environment can be effectively used within a play area. Environmental print taken directly from the children's local community can be used within the play setting to give play meaning and purpose. Children can collect the print themselves. For example, they can gather forms from the post office, menus from cafés, catalogues from DIY, gardening, electrical, toy and clothes shops and use them in their play area so that they are involved in recreating the environment they see and experience within their own nursery or classroom.

In addition to using environmental print within a role play area, there are many other opportunities for extending children's interaction with the texts that surround them. Figure 4.2 gives some examples of the ways in which nurseries and schools in the Sheffield area have created this rich world of literacy experiences.[1]

It is not enough, however, simply to provide these experiences; adults must also interact with children in order to extend their learning and enable them to fully access the print which surrounds them. The final section of the chapter outlines ways in which adults may successfully do this.

The adult's role in promoting environmental print

Babies and young children learn about literacy through the literacy encounters in their everyday lives, particularly when there is active engagement with someone more skilled than themselves. They are, in these early stages, forging the 'roots of literacy' (Hannon, Weinberger and Nutbrown, 1991, p. 5). Adults facilitate young children's understanding of the literacy process by talking, listening to and extending their responses and interactions. Babies and young children interact with a range of adults: parents and carers, childminders, nursery nurses, health visitors, crèche workers, playgroup leaders and workers, babysitters, relatives, neighbours and community workers. All these adults have a role to play in children's language and literacy development.

A child's first interaction with a supportive adult is with their parent or parents. Research over the last two decades by Newson and Newson (1977), Brice-Heath (1983), Davie, Butler and Goldstein (1992), Hannon (1995) and Weinberger (1996) indicates that parents and families are 'powerful influences on children's literacy development' (Nutbrown and Hannon, 1997, p. 8).

Payton (1984) observed and recorded in detail her daughter's literacy development before starting school. She found that her daughter,

Word walk	This involves parents and carers and their children collecting words and print from the local environment. The adult encourages each child to look for words and to collect print, e.g. sweet wrappers, crisp packets, bus tickets. (Health and safety must be considered.) The walk can be taken around the school, in the school grounds or in a specific local area such as the shops. The word walk can be structured or unstructured, as appropriate to the age and needs of the children. Some suggestions are to: • walk around the nursery, school or classroom and see how many words you can collect • collect a word beginning with the sound a, b, r, ch, sh, etc. • collect the following – a road name, a shop name, a message, a logo. The words collected can be recorded by the children using a clipboard and pencil/pen, the collection can then be talked about, categorised, developed and displayed in the early years setting. Photographs of the walk can be taken in order to make a book of the event.
Alphabet book/ display/sound table	The world a child lives in is full of children's culture (cartoons, comics, sweet logos, clothing labels, fast food packaging). The children read this print as part of their everyday lives. This is a rich print source to use in the nursery or classroom. Children can be asked to bring in pieces of print they are familiar with, e.g. sweet and food wrappers. These can be used in a display about food or on the sound table which focuses on a particular sound or placed in a scrapbook – h for Hula Hoops, k for Kit Kat, m for Mickey Mouse, Milky Bar, McDonalds, p for Polo Mints, as suggested by Ann Ketch (1991).
Newspaper letters, words and sounds	Newspapers and magazines are a source for many different styles of print. Children are asked to look through them collecting a sound (e.g. th) or a letter (e.g. h) or a word (e.g. the) which the child cuts out and glues onto a piece of paper or highlights using a highlighter pen. This helps to develop phonemic and word recognition.
Print journeys	This involves spotting and recording print that can be seen on a journey from the top of a bus, from a train or a tram, e.g. shop signs, road names, road signs, litter bins, school sign, traffic signs, pedestrian crossing, advertising hoardings.
Shopping for print	A visit to a shop where a range of logos, packaging and advertising is found. These can be collected or drawn and copied so that the print, text, logos, adverts can be recreated in art and technology sessions, e.g. designing and making food, washing powder packages, advertising signs to be used in the play area.

Figure 4.2. Using environmental print in an early years setting

A print picnic	A picnic is held to celebrate print. An invitation to the picnic is written first, a written reply allows a child to attend. Children are asked to wear clothes with print or words on. The food that is eaten is made of letters or has writing and words on, e.g. alphabet spaghetti, cakes and buns with a message (child's name) written on, the tablecloth and napkins have the alphabet written on, pass the parcel is played, the forfeit has to be read, word games like junior scrabble, word snap, hangman, magnetic letters are played. The going home party bag is full of reading and writing activities, e.g. a crossword book, a word search, a story book, a comic, a notepad and pencil to write with.
Literacy packs	These are literacy-related activities in waterproof folders which parents and carers can borrow to use with their child at home. They can include environ-mental print. A **shopping pack** could include: • a handwritten shopping list • a photograph of shops and their name signs • a catalogue • a purchase receipt • non-fiction information book about different types of shops • a story about shopping, e.g. *The Shopping Basket* by John Burningham • Notes for parents about how to use the resources with their child. A **writing pack** could include: • forms • a notebook • an old diary • an old calendar • paper of different colours, sizes and shapes • envelopes • pens and pencils • a story about writing, e.g. *The Jolly Postman* by Janet Ahlberg • Notes for parents with suggestions of how a child can use the pack and other writing-related activities.
Print games	• 'I see' – a game similar to 'I Spy' where the focus is signs or letters in the environment. It can be played at Group Time in the nursery or by parents on a car journey. • Matching and Snap game – logos from cereal packets, etc. can be cut out and glued onto card and used as a recognition game. • Track game – a board game where a child stops on a space and picks up a card which could have a sweet wrapper stuck onto it or a photograph of some environmental print, e.g. road or name sign. The child needs to read the print in order to continue the game.
Posters and labels	Adults and children can make posters which make use of familiar signs and logos. Cutting out the letters in a child's name out of the large print found on boxes can produce a name label for a child's bedroom.
Number plates	In the early stages it is difficult for children to distin-guish between numbers and letters as they can both look like a black pattern to a child. By looking at parked car number plates an adult can talk about the

Figure 4.2.   Cont.

Number plates cont.	concept of what a number is and what a letter is and the difference in a pattern. The child can then copy the numbers and letters onto a clipboard if they wish to.
Environmental print day	This focuses on household print within the home and how it can be used for literacy development by parents. Parents and children can be asked to bring examples of print from their home into the nursery or classroom. Print-related activities are set up for parents to use with their children. Nursery staff are able to share how everyday household products can be used in early literacy development.
Outside play	Environmental print is incorporated within the playing environment, children can make signs and labels to use in their play, e.g. number plates for the bikes, trikes and pedal cars, a petrol pump with the price and a numbered dial, road signs and markings on the ground and at the side of the road, bus stop sign, road name sign, shop signs.
Sand	Plastic letters (upper and lower case) and packaging can be used in the sand to make words. An adult can talk about the letters and the words as the children play.
Water	Empty plastic packaging could be used in the water tray and used to stimulate discussion about print. Sponge letters floating in the bath or in a water tub can be played with and made into words.
Magnetic letters	These sticky letters can be used to copy words seen in the environment, e.g. a logo, a sign in the classroom.
Writing table	A table supplied with a range of resources, e.g. paper, envelopes, greeting cards, notebooks, pencils, pens, etc. will enable the children to express their knowledge of print as a form of communication. Using environmental print in the area can provide a stimulus for children, e.g. forms to fill in.
Role play	Literacy materials can be incorporated into all role play areas so that children can use print in a relevant and purposeful form of communication, e.g. forms in the post office, a menu in a café, appointment book in a doctor's surgery, a recipe book, calendar, notepad and pen in a home corner.
Interest reading workshop	This is a time when parents can work with their child with reading activities on a one-to-one basis. The reading materials can be developed around a specific interest of a child, e.g. football, ice hockey, swimming, bugs, snakes, Disney characters. Reading material which includes non-fiction and environmental print, e.g. football programmes, cinema tickets, maps, comics, nature magazines, catalogues can be used for reading and writing activities. This can be useful to help reluctant readers.

Figure 4.2.   Cont.

Community photographs	A collection of photographs showing print and the community languages of the local area can be taken, e.g. road names, shop fronts, door numbers, doctor's surgery, takeaway shop, school sign; these can all be used with children to stimulate discussion and to help them recognise that print is important and tells them about their community.
Jigsaws	Photographs, postcards, carrier bags, leaflets, etc. can be collected, cut up and made into jigsaws for the children to complete. They will enjoy trying to recognise the logos.
Community links	This is a planned visit to a local supermarket, shop or factory in which the staff talk with the children about the store or factory and how they use print to package, store, advertise and sell their products. The supermarket, shop or factory can be recreated in the school or nursery by the children. The supermarket, shop or factory's staff can then visit the children's shop or factory to buy goods.
Storysacks	A Storysack is a large cloth bag containing a good quality young child's fiction book with supporting materials to stimulate reading. To bring the books to life, soft toys of the main characters, artefacts relating to items in the story, a non-fiction book relating to the fiction theme, an audio tape and a language game based upon the book are included. Environmental print such as a menu, a recipe, tickets, signs, bus timetable, letters could be included in the sack when appropriate to develop the story. A card is included with suggestions for parents to develop listening, reading and writing skills using the contents of the Storysack.

Figure 4.2. Cont.

Cecilia, had been actively involved with the printed word long before she was able to read the print. In evaluating her role as a parent, Payton found that the contextual talk and conversation she provided helped her child to use her cognitive processes and gain meaning of the print around her. Payton analyses the processes which enabled Cecilia to gain meaning from environmental print:

Cecilia has been immersed in an environment full of print (labels on clothes, grocery items, shop signs, street names, etc.) similar to the way in which she has been open to the influence of oral language from infancy. Print is passive, there to be noticed or not. That it is eventually perceived is incontrovertible. The following incident shows Cecilia's achievement and understanding. She and I were queuing at the checkout in the supermarket and as I emptied the contents of the basket onto the counter, Cecilia indicated the writing on the price ticket and correctly remarked, 'That says Co-op'. As far as it was known, Cecilia had neither previously asked nor been told the word, it appeared to be genuine inference. In many typical everyday conversations it was the day's shopping requirements, where they were to be purchased, how the journey should be made and so forth, which provided contextual information. It is argued therefore that it is these exchanges which prepared and created the necessary climate for the comment to be made, in similar manner to the way in which sense had been constructed in oral situations before. Here also the child hypothesised, analysed and finally formulated a proposal.

(Payton, 1984, pp. 27–8)

Once children arrive at an early years setting, they need to be greeted by adults who will continue this role of facilitating children's learning and extending children's encounters with print. Parents and early years workers need to knit together their separate contributions and

Supplying	Providing experiences, opportunities and resources inside and outside the home and early years setting that will enable children to interact with environmental print.
Supporting	Valuing children's literacy learning, whether it is a spoken comment about a sign or a letter or their mark-making on a piece of paper. Helping children to interact with environmental print by asking questions about its meaning. Intervening to extend their learning where appropriate.
Scaffolding	Helping children to achieve tasks that they may not yet be able to do on their own, e.g. read the signs around them. Talking with children about the signs and symbols they see. Asking questions and commenting about the print around them so that children start noticing the print and use the context to make meaning of the printed matter around them.
Sharing	Sharing photographs, books, etc. which feature environmental print. Sharing experiences of print in the environment, e.g. talking to children about interesting signs they have seen in the street and so on.
Showing	Providing a role model for children. Demonstrating ways of using environmental print, e.g. 'Look, this sign tells me that I should wash my hands now . . .'. Showing the importance of using the print around us to fulfil particular tasks, e.g. reading recipes when cooking.
Saying	Praising children's efforts to gain meaning from the print around them.
Seeing	Observing children's development closely in order to plan effectively for their future development. What print are they noticing in the early years setting/outside? How can we build on that?

Figure 4.3. Roles of the adult in developing children's engagement with environmental print

value the ways in which each party approaches the task of educating young children.

There are a number of models available which attempt to provide a framework for adults' involvement in children's development (Nutbrown and Hannon, 1997). In Chapter 12 of this volume, Mary Brailsford, Diane Hetherington and Evelyn Abram introduce a model of adult support in literacy development which is based on seven s's. The adult is seen to have a number of roles: supplying, supporting, scaffolding, sharing, showing, saying, seeing. The table in Figure 4.3 adapts their model in order to suggest how the adult can support children's engagement with environmental print.

Conclusion

It is clear that we live in a society in which the nature of printed text is changing rapidly (Kress, 1997). As we approach the twenty-first century, we are becoming increasingly more sophisticated in our understanding of printed and tele-visual texts and environmental print is becoming steadily more important in our lives. Early years settings need to ensure that they reflect these changes and are responsive to the range of texts that children encounter in their everyday environment. Providing experiences with texts that children recognise and are familiar with can help them to feel comfortable and confident in their literacy practices. Environmental print provides an important means of bridging the gap between home and nursery or school experiences.

Note

1. Thanks to the staff and the children in the following nurseries, schools and projects in which the literacy activities outlined here were developed:

   Ballifield Nursery First and Middle School, Sheffield
   Halfway Infant School, Sheffield
   Sharrow Nursery and Infant School, Sheffield
   The REAL Project (Raising Early Literacy Achievement), a joint project between Sheffield University and Sheffield Local Education Authority
   The National Storysack Project (Basic Skills Agency).

Suggestions for further reading

Hall, N. (1987) *The Emergence of Literacy*, London: Hodder & Stoughton.
Hall, N. and Robinson, A. (1995) *Exploring Writing and Play in the Early Years*, London: David Fulton.

Nutbrown, C. and Hannon, P. (eds.) (1997) *Preparing for Early Literacy Education with Parents*, Nottingham: REAL Project/NES Arnold.

References

Barratt-Pugh, C. (1997) Why says 'Happy New Year', Learning to be Literate, Reading and Writing with Young Children, in L. Abbott and H. Maylett (eds.) Working with Under-3s: Responding to Children's Needs, Buckingham: Open University Press.

Brice-Heath, S. (1983) *Ways with Words: Language, Life and Work in Communities and Classrooms*, Cambridge University Press.

Bruce, T. (1997) *Early Childhood Education*, 2nd edition, London: Hodder & Stoughton.

Davie, R., Butler, N. and Goldstein, H. (1992) *From Birth to Seven: A Report of the National Child Development Study*, London: Longman/National Children's Bureau.

Frith, U. (1985) Developmental Dyslexia, in K. E. Patterson *et al.* (eds.) *Surface Dyslexia*, Hove: Lawrence Erlbaum Associates.

Goodman, Y. (1980) The roots of literacy, *Claremont Reading Conference Yearbook*, Vol. 44, pp. 1–32.

Hall, N.(1987) *The Emergence of Literacy*, London: Hodder & Stoughton.

Hall, N. (1988) Write from the start, *Child Education*, April.

Hannon, P. (1995) *Literacy, Home and School: Research and Practice in Teaching Literacy with Parents*, London: Falmer Press.

Hannon, P., Weinberger, J. and Nutbrown, C. (1991) A study of work with parents to promote early literacy development, *Research Papers in Education*, Vol. 6, no. 2, pp. 77–97.

Ketch, A. (1991) Delicious Alphabet, *English in Education*, Vol. 25, no. 1, pp. 1–4.

Kress, G. (1997) *Before Writing*, London: Routledge.

Newson, J. and Newson, E. (1977) *Perspectives on School at Seven Years Old*, London: Allen and Unwin.

Nutbrown, C. and Hannon, P. (eds.) (1997) *Preparing for Early Literacy Education with Parents*, Nottingham: REAL Project/NES Arnold.

Payton, S. (1984) Developing awareness of print: a young child's first steps towards literacy, *Educational Review*, no. 2, University of Birmingham.

Weinberger, J. (1996) *Literacy Goes to School*, London: Paul Chapman.

Wray, D., Bloom, W. and Hall, N. (1989) *Literacy in Action*, London: Falmer Press.

5

Early Reading Development

Guy Merchant

Understanding the complexities of learning to read is as important to early years practitioners as it is to their colleagues working at Key Stages One and Two. As we shall see, a substantial amount of literacy learning takes place before children begin their compulsory schooling. This chapter explores how reading develops and how those working in under-fives settings can support young children in the early stages. It begins by looking at the reading process, first by providing an overview of practice and research in early reading and then by examining the kinds of understanding and skills that form the foundations of literacy. This leads on to a consideration of the reading experience and how this can be structured to provide meaningful learning in young children. Here I will emphasise the value of introducing young learners to a wide range of texts and outline how key skills and understanding can be developed. I conclude by looking at the importance of story in the early years.

Changing perspectives – from reading readiness to emergent literacy

It is now widely acknowledged that children growing up in our print-rich society begin their literacy learning well before the start of formal schooling. Researchers and writers have shown how babies and toddlers interact with print and begin to display literate behaviour at a very early age (Bissex, 1980; Butler, 1988; Crago and Crago, 1983; Wade and Moore, 1996). To build on this learning, early years workers now recognise and value those understandings about literacy that are established at home and in the child's primary social networks.

Our thoughts about educational practice and early reading have evolved considerably over the last half-century. Learning to read, once associated with the onset of compulsory schooling, begins with young children's early experience of print. Current thinking has encouraged us to re-evaluate our definition of what reading actually is, as well as the ways in which early learning in literacy can be developed.

Previously, the teaching of reading was seen as an essential act of formal learning, strictly controlled by the qualified professional in the school setting. Characteristically, this was associated with structured reading tasks like developing alphabetic knowledge and memorising 'sight' vocabulary. This kind of instruction coincided with entry to school. Although current practice still emphasises the importance of formal teaching and learning (The National Literacy Strategy: DfEE, 1998) it places it in the wider context of literacy development.

The traditional view suggested that success in early reading is built on well-established pre-reading behaviours. So, importance was given to visual and aural discrimination in determining 'reading readiness'. An influential text for teachers suggested that a 'child must be mentally and physically ready for reading, and emotionally settled at school' (Dean, 1968, p. 45). It was also claimed that children should have developed a 'fair vocabulary' before learning to read. Although precisely what constituted a 'fair' vocabulary or an acceptable level of language development for beginning reading remained problematic. Even motor skills were seen as an ingredient in reading readiness, since 'handling books requires fairly fine muscle control' (Dean, 1968, p. 45).

The idea of reading readiness was loosely based on a model of psychological development that claimed that children could not or would not learn to read successfully until certain prerequisite skills were established. Further, it was suggested that these skills were governed by a process of maturation, and that adult intervention could not speed up that process (Moyle, 1976). Children's early experiences of literacy were overlooked in the enthusiasm to identify the mental and physical prerequisites for the successful learning of decoding skills.

The influential work of Smith (1971) and Goodman (in Gollasch, 1982) drew professional attention to the idea of reading as an active search for meaning. Although meaning-based approaches are not without their critics (for example, Beard, 1993), for those working with the under-fives they draw attention to the importance of early encounters with print and with the distinctive features of written language as children learn how texts, words and letters can convey meaning. This broader conception of reading encouraged professionals to give more value to the richness of experience and knowledge about literacy that children have gained before they begin formal schooling. The work of Brice-Heath (1983) and Hall (1987) in studying pre-school 'literacy events' have helped us to reframe our definition of what constitutes early literacy. Summarising this new way of thinking, Stierer *et al.* (1993) assert that young children:

have spent a lot of time studying literacy-based elements in their environment and observing people using literacy, and ... they will have put some powerful effort into unravelling the phenomena of reading and writing.

(Stierer *et al.*, 1993, p. 5)

So, we no longer need to define literacy simply in terms of the formal instruction of decoding skills. Instead we can consider how we build concepts about print and meaning, about the use of different kinds of texts and how we can develop 'readerly' behaviour – children's first steps in becoming members of the community of readers. This developmental model of reading and writing is known as 'emergent literacy' (Hall, 1987; Clay, 1991). For a definition of emergent literacy we refer to Riley (1996) who suggests that it is:

concerned with the earliest phase of understanding about print that enables the child to generate hypotheses about the nature of reading and writing.

(Riley, 1996, p. 89)

Ideas about emergent literacy have helped adults working in the early years to move towards a clearer conception of their role than that suggested by the advocates of reading readiness. The importance of pre-school literacy events, the need for adults to model the processes of reading and writing, and the significance of drawing on children's early experience of print, underpin work with the under-fives. Adults are active participants in emergent literacy rather than passive observers of maturational processes.

What we know about the reading process

For most of us, the skills of reading have become so well learnt that they seem routine and automatic. In fact it is quite hard for adults to explain how they read. As with driving a car or using key strokes and mouse-clicks on a computer, it is only when you try to instruct others that you realise how habitual the activities have become. This sort of learning is very useful since it allows our attention to focus on distinct yet related functions. When we have routine control of stopping, starting, gear changes and steering, we can give our full attention to the flow of traffic or find our way through an unfamiliar city. Similarly in reading, our ability to recognise words rapidly and automatically allows us to pay attention to the construction of meaning in unfamiliar texts.

Current theory and research suggest that skilled readers are active in their search for meaning (Stanovich, 1980), and that they depend upon rapid whole word recognition, fixating on each word in turn as they read continuous text (Just and Carpenter, 1985). Skilled readers are also familiar with different kinds of texts, the purposes they fulfil and the different kinds of reading that they entail. So they will not be looking for evocative prose, and lengthy sentences with carefully chosen descriptive adjectives in the handbook for the microwave oven; nor will they expect that reading the latest best-seller will help them in assembling flat-packed furniture. The skilled reader has quite specific expectations of texts and uses a variety of reading skills appropriately. Reading, then, is a highly complex process that involves orchestrating skills and knowledge at a number of different levels. So, how do young children develop these skills and gain access to the community of readers?

Research and theory about learning to read has generated much heated debate and our attempts to turn ideas into practice have often resulted in an over-simplified view of reading (Wray, 1994). Advocates of meaning-based approaches (Smith, 1971; Gollasch, 1982) have been criticised by those who favour a more structured, skills-based approach (Beard, 1993, McGuiness, 1998). This debate has generated contrasting models of the reading process. These are commonly described as either 'top-down' or 'bottom-up'. 'Top-down' approaches emphasise the prime importance of making meaning – dealing with the larger units of context and understanding before addressing reading at sentence level, then focusing on words and lastly individual letters. In contrast, 'bottom-up' approaches begin with the smallest units of language, building up from individual letters, to whole words, sentences and so on to finally arrive at meaning.

More recent work suggests that this is a rather artificial distinction. Skilled readers, as we have seen, operate rapidly and flexibly at a variety of different levels. So, for instance, they may not depend heavily on the 'sounds' that letters represent, but use this knowledge when they need to (in using dictionary and reference skills or when reading car number plates). Skilled reading is typified by the rapid deployment of appropriate strategies. It follows that learning to read must be concerned with practising and perfecting these strategies in the pursuit of gaining meaning from text. Young children should be introduced to all the aspects and levels of the reading process. In other words, they should be introduced to the function and meaning of the printed word as well as to the formal technicalities of reading.

So far we have talked in a rather general way about the knowledge and skills involved in reading. We now go on to explore five aspects of learning to read that are of central importance to those working with young children in the early years. It is important at this point to re-state the fundamental principle that reading is about the active construction of meaning. As we focus on distinct areas of reading we need to bear in mind how these are taught within a context of meaningful literacy activity. The five areas are: literacy awareness, syntactic awareness, word recognition, phonological awareness and orthographic awareness.

The first area, **literacy awareness**, is concerned with the young child's understanding and experience of print – in other words, the sorts of knowledge about the written word that are a central part of emergent literacy (see above). Important learning about the place of literacy in our society is derived from the child's everyday experience. We live in a world that is rich in print. From an early age, many children will have learnt how familiar logos and slogans appear on the packaging of their favourite food or drink, or how the curves and lines of particular letters represent their own name. They will have seen text on page and screen and have some knowledge of how their parents or other adults make use of print at work or in leisure time. In the early years we build on this knowledge by using and discussing the print environment both inside and outside the classroom. Taking children on a 'print walk' provides an opportunity to draw attention to different kinds of signs and notices and the messages they convey, as Elaine Hallet suggests in Chapter 4. You will also be able to draw children's attention to a variety of scripts, some of which may represent different languages. The kind of talking about literacy that we generate through these kind of activities is central to children's early development.

An important aspect of literacy awareness is the development of concepts about print (Clay, 1985). Clay uses this term to describe children's knowledge of the conventions of print and written text. So this includes understanding where to begin to read a book, the directional concepts of top-to-bottom and left-to-right that are used in the sequential reading of a printed page, as well as specific concepts such as 'word' and 'letter'. It is worth acknowledging that children's concepts about print will vary according to the nature of their early experiences. Bilingual children may well be familiar with print that adopts different conventions of directionality such as texts which are read from right to left (for example, Arabic or Urdu). In a similar way, home environments in which children witness regular use of specific kinds of texts such as reference material or on-screen print are likely to promote different kinds of literacy awareness.

Understanding and experience of literacy will help young children to:

- understand the functions of different kinds of text (e.g. labelling, giving directions or providing entertainment)
- understand that print communicates meaning
- understand how print corresponds to spoken language and the ways in which we can talk about text
- distinguish print from pictures and other visual symbols
- understand the concept of directionality in text (whether on page or screen)
- be aware of the differences in directionality in different written languages
- be aware of the left-to-right directionality in English
- know some of the language of reading (for example, front, back, line, word, space, letter, etc.).

The second area of early reading is **syntactic awareness** or knowledge of grammatical structure. This is not about 'naming the parts' (as in the study of grammar as a topic in its own right), but about becoming familiar with the patterning and sequence of language. Although this awareness is part and parcel of oral language development, it also extends beyond it. Children will begin to be introduced to the distinctive patterning of written language often through the repetition of phrases and sentences in their favourite stories. They will get to know about 'the voice' associated with the written form and the grammatical 'completeness' that characterises the more formal language structures of most written text.

The third area of early reading is **word recognition**. Through early encounters with print, young children will learn that certain combinations of letters are used to represent familiar words. Developing out of the kinds of understanding outlined above they will begin to recognise the printed form of their own name, the title of a favourite story or the brand name of their breakfast cereal. Although this sort of awareness should be encouraged, the emergence of early word recognition does not suggest that children should immediately be moved to learning lists of key words. Research seems to suggest that at this stage children are recognising words as visual shapes rather than as combinations of letters. So, in experimental conditions where researchers have altered the style of the script, the alignment or the letter spacing of words they have found that young children can no longer recognise familiar words. Frith (1985) uses the term logographic reading to describe this attention to visual patterning as opposed to letter patterning. Logographic reading, then, is an important aspect of emergent literacy, but should not be mistaken for the kind of word recognition that skilled readers engage in.

We now turn our attention to the area of **phonological awareness**. Phonological awareness can be described as knowledge about the sound structures of the language and how words can be broken down into or built up from individual units of sound (or phonemes). Research has shown how an ability to rhyme, alliterate and identify syllables in words is influential in later reading success (Bryant and Bradley, 1985; Goswami and Bryant, 1990). For most beginning readers, phonological awareness provides a good foundation on which to build later work on sound–symbol correspondence – or what most of us still describe as 'phonics teaching'. So, using nursery rhymes, enjoying and repeating alliterative phrases, playing I Spy and enjoying clapping games are not only commonplace elements of good early years practice, they are actually vital in the early stages of reading.

The final area of early reading is **orthographic awareness**. Orthographic awareness is defined as knowledge about the writing system and how letters and letter strings are used to represent words. Various studies have demonstrated how an awareness of orthographic patterning is important in beginning reading. Recent work by Riley (1996) suggests that an ability to identify and label letters of the alphabet at entry to school is a good predictor of early reading success. Building on young children's experience of the print environment is a useful starting point here. Collecting and classifying words and letters from magazines, advertisements and food packaging can be used to develop early orthographic understanding. Learning from the 'M' of McDonald's or the 'K' of Kellogg's as well as from the letters of children's own names can become an interesting way of introducing the letters of the alphabet.

These five areas of early reading will be developed on transition to Reception classes. Here, teachers following the guidance of the National Literacy Strategy (DfEE, 1998) will be carefully planning their work in order to build on children's emergent literacy. In most cases this will involve identifying learning objectives at text level (comprehension and composition), sentence level (grammar and punctuation) and word level (phonics, spelling and vocabulary). Figure 5.1 shows how the five areas of early reading development feed into this work.

Developing early reading – the reading experience

Successful work with the under-fives will be based on an understanding of early literacy experience and the five areas of the reading process I have outlined above. It will also take into account how progression in this learning feeds into the structures of the formal cur-

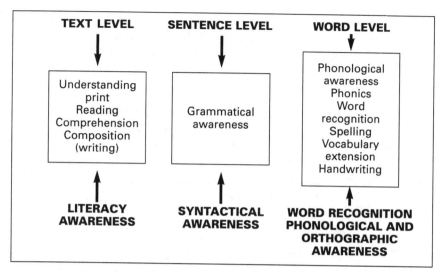

Figure 5.1. Mapping the 5 areas of early reading on to the 3 levels of the National Literacy Strategy

riculum at Key Stage One. Learning experiences that involve interaction with meaningful and appropriate texts are the most important starting point. Here I begin by looking at working with text, and then show how the five aspects of reading can be developed through specific activities. The section concludes with a specific focus on the role of story in early years education.

Working from text

The benefits of an early introduction to print in books is well documented (Butler, 1988). Research work by Wade and Moore (1996) looks at how introducing books to young babies has long-lasting benefits that can be traced through entrance to nursery and later on in school performance. Good books for the very young encourage enjoyment and interaction through a rich interplay between visual and print features. Advances in book technology have built on the fascination with novelty, prediction and surprise as children are encouraged to interact with books by turning wheels, lifting flaps, and examining cutouts or pop-ups. For the very young, there are an increasing number of 'indestructible books' on the market – made out of cloth, board and synthetic materials. Books for the young can also appeal as simple but memorable stories, sometimes referring to the shared experiences of young children (for example, meal times, having a bath, etc.) and sometimes introducing them to the imaginative realm. At this stage they will also experience the intimacy of sharing a book with an adult, a friend or sibling as well as learning about the physical characteristics of books and how to handle them. In short they will learn that books are valuable, useful and enjoyable. Whitehead (1996) draws our attention to the ways in which early encounters with books form the foundation for the development of concepts about print:

> Babies and older toddlers respond to pictures and to print in books in a variety of ways; at first with eye-gaze, smiles, gurgles and squeals, scratching at the paper, pointing and bouncing with enthusiasm. Eventually this develops into naming, joining in with the words, turning the pages and initiating real discussions about character, motives and plots, as well as linguistic talk about letters, sounds and the conventions of print.
>
> (Whitehead, 1996, p. 66)

A lot of this early learning takes place in the context of the home. In order to recognise and build on such learning, strong, professional relationships with parents and care-givers are essential. Continuity of experience between home and school is important. Establishing a good relationship in the early years is a strong foundation for the home–school partnership as it develops. The growing recognition of the importance of this partnership in the development of literacy is well documented (see Hannon, 1995). Chapter 11 in this volume provides an overview of this area.

Enriching children's experience of text will mean introducing them to new kinds of books and talking about them. Under-fives settings need to be resourced with a broad range of good quality book materials. These will need to be updated regularly and stored in such a way that they are readily accessible to children. Book provision needs to include different kinds of texts (fiction, non-fiction, poetry and rhyme) as well as different formats. In choosing books we need to bear in mind the interests of the children we are working with as well as the ways in which print and illustration construct positive role models of different groups in society.

Experience of text in book form will be complemented by an introduction to a broader range of work on print. Developing the understandings that print carries meaning must take into account the fact that these meanings relate to social practices. So as well as book-based work, attention can be given to signs, labels and notices. Literacy within the child's experience may include food and toy packaging, advertisements and catalogues, train tickets, football results, magazines or comics. This sort of variety of text should be part of the print environment of the nursery and children should be encouraged to talk about and compare different kinds of print.

Attention should also be given to providing an inviting and stimulating environment for looking at books. Many rooms will be arranged so that there is a quiet, comfortable area that provides an attractive environment for reading. This will need to be changed from time to time so that children's interest in visiting the area is maintained. Display will be an important aspect of creating this environment. It may be decorated with children's work, or show images of children and adults enjoying books. When using images of people reading, try to include pictures of friends and adults that the children know. Those responsible for the reading area will also want to ensure that pictures of readers do not give the impression that reading is a female activity or excludes particular social or ethnic groups.

Favourite books will also be featured in the reading area alongside different kinds of print and examples of writing in different languages. The area might also include simple books made by individuals or groups of children or photograph albums with simple captions that record everyday events or special occasions. Another aspect of provision will be ICT materials. Audio tapes with listening centres may be provided and where possible children should have access to computer-based text. As well as a reading area, the nursery or playgroup should make good use of all opportunities to create a print-rich environment. Role play areas can provide many good opportunities for spontaneous literacy activity (see Chapter 7). They may reflect elements of a story that has been read and include props that will allow for the acting out of various roles and key events. Alternatively, they can draw on children's experience of popular culture (Marsh, Payne and Atkinson, 1997) or social settings such as shops, cafés or opticians. In this sort of imaginative play, it is important to provide the resources that encourage print-related activity.

Although the physical environment is important, it is no substitute for sharing text through talking and reading. Young children should have plenty of opportunities to see adults (including their own parents) involved in reading, but there will also be more formal occasions on which adults read aloud to children and engage them in talk about a specific text. On such occasions, adults will be reading to children from a range of different texts, modelling the sorts of reading behaviour they use as well as how they construct the meaning of the text as a whole. They may use large format books (big books) which allow for discussion of specific features of a shared text. In these sessions adults will be building on children's understandings about literacy and drawing children's attention to illustration and print. They may also focus on specific features, such as repeated words or phrases or individual letters. At this stage they will be familiarising

children with the technical language for talking about print (for example, page, line, word, space, letter). In the context of this sort of work
on text children will be encouraged to recognise 'some familiar words
. . . [and] . . . letters of the alphabet by sound and shape' (QCA, 1998,
p. 3).

Developing the five aspects of reading

Working from texts will provide specific opportunities for developing the five aspects of early reading referred to above. Although these
opportunities may arise quite spontaneously in our work, there are
other times when specific activities should be carefully planned. This
section gives an overview of the kinds of activities that form an essential part of good early years practice in literacy.

The kind of approach that has been outlined provides plenty of
scope for the development of **literacy awareness**. As well as listening
to stories and rhymes, revisiting their favourites and beginning to join
in and respond to these readings, young children should be introduced to print in different forms. This may involve talking about the
written word on posters, leaflets, in catalogues or on packaging.
Collections and displays of these kinds of texts will involve children
in actively looking at print in the environment and discussions will
begin to introduce the terminology of literacy (concepts about print)
– picture, symbol, word, letter and so on. In working with print, children will be encouraged to point to words as they are read, so that
they can see the one-to-one correspondence between printed word
and spoken word. They can also be introduced to large print on the
computer screen in a similar way. With continuous text, such as an
enlarged nursery rhyme, pointing to each word in turn will demonstrate the left-to-right orientation of printed English and the 'return
sweep' that takes the reader from the end of one line to the beginning of the next. Here the adult may use prompting questions such
as:

- Where do I start to read this rhyme?
- Which word should I point at to begin?
- Where do I read next? (after the end of a line)

Developing **syntactic awareness** will be achieved through focusing
on the patterning and sequence of written language. Clark (1988)
shows how young children become familiar with the language of
books through revisiting favourite texts. She recorded children in a
nursery school as they retold these stories. Her observations show
how they have learnt to handle books and understand that 'book lan-

guage does not vary with retelling' (Clark, 1988). More importantly for our discussion here, her observations show how young children begin to use vocabulary and grammatical features that are associated with the written form and that in doing this they use a 'special voice'. To promote this sort of learning we will need to make sure that children have a rich diet of reading material and that favourite titles are available in the story corner, so that children can consolidate their learning about the language of books. As we shall see in the following section, books with a predictable, patterned structure are particularly supportive in this context.

In their reading and re-reading of texts, adults will want to draw children's attention to grammatical structure. One way of doing this is to deliberately omit a word as you are reading and ask for suggestions, for example, 'Jack and Jill went up the hill to . . . a pail of water'. A bell or chime may be used to help focus children's attention on the missing word. A more sophisticated approach to this game is to use a Post-it or mask to cover the missing word on an enlarged text or big book. You may claim that you don't know the hidden word and ask children to agree on one that 'fits' or 'makes sense'.

Encouraging early **word recognition** should build on children's interest in the printed word. It is important to re-state that it is not, at this stage, about learning to recognise specific key words out of context through flash cards or other methods. The essential learning is that a commonly occurring word has a familiar shape in print. Using labels of children's names to indicate the activities that they are involved in is an example of this. It has a real function in terms of organisation and encourages word recognition. Talking about children's favourite food, films or toys can lead to collecting and displaying posters, advertisements and packaging to draw attention to common words. Parents can become actively involved in this sort of work, which can be an excellent way of introducing talk about print at home and in the nursery. Simple word recognition can also take place in the context of shared reading. For example, matching word cards will help children to recognise the names of characters in the stories they read.

The use of rhyme, song and poetry has particular significance in the development of **phonological awareness**. Here we are helping children to identify the sound patterns or phonology of the English language. In the early stages, it is important to focus on the beginning sounds of words (consonant onsets), words that sound similar because they rhyme and the division of longer words into syllables. Activities that concentrate on identifying and reproducing these sound patterns are important. We are not concerned at this stage with matching spoken sounds to letters of the alphabet. Listening for pairs of words that rhyme – for example, in the counting rhyme *One Smiling Grandma* (Linden, 1996) – and talking about the alliteration in this and other rhymes is an important starting point. Collections of objects that begin with the same initial sound will be useful to establish. Young children will also be keen to play games like I Spy, particularly where the game focuses on objects in the immediate environment. Alliteration (words that begin with the same sound) can be discussed by using published rhymes or those composed in the nursery setting. Using children's names to create alliterative phrases is always an enjoyable activity (for example, 'Sam sitting still' or 'Rihana running round'). Songs for young children, clapping and skipping rhymes also help to show how words can be broken down into syllables. Again, these should be a regular feature of the early years curriculum.

Research suggests that children who can label the letters of the alphabet on entry to school are likely to make good progress in early reading (Riley, 1996). **Orthographic awareness** will be developed by talking about the visual features of print. The terminology of letter, sound and spelling can easily be introduced to the under-fives. Children working with alphabet tiles and magnetic letters will be slowly and systematically introduced to the alphabet and the most common sounds that the letters represent. They will be shown alphabet books and may be involved in producing their own as an individual or collaborative task. Alphabet friezes and simple matching games will be used to develop orthographic awareness, and children will be encouraged to focus their attention on letters as they experiment in their own writing.

The power of story

The work of Meek (1988) has been particularly influential in drawing our attention to the role that narrative texts play in supporting young readers. Godwin and Perkins (1998) detail the ways in which story influences personal, linguistic and conceptual development, but here we restrict ourselves to the relationship between story and early reading development.

As well as being an important and enjoyable social experience, story introduces young children to carefully chosen vocabulary, distinctive patterns of language and predictable narrative events. So, for example, the language patterning and illustration of *Brown Bear, Brown Bear What Do You See?* (Martin, 1995) helps children to predict the text to a high degree of accuracy without depending on word-level decoding. In addition to this, the question and answer format of the written text helps children to draw on implicit grammatical understanding (syntactic awareness). In a similar way, the repetitive language of a traditional story like *The Gingerbread Man* is simply structured and is punctuated with the chorus of 'You can't catch me, I'm the gingerbread man!' which is easily committed to memory. This helps young children to model the reading process as they revisit this story either with an adult or on their own.

The list-like formula that characterises stories like *A Dark, Dark Tale* (Brown, 1981) or *Bringing the Rain to Kapiti Plain* (Aardema, 1981) is also a useful device which encourages children to join in when they are read aloud and supports children's early attempts at independent reading. Another popular device is the use of rhyme which again aids prediction and supports recall as well as building on children's developing phonological awareness. Much of the work of the Ahlbergs makes use of rhyme and humour in ways that support the young reader (for example, *Peepo!*, Ahlberg and Ahlberg, 1985).

Under-fives will enjoy a rich diet of stories. Regular story sessions can be used to introduce children to new stories and to revisit old favourites. As Browne suggests,

> At story time, the teacher's enthusiasm for books is transmitted to children. The teacher is modelling how to read, the way words tell the story, the function of illustrations, and the movement of text across and down the page.
>
> (Browne, 1998, p. 29)

Other adults and even older children can sometimes be encouraged to read aloud or talk about what they enjoy reading. This sort of experience can be enriched if you are able to involve someone who speaks a community language and can introduce children to stories from another culture in another language. Work of this kind is important for all children growing up in a multi-cultural society but will be particularly important for children who speak the same language as the storyteller.

Story sessions can be followed up with a variety of kinds of activity. It is important to encourage children to respond to what has been read to them. Through the questions children ask both during and after the story we are able to monitor and extend their understanding; not simply of the story itself but of the ideas, issues and concepts that it suggests. In doing this we are establishing the practice of talking about reading which, as Aidan Chambers observes, is helping children 'to be articulate about the rest of their lives' (Chambers, 1993, p. 10). On other occasions the adult may provide a model for this sort of oral response by giving her own comments on the story and asking for children's views. This should not be seen as a mechanical exercise in assessing children's comprehension but more as an open-ended discussion arising from the reading.

It is also useful to think about other ways of responding to stories. Painting, printing and modelling are exciting ways to develop work on favourite characters. Through dressing-up and role play children can re-enact and adapt the stories they have heard. Story can also be used to give form and purpose to table-top play, as well as small and large construction activities.

It is important to ensure that books that have been read aloud are accessible to children so that they can revisit them in their own time and at their own pace. Versions of the story on audio tape are a useful resource to collect. Recent work on 'Storysacks', in which a book is accompanied by games, relevant objects and soft toys, has been particularly successful in involving parents in early reading activity.

We can see, then, how story draws on children's literacy awareness as well as their developing syntactic, phonological and orthographic understanding and supports their early attempts at constructing meaning from the printed word.

Conclusion

Adults working with children in the early years have a vital contribution to make to the development of early reading. By creating a supportive environment for early literacy learning, by establishing good links with parents and care-givers and by direct teaching they can help to lay the foundations for later success. Effective practice will:

- build on children's early literacy experience at home
- recognise the importance of the child's immediate print environment
- broaden children's experience of the range and function of different kinds of texts
- introduce children to good quality story and rhyme on a regular basis
- ensure that reading is seen as active meaning-making
- encourage children to enjoy the printed word
- develop children's literacy awareness, word recognition, syntactic, phonological and orthographic awareness
- recognise the importance of play in rehearsing and consolidating literacy learning.

Above all, the importance of the adult's responsibility to value the

child's early literacy learning and to extend this by creating a stimulating print environment must not be underestimated, for it is at this
key point in a child's life that fundamental attitudes and understandings are established. This is an exciting challenge which, if met
with enthusiasm, can provide both child and teacher with opportunities for meaningful interactions in the classroom.

Suggestions for further reading

Adams, M. J. (1990) *Beginning to Read*, Massachusetts: MIT Press.
Godwin, D. and Perkins, M. (1998) *Teaching Language and Literacy in the Early Years*, London: David Fulton
Whitehead, M. (1997) *Language and Literacy in the Early Years*, 2nd edition, London: Paul Chapman.

References

Beard, R. (ed.) (1993) *Teaching Literacy: Balancing Perspectives*, London: Hodder & Stoughton.
Bissex, G. L. (1980) *Gnys at Wrk: A Child Learns to Read and Write*, Harvard: Harvard University Press.
Brice-Heath, S. (1983) *Ways with Words: Language, Life and Work in Communities and Classrooms*, Cambridge University Press.
Browne, A. (1998) Enjoying books in the early years, *The Primary English Magazine*, Vol. 3, no. 4, April, pp. 29–31.
Bryant, P. and Bradley, L. (1985) *Children's Reading Problems*, Oxford: Blackwell.
Butler, D. (1988) *Babies Need Books*, Harmondsworth: Penguin.
Chambers, A. (1993) *Tell Me: Children, Reading and Talk*, Stroud: Thimble Press.
Clark, M. M. (1988) *Young Literacy Learners – How We Can Help Them*, Leamington Spa: Scholastic.
Clay, M. M. (1991) *Becoming Literate: The Construction of Inner Control*, London: Heinemann.
Clay, M. M. (1985) *The Early Detection of Reading Difficulties: A Diagnostic Survey with Recovery Procedures*, 3rd edition, Portsmouth: Heinemann.
Crago, M. and Crago, H. (1983) *Prelude to Literacy*, Illinois: Illinois University Press.
Dean, J. (1968) *Reading, Writing and Talking*, London: A & C Black.
DfEE (1998) *The National Literacy Strategy*, London: HMSO.
Frith, U. (1985) Beneath the surface of developmental dyslexia, in K. E. Patterson, M. Coltheart and J. Marshall (eds.) *Surface Dyslexia*, London: Lawrence Erlbaum Associates.
Godwin, D. and Perkins, M. (1998) *Teaching Language and Literacy in the Early Years*, London: David Fulton.
Gollasch, F. V. (ed.) (1982) *The Selected Writings of Kenneth S. Goodman*, London: Routledge and Kegan Paul.

Goswami, U. and Bryant, P. (1990) *Phonological Skills and Learning to Read*, Hove: Lawrence Erlbaum.

Hall, N. (1987) *The Emergence of Literacy*, Sevenoaks: Edward Arnold.

Hannon, P. (1995) *Literacy, Home and School: Research and Practice in Teaching Literacy with Parents*, London: Falmer Press.

Just, M. and Carpenter, P. (1985) *The Psychology of Reading and Language Comprehension*, Newton, MA: Allyn and Bacon.

McGuiness, D. *Why Children Can't Read*, Harmondsworth: Penguin.

Marsh, J., Payne, L. and Atkinson, S. (1997) Batman and Batwoman go to school, *The Primary English Magazine*, Vol. 5, no. 2, pp. 8–11.

Meek, M. (1988) *How Texts Teach What Readers Learn*, Stroud: Thimble Press.

Moyle, D. (1976) *The Teaching of Reading*, 4th edition, London: Ward Lock.

Riley J. (1996) The ability to label letters of the alphabet at school entry: a discussion of its value, *Journal of Research in Reading*, Vol. 19, no. 2, pp. 87–101.

QCA (1998) *Desirable Outcomes for Children's Learning on Entering Compulsory Education*, London: HMSO.

Smith, F. (1971) *Understanding Reading: A Psycholinguistic Analysis of Reading and Learning to Read*, London: Hodder & Stoughton.

Stanovich, K. (1980) Towards an interactive-compensatory model of individual differences in the development of reading fluency, *Reading Research Quarterly*, Vol. 16, no. 1, pp. 32–71.

Stierer, B., Devereux, J., Gifford, S., Laycock, E. and Yerbury, J. (1993) *Profiling, Recording and Observing: A Resource Pack for the Early Years*, London: Routledge.

Wade, B. and Moore, M. (1996) Home activities: the advent of literacy, *European Early Childhood Education Research Journal*, Vol. 4, no. 2, pp. 63–76.

Whitehead, M. (1996) *The Development of Language and Literacy*, London: Hodder & Stoughton.

Wray, D. (1994) Reviewing the reading debate, in D. Wray and J. Medwell (eds.) *Teaching Primary English: The State of the Art*, London: Routledge.

Children's literature referred to in the text

Aardema, V. (1981) *Bringing the Rain to Kapiti Plain*, London: Macmillan Children's Books.

Ahlberg, J. and Ahlberg, A. (1985) *Peepo!* Harmondsworth: Puffin Books, Penguin.

Brown, R. (1981) *A Dark, Dark Tale*, London: Andersen Press.

Linden, A. M. (1996) *One Smiling Grandma*, London: Mammoth.

Martin, B. (1995) *Brown Bear, Brown Bear, What Do You See?* Harmondsworth: Puffin Books, Penguin.

6

Developing Writing

Ann Browne

About writing

What writing is for

Writing is an act of communication and can convey a variety of messages in many different ways. It can be used to establish contact with others, give information, persuade, entertain and exchange ideas. At times writing may be used to conduct an internal dialogue or record information rather than to communicate with others. Writing things down can help to clarify and organise one's thoughts and make sense of experiences (Kress, 1997).

Types of writing

Britton (1972) suggested that there are three main types of writing which each have different functions. These are expressive, transactional and poetic. Expressive writing is personal and most closely resembles speech. It is used to express the writer's thoughts, feelings and experiences in a relatively unstructured way and it is found in diaries, letters to friends and jottings. Transactional writing is used to 'get things done'. It is used to give instructions, persuade, advise, record, report and inform and is generally impersonal. Poetic writing is valued for its artistic merit including the form, style and choice of vocabulary It is carefully composed and crafted since it is often used to entertain and interest others.

Young children's spontaneous, early writing is usually in the expressive mode. They often use writing to represent something that is significant to them. They may attempt to write their names, use writing to identify family members or label important possessions. They use writing to convey something about themselves and their experiences. Young children may tell adults that their writing 'is about my dog' and a little later, when they read back what they have written, demonstrate how they are using writing to communicate personal information such as, 'I like playing with my dog'. Teachers of very young children capitalise on these personal written communications and children's understanding of the connection between speech and writing by encouraging children to use writing to tell them about their favourite toys, to describe their holidays and to write their news. This kind of writing exploits the relationship between speech and writing by showing that what is said can be written down and draws attention to the communicative purpose of writing, both of which are helpful to children who are just beginning to find out what writing is for and how it can be represented.

Young children are likely to be aware of transactional writing from the print they have seen in their homes and communities. They will have seen information conveyed through shop and street signs and print on packaging. They will also have observed adults reading instructions and making lists. Early years teachers are expected to introduce children to transactional writing through a writing programme which includes opportunities for children to learn how to write factual texts. The most obvious form of information texts that very young children see and write in nursery and school are labels and notices such as, 'The Book Area', or 'Three children can play in the sand'. From this, children can gradually be introduced to more complex, extended non-fiction writing including recipes, information books and instructions.

The function of poetic or literary writing is to entertain through giving careful attention to the vocabulary, style and structure of the writing. Examples include stories, poems, plays, songs, rhymes and riddles. One of the starting points for developing poetic writing is through oral storytelling. This can be based on personal experience. When we talk, we often share experiences with others in story form. 'Last Tuesday, just as I was going out, the telephone rang and. . .' is the beginning of a story, even though it is an account of a real event. Children are familiar with this way of using language from their own oral experiences. However, stories in books are not just anecdotes in story form or talk written down. They are usually third person, fictional narratives which have been composed and crafted with care in order to entertain others. They are carefully organised and come to a satisfying conclusion. Children's ability to tell good stories and use poetic language can be developed by sharing and discussing books with them, giving them opportunities to compose stories using puppets and small world equipment and developing their delight in language through singing and saying songs and rhymes.

What is involved in writing

The act of writing involves three important elements: composition, transcription and review. All writing passes through these three stages at least once. Simple writing, such as a telephone message, is given some thought (composition), is written (transcription) and is quickly read through to make sure that it is clear (review). More significant writing, such as a letter to a newspaper, may go through each stage several times. As composition, transcription and review represent the process of writing that all writers use, it is important that children are given the time to explore each of these aspects.

Composition involves making decisions about the content of writing. There are two parts to this. First, generating ideas about what one wants to write and second, selecting the ideas that will be used. Composition is not just about writing; it is also about thinking. It begins with understanding what is to be written, to whom and in what way. Teachers need to help children understand that writers consider what they write and can change and delete what is written.

Transcription is the process of converting what has been composed into marks on the page. It is dependent on composition since the way in which some aspects of transcription are used depends on the content of what is written and the audience and purpose for the writing. Transcription includes spelling, handwriting, punctuation, grammar and layout. It is a time-consuming part of writing and can be difficult for young writers. They need to learn a great deal about writing before they can transcribe accurately. They need to know how to form twenty-six upper and lower case letters, how to combine these to create words and how to arrange writing on the page. Children want and can write before they have control of the writing system and adults should encourage them to do so. As they become more aware of writing and receive guidance about writing, their transcription skills will develop. Focusing too much on transcription deflects attention away from composition and may damage children's enthusiasm for writing.

Very little writing is perfect after a first draft because writing what one intends in the best possible way is difficult. Reviewing usually involves changing aspects of composition and transcription in order to improve what has been written. Introducing young children to this last part of the process of writing is often neglected in the early years. Teachers are often reluctant to ask children to re-read and alter their writing. They may think that, because children have put a great deal of effort into composing and transcribing, asking them to alter what they have written could be tedious and deflating. This is true and so not every piece of writing needs to be revised. However, if children have spent time and taken care with a piece of writing there is good reason for them to review what has been produced. Encouraging children to re-read what they have written and discuss their writing indicates to them that what they have done is important and affords the child the opportunity to enjoy and take pride in what has been written.

The conditions for writing

All writing takes place in a context. It is undertaken for a reason, with an audience and outcome in mind. It is then composed and decisions are made about content, structure, style and vocabulary. It is transcribed and attention is given to spelling, punctuation and handwriting and finally it is reviewed. Purpose, audience and outcome have an important effect on what is written and how it is written.

Purpose describes the author's reason for undertaking a piece of writing. In the world outside nursery and school this will generally coincide with one of the many functions of writing but, in the classroom, there may be a difference. This is because at school many writing activities are initiated by the teacher and children write because they have been asked to rather than because they have an important personal reason for doing so. Whenever possible, children need to engage in writing activities that have a purpose that they recognise as relevant. They need to be involved in writing that explores the different uses of writing.

Since writing is a communicative activity, what is written has both an author and an audience. Before beginning to write, authors need to know not only why they are writing but also who will read their writing. We write for ourselves, family members, friends and people who are unknown to us. The tenor of the relationship between authors and audiences can be friendly, hostile, intimate, correct, cautious or polite. Knowing about audience affects what is written, how it is presented, the time that is spent on it and the choice of writing implement. When writing to an unknown audience, or formally to a known audience, writers may take a great deal of care to organise the content, present information clearly, ensure that the writing is legible and that words are used accurately and spelt correctly. Children need to experience as wide a range of audiences as possible in order to learn how to write in different ways and to suit their writing to the situation and the reader.

Outcome means what happens to writing when it is finished. It is linked to why the writing was undertaken and who it was intended for. Writing can be read by others, replied to, kept as something worth re-reading at a later date or used as a starting point for a talk or a discussion. It can also be thrown away once it has served its purpose. Making this clear to children can help them to realise that writing does not always have to be undertaken with trepidation. The apparent permanence of writing can lead to anxieties that curtail risk-taking and experiment and lead to the 'getting it right first time' syndrome. Experimenting with writing on pieces of paper rather than practising writing in exercise books makes it easier to display, share what has been written with others or discard what is not wanted.

Early writing development

At one time it was common to see children being prepared for writing through *pre-writing* activities such as tracing and copying handwriting patterns and words, using chunky crayons and large pencils. These were intended to introduce children to the writing system, letters and directionality, and to develop the motor skills needed to control writing implements. Pre-writing was followed by set writing tasks. These usually began with children being asked to draw a picture. The content of the picture was then explained to the teacher who wrote down what was said and the children then copied or traced over the words (Beard, 1984). Practices such as these emphasised correct letter formation and spelling and often neglected to widen children's understanding of the uses of writing. They reflected the belief that children have to be taught and then practise transcription skills before they can begin to write independently.

It is now accepted that even very young children know a great deal about writing and that they can and do produce unaided writing that demonstrates their understanding of the system and the function of writing (Clay, 1975; Ferreiro and Teberosky, 1983; National Writing Project, 1990). Children learn through their experiences, experiments and observations. From the earliest stages, all children gain some experience of writing through seeing those around them producing and using writing. As children see others write and as they notice examples of writing in their environment, they often begin to experiment with producing marks that are intended to represent writing. They try out the patterns of writing initially because it seems to be a satisfying activity (Dyson, 1983) and then later they begin to attribute meaning to their marks. These child-initiated experiments with writing are now recognised as an early stage of learning to write. As children produce more writing and notice writing more their own writing shows an increasing resemblance to that produced by mature writers.

Their early attempts at writing reveal how they learn to manipulate the principles of the writing system which are fundamental to becoming a writer (Clay, 1975).

The very earliest signs of writing development are seen when children begin to make marks on objects. They may do this even before they are able to hold and manipulate a writing implement. The satisfaction children demonstrate from leaving a mark on furniture or walls, and their embryonic awareness that such marks are enduring indications of their actions, may be their first lesson about writing (Whitehead, 1996). More intentional marks, such as very early attempts at drawing, help children to realise that objects or experiences can be represented by symbols (Kress, 1997). Writing uses a set of symbols to represent something other than itself. To use and read writing, it is necessary to be aware that writing stands for something meaningful. Through their early experiments with making rudimentary marks on a variety of surfaces, children may be learning about the permanence of writing and how symbols can be used to stand for things, people and events. Later, when they begin to talk about what their writing says, they are demonstrating their awareness that writing represents meaning.

The writing that young children produce, that might once have been dismissed as scribble, is now seen as an important first step in the development of literacy. The examples of writing that follow show how much young children know about writing. They reveal children's awareness of some of the organising principles of writing and show how independent practice and exposure to writing enables children to refine their experiments and produce writing that gradually approximates to conventional models.

Children's earliest writing often contains shapes that are repeated. These may look like letters but can also take the form of joined-up scribble. Writing in this way shows a child's appreciation of the recurring principle of writing, which means that writing consists of a limited set of similar shapes and employs similar moves. The writing in Figure 6.1 illustrates a child's understanding of the recurring principle.

The twenty-six letters in the English alphabet can be combined to produce all the words contained in a dictionary. Fluent writers know that they can use this limited set of symbols in different ways to produce all the words and sentences that they want to write. They understand the generative principle of writing. Young children begin to discover this often using the letters of their names, which are the symbols that are most familiar to them, to write sequences of words. Although the words they produce may not look like the words chil-

Figure 6.1. The recurring principle

dren say they have written, writing in this way demonstrates children's knowledge of the generative principle and their increasing
awareness that the set of symbols used for writing is limited and regular. Figure 6.2 shows what this stage might look like.

The discovery of what is and what is not acceptable in writing represents children's understanding of the flexibility principle of writing.
English is flexible in that it contains twenty-six letters that can be represented in different ways. For example, *a* may be written as *A*. It may
also vary in size and decorative features. But there are limits to this
flexibility. Although each of the twenty-six letters can be written in
different ways, not all characters that include curved and straight lines
are acceptable as English language symbols. Although *b, d, p* and *q*,
which employ the same shapes but are orientated differently, are all
acceptable as letters, *a* does not become a letter shape if it is turned
around. The writing in Figure 6.3 shows a child exploring the flexibility principle. She is reversing letters and includes some numbers
(which she called letters) in her writing, as well as using conventional
letter shapes. She is aware that writing consists of a range of signs
but as yet is uncertain about 'what this range is' (Clay, 1975, p. 43).

The conventions of writing include the way in which text is
arranged from left to right across the page and from top to bottom
down the page in English. Other text features such as book titles and

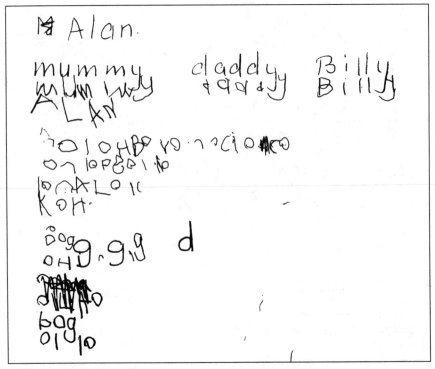

Figure 6.2. The generative principle

headings are organised in particular ways. Children learn about page arrangement principles as they gain increasing experience of reading writing and they demonstrate their ability to use this principle in the writing they produce.

Each of these manifestations of the principles of writing represents an important achievement in learning to write. When teachers are aware of the significance of these principles and recognise them in the writing that children produce they can help children to understand other principles and progress towards conventional writing through their teaching.

During their time in the nursery and reception class children's writing might appear as

- drawings
- random scribble
- scribble in lines
- letter-like shapes mixed with real letters and numbers
- groups of letters
- letters standing for words with recognisable connections
- sequences of complete words which are not spelt correctly.

Figure 6.3. The flexibility principle

All of these are normal. Willingness to write, intention to mean and gradual changes which show progress towards conventional writing are evidence of successful learning in the early years.

Understanding that learning to write is a developmental process and that composition or the intention to mean emerges in advance of transcription has influenced what and how teachers teach children about writing. Practitioners now place less emphasis on children producing correctly transcribed writing through copying or using word books. Instead the early writing curriculum now includes many opportunities for young children to experiment with and see demonstrations of writing. Using the writing that children produce independently adults work with children to extend their knowledge about writing and their ability to write. They respond to what children can do, discuss the content of what has been written and then give them guidance about transcription (Graves, 1983, Temple *et al.*, 1988).

Writing experiences and activities

Nursery and reception classes incorporate many opportunities for writing development into their normal provision and daily routines. Children learn letter names and sounds and identify words through listening to and sharing stories, poems, rhymes and songs. Through their encounters with books and print in the classroom, they begin to scrutinise letters and words in a meaningful context. Activities such as story sessions, literate role play and the provision of enticing reading and writing areas help children to see writing as a natural part of their daily lives. They enable children to appreciate the purposes of writing, to explore literacy and experiment with composition and transcription. When children incorporate writing into their play and write freely in the writing area they are discovering that they can contribute to and access the literate world and their confidence as literacy users grows. Through their active involvement with reading and writing, they are discovering that they can manipulate literacy for their own immediate purposes. Provision of this kind also gives children time and space to explore writing at their own pace and at a level that is appropriate to their existing abilities. When the emphasis is on experimentation and enjoyment, the possibility and experience of failure is reduced.

The curriculum for young children needs to be planned and sequenced so that it acknowledges children's existing abilities and extends these during the time they spend in nursery and reception classes. Teachers can present children with an appropriate and stimulating curriculum by providing models of literacy, devising activities which can be undertaken independently, teaching children about writing during discrete writing activities and planning varied ways for children to practise their developing skills.

Children need opportunities to explore the uses and the system of writing before and in addition to direct instruction about writing. Once children have been shown a model of writing and maybe had the opportunity to practise with guidance from an adult they are in a position to experiment further. Providing resources and reminding children that these are available encourages children to explore, gain practice and extend their skills in their own ways and at their own pace. Opportunities to explore writing independently should be freely and frequently available to children since they enable children to 'use writing in a variety of ways', 'for a range of audiences', 'experiment with writing' and engage in 'independent writing' (DfEE, 1998, p. 19).

Writing across the curriculum

In order that children see writing as an integral part of their lives, all activities can be resourced with writing materials. This provides opportunities for children to experiment with writing in many different situations. Paper and coloured pencils can be placed in the construction area so that children can record their plans for the models they intend to build. Pieces of card and felt tips can be used to label models with the maker's name or other notices. Large pieces of paper on an easel or smaller pieces on a clipboard can be used to record children's findings as they experiment with sand and water. Displays can be accompanied by paper and pens so that children can add their own thoughts, reply to questions or comment on the work that has been included. The results of matching, sorting and classifying activities can be noted. Sequences of notes and instruments can be written down so that the children's tunes can be played to the class during circle time. Pictures, cut out of catalogues, can be stuck into a blank book by children and an explanatory text added later when they are working in the writing area. Plastic, wooden and foam letters can be used for sorting and matching activities so that children become familiar with the shapes of upper and lower case letters, as well as learning their names and sounds. During outdoor play, children can be given buckets of water and large paintbrushes or chalk to write on the playground and the outside walls of the school. Plasticene, clay and individual trays containing small amounts of sand, damp cornflour or rice can be used to practise making letter shapes and patterns. When they paint and draw, children are learning about the representation of objects and experiences as well as developing increasing control of writing implements and using the shapes and strokes found in letters.

Writing books at home

Most children begin to learn to write before they enter nursery or reception classes. This can be capitalised upon by asking parents and carers to make a book with their child at home to bring to the nursery or reception class when the child starts. A common format for such books is to mount photographs of the child at different ages and engaging in favourite activities in a blank book. Together, the child and the adult compose sentences that will tell the teacher and other children in the class about some of the child's interests, achievements, likes and dislikes. If carers are not able to participate in this activity, a member of the nursery or school staff can make a book for the child at school or during a home visit. Making a personal book that will be read many times by others and by the child provides many lessons about writing. Children learn about authorship, audience, the functions of writing, composition and transcription as well as the need 'to think about and discuss ... ahead of writing' (DfEE, 1998, p. 19). At a later stage, children can use their personal books for reference if they want to spell their names or words that are important to them.

The writing area

This is an important part of the provision for exploring writing in early years classrooms. It needs to be well equipped with a wide range of paper, card, prepared blank books and writing implements. Other resources such as folders, a stapler, hole punch, glue, Sellotape, paper clips and scissors give children additional ideas for the type of writing they do and how they present it. Reference materials such as displays of letters, writing styles and scripts in many languages, alphabet books, simple dictionaries, word lists and a noticeboard are also useful.

The children should be able to use the writing area independently and purposefully. They will be helped to do this if they are shown how to use the resources. The children can also be involved in organising the area. Working with an adult, they can compose notices and labels for the equipment. These could be transcribed by the teacher in a shared writing session or by the children themselves. Some of the writing that is produced in the writing area can be shared with the class, responded to and displayed.

Writing areas give children the chance to experiment with writing regularly and when they choose. They can write for their own purposes, at their own pace and without needing adult attention. They can also explore the different uses and formats for writing as they use envelopes and blank books, write lists and letters and make cards. The writing area can provide opportunities for children to practise activities that have been introduced by the teacher. For example, if the children have been introduced to letter writing during shared writing or have been making greetings cards they may spontaneously practise these in the writing area.

Reading and the reading area

Reading areas filled with carefully chosen books including a selection of enlarged texts, non-fiction and books made by the teacher and the children provide examples of writing being used for many purposes. Other reading resources also help to develop children's writing abilities. Tapes and story props give children additional opportunities to become familiar with the way that stories and non-fiction are written. Sets of props or puppets give children valuable practice at rehearsing plots and investing characters with personality traits. Sequencing activities using illustrations and words taken from a book, or sets of photographs and sentences recounting an activity the children have undertaken, help to develop familiarity with story structure and narrative language. After the children have sequenced the cards, they can use them as the framework for narrating a story or event to other children or an adult. Sequencing cards based on favourite books can also be made by the children. These experiences can add substance to the content of children's written stories.

Saying and learning nursery rhymes and encouraging children to join in the repeated refrains of stories is an excellent way for children to develop phonemic awareness (Goswami and Bryant, 1990). They provide an opportunity for adults and children to discuss rhymes and, if these are written on a chart, look at the letters and letter strings that comprise the rhyme. Children who can identify onsets and rimes are taking their first steps in developing phonic knowledge, which helps them with their early attempts at spelling.

Sharing an enlarged text with the class or a group of children provides another demonstration of the uses of writing, the enjoyment it can bring and the way it is constructed and arranged. Shared reading and storytimes offer the opportunity to introduce children to words and letters and to talk about content and illustrations. Not only does this help children to learn about writing, it also provides models of how to write.

Once children are ready to focus a little more on the writing, the teacher can introduce activities based on books which reinforce learning about letters, sounds and letter patterns, all of which help with spelling. The group can be asked to look out for a particular letter as the teacher reads. They may be looking for the first letter of someone's name or a letter that frequently appears in the text. They can be asked to look for lower or upper case versions. Enlarged texts can also be used to demonstrate punctuation marks, to reflect on how texts begin and end, to explore character and to recognise how books are often composed of a sequence of events. Because shared reading teaches children so much about reading and writing, it can be tempting to overuse the teaching opportunities it presents. We need to be careful not to do this and to always remember that the main reason for sharing books is to enjoy a good read and that teaching should take second place to this.

Displays of print

Early years settings contain a considerable amount of writing. Cupboards, equipment and specific areas of the classroom are labelled. Lists, charts and children's writing are displayed. Displays of craft and art work are accompanied by explanations and titles. All these examples of print provide children with models for their own writing. Children can write captions and other contributions for displays. Questions and answers written in speech bubbles can help children to recognise the connection between speech and writing. Interactive displays that are related to letters and sounds support writing as well as reading. They help to reinforce the link between letter sounds and letter shapes and teach children about letter formation. They can include chalks and a chalking board, plastic letters and other resources that encourage children to explore and make letter shapes.

Early years settings usually have a commercial alphabet frieze which can be used to show children how letters and some words are written. Even more valuable are alphabet friezes and books that are made by the class. They can be made relevant and interesting to children by concentrating on topics such as food, flowers, countries or children's names. When children are involved in producing the environmental print in the classroom, they become more aware of the writing that is displayed and are more likely to refer to it when they are writing alone.

Visits

Taking groups of children on visits provides them with models of literacy in the real world. Outings to local shops or a walk in the locality will reveal writing in use and demonstrate many of the functions and purposes of writing. Street signs, advertisements, shop names, newspapers and magazines in the paper shop, menus, order pads and bills in the takeaway are just some of the types of writing which may be seen. An outing can be prepared for by making a list of things to take and a list of people who will be going. A shopping trip may require a written shopping list. After a visit, children can try to incorporate the environmental print they have seen into their modelling, construction and imaginative play in the classroom. If appropriate, the teacher and children can write a letter together in a shared writing session to thank the shopkeepers they visited. Alternatively, the children can write their own 'thank you' notes. Visits and follow-up activities stimulate discussion about language, its functions and its appearance and can raise children's awareness of writing.

Imaginative play areas

These are an important resource for all sorts of learning in the early years classroom and need to be organised as carefully as any other planned learning activity. Adding literacy materials which encourage children to read and write provides opportunities for them to explore print in many forms. Books, magazines, brochures, telephone directories, calendars, diaries, maps, notices, forms, notepads, envelopes and a range of writing implements all have a place in the home, café, shop or garage. In dramatic play, a few well-chosen props can be used by children to re-enact familiar stories and explore sequence and characterisation. For example, a crown and some cloaks might be sufficient for children to become Princess Smartypants (Cole, 1986) and her unfortunate suitors. Children's exploration benefits from adults who spend time modelling literate behaviour in play areas. They quickly imitate adult writing and reading behaviours and incorporate these into their play. To remain effective, the focus and the resources in role play areas need to be changed regularly. Involving the children in making changes draws their attention to what they can use and how.

Shared writing

In shared writing sessions the teacher records what the children compose. The teacher writes on a large flip chart so that the children can see how words are written down, how they are arranged on the page and how they are spelled. They can also see how individual letters are formed. The adult can negotiate the children's suggestions and, in doing so, draw attention to how what is written has to be appropriate to the function and audience. As the children make their suggestions, the adult may need to make some revisions. This gives children a valuable message about the impossibility of producing perfect writing at a first attempt and shows them that it is important to review what has been written. A variety of text types, such as informative captions for displays, letters and stories, can be composed in this way.

Sometimes shared writing sessions are used to create stories modelled on known texts. This teaches children about story structure, plot and sequence. The characters or the objects in the story may be changed, but the language and the structures of the original text remain the same. For example, the model provided in *Where's Spot?* (Hill, 1980) could be used to write a book entitled 'Where's the Teacher?'. Information texts, rhymes, poems and songs can also be used as models. When the writing is complete it can be made into a book for the class or copied out and displayed.

Direct teaching

Much of the direct teaching that takes place in the early years will occur when adults respond to and discuss children's writing. This may have been produced spontaneously or during one of the planned opportunities for writing. All the writing that children produce needs to be treated seriously. It merits comment that focuses on the content and the author's intention. Responses such as 'lovely writing' are insufficient as they do not do justice to the effort that the child has expended and do not give feedback that is helpful for the future. Using one's knowledge of the child's previous experience and understanding adults can extend what children know and can do by acting in the following ways:

- Respond positively and with respect to what children have done.
- Ask the child to read back or tell you what she has written.
- Talk about the content.
- Comment on any significant aspects of the transcription.
- Respond in writing with a comment, a question and a correct version.
- Write a reply if a child has written to you.
- Display the writing on the writing noticeboard.
- Use the writing if it is a notice or story or has been produced for a play area or a display.

Writing for a range of audiences and purposes

Writing non-fiction usually takes place across the curriculum as part of learning about other things. It is rarely undertaken for its own sake. Its central function is to convey information clearly and accurately and it often includes lists, headings and diagrams. Children's appreciation of the characteristics of non-fiction writing can be extended when adults share factual books with them and instigate discussions about the way the information is presented. Shared writing can also be used to demonstrate how information texts are organised. When children are asked to write factually they will be helped if the teacher is clear about the purpose, audience and structure of the writing and makes this explicit. Placing writing resources alongside the many activities that are arranged in the class encourages children to use writing to record information.

Developing transcription

The National Literacy Strategy Framework for Teaching (DfEE, 1998) identifies the following as areas for attention before children are five:

Grammar and punctuation

• Know that writing is ordered from left to right.

Spelling

• Recognise letters of the alphabet.
• Write initial letters of words.
• Distinguish between letter sounds and names.
• Be aware of alphabetical order.

Handwriting

• Form lower case letters correctly.
• Form upper case letters correctly.

As these concerns are returned to in years 1 and 2, it is not expected that children's command of them will be complete at the end of the Reception year. Some of the activities described in this chapter address these aspects of writing directly; for example, sorting and painting. In addition, children's competence in the transcription skills of writing does develop as they engage in writing and receive adult support.

Conclusion

During their time in nursery and reception classes professionals help children to:

• understand the purposes of writing
• understand that what is said can be written down
• understand that speech sounds can be represented by letters
• become more familiar with writing implements and other resources for writing
• develop the skills needed to form letter shapes
• use writing in play and for their own purposes
• write their own names
• read or tell what they have written
• become familiar with different types of writing

through providing them with opportunities to:

- browse, share and read books
- see writing as a natural accompaniment to a range of activities
- experiment with writing
- talk about writing with others.

The aim of practitioners who work in early years settings is to help children to become writers. This goes beyond merely teaching children to write. It involves developing children's confidence and understanding of writing as well as their skills. Practitioners who create a language-rich environment and provide activities and experiences that enable children to explore writing are helping children to establish the foundations for writing and become able and committed writers.

Suggestions for further reading

Campbell, R (1997) *Literacy in Nursery Education*, Stoke on Trent: Trentham Books.

Godwin, D. and Perkins, M. (1998) *Teaching Language and Literacy in the Early Years*, London: David Fulton.

Temple, C., Nathan, R., Burris, N. and Temple, F. (1988) *The Beginnings of Writing*, 2nd edition, London: Allyn & Bacon.

References

Beard, R. (1984) *Children's Writing in the Primary School*, Sevenoaks: Hodder & Stoughton.

Britton, J. (1972) *Language and Learning*, Harmondsworth: Penguin.

Clay, M. (1975) *What Did I Write?* London: Heinemann Educational.

Cole, B. (1986) *Princess Smartypants*, London: Picture Lions.

DfEE (1998) *The National Literacy Strategy Framework for Teaching*, London: HMSO.

Dyson, A. H. (1983) The role of oral language in early writing processes, *Research in the Teaching of English*, Vol. 17, no. 1, pp. 1–29.

Ferreiro, E. and Teberosky, A. (1983) *Literacy before Schooling*, Portsmouth, NH: Heinemann Educational.

Goswami, U. and Bryant, P. (1990) *Phonological Skills and Learning to Read*, Hove: Lawrence Erlbaum Associates.

Graves, R. (1983) *Teachers and Children at Work*, London: Heinemann Educational.

Hill, E. (1980) *Where's Spot?* Harmondsworth: Puffin Books.

Kress, G. (1997) *Before Writing*, London: Routledge.

National Writing Project (1990) *Perceptions of Writing*, Walton-on-Thames: Nelson.

Temple, C., Nathan, R., Burris, N. and Temple, F. (1988) *The Beginnings of Writing*, 2nd edition, London: Allyn & Bacon.

Whitehead, M. (1996) *The Development of Language and Literacy*, London: Hodder & Stoughton.

7

Young Children, Play and Literacy: Engagement in Realistic Uses of Literacy

Nigel Hall

Introduction

It is not so long ago that literacy and the early years existed in a rather strange relationship. Even in the middle of the 1980s it was common to meet nursery nurses who in their training had been told not to put print in the nursery because it would confuse the children. The early years was supposed to be a time when children were children, rather than pupils.

There are, of course, many and complex reasons why literacy was not a major feature of experience in early schooling (see Hall, 1987 for a review) but the notion that children could not cope with literacy, were confused by it, or needed massive formal pre-literacy experience, has now been shown to be ridiculous. Children are hardier souls than had been imagined and are well used to dealing with many complex and confusing aspects of the real world. Having full knowledge of the real world is not a necessary conditioning for operating in it, as ought to be clear to all adults who each day switch on lights without understanding electrical principles, drive their cars without a full knowledge of the internal combustion engine and cook food in a microwave without understanding radiation.

However, as recognition has grown that literacy is accessible to young children, so literacy has been hijacked by a political system which sees the appropriate experience of literacy for young children as being the analysis of literacy as an abstract object rather than the provision of opportunity for using literacy in semi-authentic and authentic ways. One consequence of this approach is that there is a deep schism between the way literacy is treated in education and the way literacy is used in everyday life, that everyday life which young children normally inhabit.

The claim in this chapter is that whatever abstractions about literacy might be necessary or imposed upon children, they still need space and time to explore the use of literacy as something meaningful and purposeful in people's lives, and that it is socio-dramatic play which offers powerful opportunities for achieving this. Socio-dramatic play has the potential to link the world of in-school literacy with world of out-of-school literacy. In order to make this clear, the first requirement is to explore briefly the characteristics of literacy in everyday life and literacy within education.

Literacy in and out of education

I want first to examine some features of real-life literacy experiences. Literacy is almost always highly meaningful to people. It is usually related to their lives, their interests and their concerns. That is not to say that literacy objects are always welcome; certain forms, demands and claims may upset us more than they make us happy, but nevertheless they relate to aspects of our lives we understand (Barton and Hamilton, 1998). In everyday life literacy makes things happen; it is a means to many kinds of ends: we read labels to ensure that we eat the right food, we follow instructions to make sure we reach the right places, and we write letters to make sure our views are known. Our literate behaviour is judged as a success by whether it does make things happen. In connection with this, literacy is used for a huge range of purposes and involves a wide range of sources and audiences. Our literate behaviour is intimately related to our social pasts and our social futures. Much of it emerges from prior experiences: letters we have received, places we have been, people we have met, and things we have done. Much of this will also connect to future expectations for our lives. Because of this intimate link between our particular lives and literacy, the uses of and values about literacy will vary from person to person, community to community and culture to culture (Minns, 1990). Finally, while we do sometimes engage in literacy for literacy's sake, more often literacy is embedded in the pursuit of other ends. Literacy acts are made meaningful by being part of longer and larger events; these acts contribute to the successful conclusion of the event: getting fed, obtaining a mortgage, going on holiday or finding a job.

How does this compare with children's experiences of literacy as they move into early years education; is it similar or considerably different?

Literacy in early years education, and especially in the new world of literacy hours, is almost always imposed upon children; it turns them into responders rather than initiators and is seldom related to the children's own lives. It is frequently exercise-based rather than used to make things happen in the world, and success is therefore predicated on achieving the task rather than using literacy to do something meaningful. The exercises are ends in themselves as far as children's experience is concerned. The past and future of literacy in education is not based upon personal lives but in relation to difficulty and an additive notion of knowledge. Tasks tend to be fairly uniform in difficulty as they are designed to meet very specific objectives, something that also governs interpretations, choices, modes of practice, and assessment. Literacy tasks tend to be single acts rather than parts of larger events. Instead of the rich, varied and purposeful uses of literacy found in people's lives, educational practices usually involve a limited range of specially privileged purposes and audiences and make relatively constant demands upon users.

As children move into formal schooling so these elements begin to dominate and are institutionally sanctioned by documentation and assessment practices. However, it would be unwise to believe that pre-five experiences are not subject to the same overall constraints. While baseline assessment models (QCA, 1998) and 'Desirable Outcomes' (SCAA, 1996) pay lip service to the real uses of literacy and language, most of the elements still derive from a narrowly conceived perspective on literacy which is revealed clearly by assessment practices. Reading is solely related to book use, and the multitude of everyday reading experiences and their purposes gets no mention at all. In the baseline assessments for writing none of the four items has any relationship to purpose or meaning. Of course, the baseline assessments are for children once they have started formal schooling, but it is going to be a rare nursery school that will not see these as aims for their own work.

In pointing out these differences between in-school and out-of-school uses of literacy I am not seeking to claim that one is right and one is wrong; both are facts of life, and the complexities of managing large numbers of children and meeting a number of aims inevitably impose differences on how literacy is used within education. However, the costs of such an analytic curriculum is increasing the distance between experiences of literacy in school and experiences out of school. It is in this context that socio-dramatic play has such a potentially powerful role in helping children develop knowledge of the 'who', 'when', 'why', 'where' and 'what' of literacy as well as the 'how'.

The relationship between literacy and play

Socio-dramatic play can provide opportunities for young children to act appropriately as users of literacy rather than simply as analysers of literacy. Why is this so? If we examine the nature of socio-dramatic play it is easy to see that it shares more characteristics with the ways in which literacy is used outside school than the way it is used inside it.

The first point is that it involves children's choices. It is rare that young children's play is completely controlled by adults. Of course, in early years education adults may intervene by designating partic-ular play centres as hospitals, garages, fire stations, homes, space rock-ets, the three bears' cottage and so on, and they may provide or invite specific kinds of resources that they feel are appropriate. However, once inside such a centre, the particular choices made and the spe-cific ways in which the play proceeds are usually determined by the children. It is, therefore, always meaningful to children and their lives.

The second point is that socio-dramatic play is usually based around events rather than single acts. If a play centre is an airport, then to play airports somethings has to happen – a crash, going on holiday, or a customer losing luggage. Thus anything that happens within these events gains its meaning from being situated within that event. Writing out a ticket for a passenger is not an act of writing in its own right; it gains its meaning from the circumstances of the 'going on holiday'. It is contextualised because it is a means to an end rather than an end on its own. Because in play literacy acts crop up within meaningful events, they tend to relate to a variety of purposes, be addressed to a variety of audiences, and utilise a variety of resources.

Thirdly, play gains its meaning not from whether it is likely to be examined, marked or even approved by adults, but by whether it works as a meaningful script for the children.

The final aspect of play to be looked at here is its realism and authenticity. It seems something of a contradiction to see play as real or authentic; after all, it is by definition not real. However, play which was not related to reality would be as impossible as fiction not based upon reality. The very things which makes it recognisable are the 'as real' things in it. This reality can operate on many levels, from accept-ing as real particular kinds of symbolic objects to total belief in the role one is playing (although whether playing is the correct word in such circumstances is debatable).

Some important relationships between real ways in which literacy is used and the nature of play should now be clear. They are both purposeful, both offer users choices, both are meaningful in users' or

players' lives, and both embed particular acts in larger, more purposeful event-based experiences.

What happens when children, play and literacy meet?

Given the above claims, what actually happens when literacy is experienced by young children in association with play? Writing in 1998
it is possible to give some answers to this question. When I first asked
it in 1985, nothing was clear at all. To see what would happen a group
of us (later reported in Hall *et al.*, 1988) took what was, for the time,
a typical nursery school home-corner; it was rich in home objects such
as furniture and clothes but unlike most homes had no print or print
objects in it. By doing what is now commonplace and filling it with
print and print-related objects, we were able to begin to answer our
question.

What did the children show us? During the four days of observation 290 events were observed in which literacy-related behaviour
occurred. These ranged from fleeting bits of engagement to highly
organised and sustained episodes of play in which literacy was a consistently embedded feature. Children demonstrated a knowledge not
simply of some of the purposes of print but of the social contexts in
which these purposes were embedded. The children in this nursery
group were exploring the use of written language to establish ownership and identity, to build relationships, to remember or recall, to
request information, to record information, to fantasise or pretend,
and to declare. Those children were not waiting for formal education
to use literacy but they had been waiting for the opportunity to display their use of it. The play situation generated within the classroom
allowed these four-year-old children such an opportunity.

That last sentence is perhaps the really significant one. Adults
working with young children had been guilty of underestimating
what children knew. The assumption was that children knew nothing
about literacy, so no provision had been made to allow children to
demonstrate their knowledge. Without the provision the literacy-
related behaviour did not become visible, so appearing to confirm the
adults' expectations. Only when we broke that cycle did the children
inform us that they were intensely aware of the world of print, and
had quite a lot of knowledge about the 'who', 'when', 'why', 'where'
and 'what' of literacy.

What makes for a rich, literacy-oriented play area?

That children use literacy in play is now well established and many who work with young children in the UK are now well acquainted with ensuring that there are literacy-related objects in socio-dramatic play centres. However, one point must be made very clearly at this point; although this chapter is about literacy and play, and explores ways in which these two experiences can be related, I am not suggesting that all play should have literacy formally associated with it. Children need experiences of different types of play, and play for varied purposes. The suggestions in this chapter are options, not prescriptions for all play.

If the choice of the adults is to explore literacy and play together, then while simply sticking in a few print-related items may make a difference, it is better to plan both the centres and the print in ways which are likely to promote greater engagement with literacy. Part of such planning involves the selection of useful themes for play centres. The following questions will guide planning.

1. **Is the area one for which literacy is a natural partner?** Some areas have a richer potential than others. A medieval castle makes a wonderful play centre but given the rather limited literacy levels of the time, print and using print is not a major feature of castle life. Of course, the medieval castle as an historic site is a different matter, signs, guidebooks and instructions abound.

2. **Can the children visit a real area related to the theme?** Being able to visit and see the richness of print in a real environment, and maybe even see people using it, can help the children incorporate it meaningfully in their own play. This is particularly so if they are asked to search for signs, notices, leaflets (as well as people using the print) and if these are discussed back in their base.

3. **Does the area have potential for a range of roles and functions?** In other words, does the real-life equivalent of the play centre have roles equally accessible to boys and girls and all social groups, and are these roles associated with the use of print for a wide range of purposes? Will they allow the children to gain a rich diversity of experience of literacy rather than narrow it down?

Roskos and Vukelich (1991) suggest three other questions that might be worth thinking about:

- Are any literacy-related props things that the children might have encountered in their own environment?
- Does the prop serve a particular function that is familiar to the children in their daily lives?
- Can the props be used naturally and safely by young children?

When it comes to looking closely at the literacy-related features of the centre, it could be worth while drawing up a chart related to the theme which explores aspects of an area, the people who work or attend there and the kinds of literacy that relate to their roles. Play around with the example in Figure 7.1 and fill in the rest of the columns. Go for as many things as possible; in other words, brainstorm as freely as you can. The greater the number of things you can find the better will be your final selection of what might be relevant to the children with whom you work. What this brainstorming does is create a set of possibilities; they are not things you have to do, simply things from which you can choose.

Everything so far in this section is related solely to identifying themes and roles, and locating literacy potential in terms of resources and provision. Neuman and Roskos (1992), after studying children aged 3 and 4, found significant differences between play centres that did include print-related material and those that didn't. Play in the print-orientated areas was sustained for much longer periods, was considerably more complex, made greater use of the print-related material and involved a wider range of literacy-related behaviours. They found that the children's literacy talk was always situated, that is it derived its meaning from the context of the ongoing play event. They claimed that literacy talk was always accompanied by active engagement in the event itself

What	The Clinic			
Where	Doctor's room		Reception area	
Who	Doctors	Nurses	Receptionists	Patients
Literacy activities	Read charts Write notes Write prescriptions Read patient notes Read medical books			
Resources				

Figure 7.1. Planning literacy in role play areas

and that during the play the children would switch from being a learner to being a teacher; in other words, helping to clarify something about literacy for other children. They claimed that the physical presence of literacy-related objects assisted children in using more explicit language about literacy during their play.

One very important resource is not equipment or materials, but adults. For too long many adults have felt it inappropriate to get involved in children's play. Of course, sometimes it is inappropriate, but recent work suggests that there are times when, by getting involved, teachers can model, suggest and point out many things to help children understand about literacy. This does not mean formal teaching, but by taking a role within the play, or reacting to something brought to one's attention by children who are playing, adults can subtly integrate literacy into a response, provide a rationale for the use of literacy, or demonstrate that literacy has a role in the play theme.

Extending knowledge of literacy with play

In this section I want mainly to explore more specific ways in which adults can use the motivation and commitment of play and build experiences that operate as more complex events, events that can provide a better opportunity for children to experience literacy as a more means-ended and natural process. It is, however, so important to appreciate that at no time should these events be the only experiences children have with the play centre theme. Most of the time children should continue to play in whatever ways they choose. Literacy events should be developed alongside the children's choices, not instead of them.

One of the most powerful ways of developing more specific literacy practices is for the adults to introduce events and problems that are meaningful to the themes and thus also to the children. Sometimes these events can be introduced within the play centre itself. Sometimes it might be better to introduce them outside the play centre, but to relate them closely to the theme of the play. Before looking at some actual examples, it is useful to look at what is involved in creating events.

Creating events

Events are happenings which have some overall aim. Achieving this may be easy or highly problematic. For instance, in relation to the clinic example started above, events might be:

- getting planning permission to build a clinic in the classroom
- an accident in the clinic
- the doctor being unable to turn up to take the clinic
- a new staff appointment in the clinic
- a burglary in the clinic
- a complaint about the treatment.

Any such list is simply a set of possibilities. None at first sight appear to have anything directly to do with literacy, which is, of course, how most events occur in life. But, as indicated earlier in this chapter, it is the event which makes meaningful the actions within it, and some of these actions can involve literacy; others may involve different areas of experience.

Introducing events

Events are likely to be more meaningful to children if they seem to arise out of the real world, rather than obviously from the mind of an adult. For this reason using external agencies or even pretend external agencies can make a more powerful impact than an adult simply saying 'Let's imagine'. Letters that come into the classroom, people who visit, or discoveries in the classroom all provide ways of starting off events.

The events suggested above for the clinic can all be introduced in different ways. What would be the reaction if the children came in one morning and found their clinic closed, with a big sign saying, 'Police notice: closed because of vandalism'? Or the teacher introduces a letter which says that the clinic will have to close because it was built without permission, or the children arrive and several things are missing, presumed stolen?

If these are introduced directly into the play centre then observing how the children react will be interesting and informative for the teacher. However, discussing what has happened with the whole class, and exploring how they might deal with it may lead to a more intense involvement with both the event and with literacy, as happened in the two following examples.

Example: the library

This nursery class had created a local library as their play area. They had created displays, sorted and arranged books, made and used tickets for borrowers, had borrowed books, acted as librarians, and generally had a creative and interesting time. Unfortunately, all good things come to an end and the teacher was looking for a way of closing down the area before moving on to something else. The event she created for this might be characterised as the 'Closing down our library'. One morning a letter arrived in the nursery which started. 'It has come to our attention that you are running a library.' It went on to say:

> I am sorry to tell you that you must close the library down in your school by Wednesday of this week as the council does not have enough money to have a library here.

However, it left an opening, because the last sentence said, 'Please write to me if you have anything to say about the library closing.'

These children had loved playing in their library and were intensely committed to it; as can be imagined, their reaction to this letter was a strong one. Considerable discussion took place as the children thought about all the things they could do. As a result of several suggestions, the teacher offered them the chance to write to the Head of Council Library Services. The children did not sit there saying, 'We can't write, we're only four.' They did not hesitate and in their own way wrote forceful letters which made their feelings clear. They told the teacher what they had written (see Figures 7.2, 7.3, 7.4).

What do we learn from this? While the event was not introduced directly into the play it drew intimately from the experience of the play. The worlds of play and literacy were not separated but were mutually related. The children, although only four, did not see their letters as exercises in writing, they used literacy to try and make something happen in the world. The experience had an end beyond the literacy itself; the end was an attempt to secure the perpetuation of their library. Many people would think it developmentally inappropriate to have four-year-olds writing protest letters. These children were, of course, unconcerned with what others may think was devel-

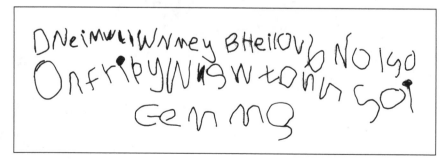

Figure 7.2. 'Don't close our library or I'll put you in jail.'

Figure 7.3. 'Please come to our school and see our library.'

Figure 7.4. 'Please don't close the library or you'll be dead.'

opmentally inappropriate, they simply got on with doing what they felt was necessary for them.

Example: the garage

My second example comes from a very sustained play experience in a reception class (Hall and Robinson, 1995). Although the average age of the children was five, one-third of them had been in the reception class only a few weeks when they participated and several were still only four at this point. The theme was a garage, and the children had visited a garage, made notes, discussed what they wanted in their garage, had started to build their garage, and had begun to produce all kinds of signs, notices, instructions for it. In an early event the children had discovered that you can't built anything anywhere, and had ended up filling in local authority planning application forms to get permission to have a garage.

This had proved no problem at all for the children but now the teacher introduced another event with a complication – applying for a job in the garage. In order to play in the garage, they had to apply. It must be pointed out that this event was introduced while the area was being built, so no child was totally frustrated by not being able to play in the garage.

As the children discussed what it meant to apply, they realised that they needed some advertisements, and in order to have advertisements they had to have some job descriptions. The children had no problem seeing this process as being a reasonable part of the reality of the experience. In order to generate a job description they had to think back to their visit to the real garage, as well as draw on their own experiences of life. As this was discussed with the whole class so the children's knowledge of who did what in a garage significantly increased. Once the discussions had taken place and the advert produced, children began applying. For the children who had only just arrived in the class, a form was produced which they could fill in. The children could either have a go at filling it all in by themselves or could dictate some of it to the teacher (see Figures 7.5 and 7.6).

In this particular class, the form-filling was an out-of-play-centre activity. It would have been just as easy for the forms to have been put into the play centre and the children could fill them in as part of ongoing play. However, in that case it would still have benefited from the whole class discussion. Why? Because in the process of discussion the whole world of working in the garage was more widely opened up for all the children. They knew much more about who worked in garages and what the working roles required. The information gained

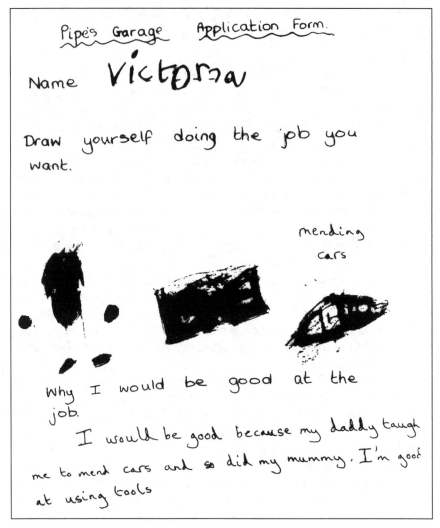

Figure 7.5. Victoria's application form.

made a difference to the repertoire of the players once they moved into the play centre.

The children in this class got involved with a huge range of forms of written language, but not once was there any indication that they saw this a chore. On the contrary, these children did not see what they were doing as writing and reading, they saw it as being involved with the garage. The garage gave sense and purpose to any reading and writing, and the literacy fed back into the garage by contributing to the children's understanding of what was involved in the world of work. Work was no longer simply a place where people performed

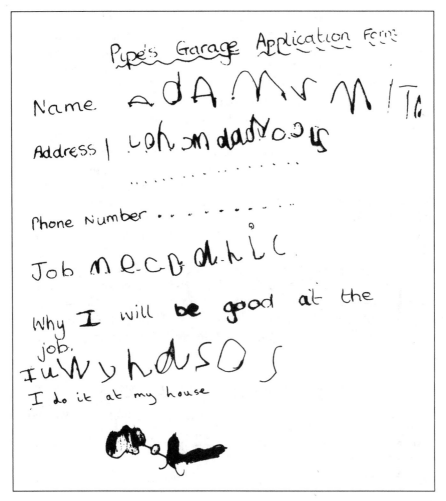

Figure 7.6. Adam's application form.

actions, but was a socially situated experience, bounded by a bureau-cracy of regulations and regulators, cohabiting with neighbours and citizens, and supplying a range of services to people in a community.

Conclusion

In the ways described above, play and literacy become working part-ners. The literacy and play exist in a reciprocal relationship that has it origin not in exercises and government agendas but in the real world that exists outside and beyond schooling. If we re-examine the claims made earlier about real-life literacy it will be seen that the chil-dren in the two examples above were experiencing literacy as something that was meaningful in their lives: it related to their situation and futures, they could make things happen by using it, it involved them with a wide range of functions, forms and audiences, and was directed towards purposeful ends. Finally, they experienced literacy as something highly challenging yet intensely enjoyable.

What emerges clearly is the socio-dramatic play provides a perfect context for allowing children to be literate people. They do not have to wait until they know all about literacy in order to use it. Even the youngest children (and in the study by Neuman and Roskos many were only three) can understand how literacy can be used to act upon the world in some way. The task for adults working with children is to create the socio-dramatic play situations in which children can find it meaningful and appropriate to act in literate ways, and in which they can reveal to interested adults the extent of their knowledge about literacy.

Creating opportunities for literacy in socio-dramatic play shows clearly that young children do not have to be protected from the complexities of literacy, they are ready to embrace them and respond to their challenges. Young children still have a lot to learn about literacy but being beginners should not preclude them from participation in realistic literacy acts.

Suggestions for further reading

Christie, J. (ed.) (1991) *Play and Early Literacy Development*, New York: State University of New York Press.

Hall, N. and Abbott, L. (eds.) (1990) *Play in the Primary Curriculum*, London: Hodder & Stoughton.

Hall, N. and Robinson, A. (1995) *Exploring Play and Literacy in the Early Years*, London: David Fulton.

Roskos, K. and Christie, J. (1999) *Literacy and Play in the Early Years: Cognitive, Ecological and Sociological Perspectives*, New Jersey: Lawrence Erlbaum.

References

Barton, D. and Hamilton, M. (1998) *Local Literacies: Reading and Writing in One Community*, London: Routledge.

Hall, N. (1987) *The Emergence of Literacy*, London: Hodder & Stoughton.

Hall, N. and Robinson, A. (1995) *Exploring Writing and Play in the Early Years*, London: David Fulton.

Hall, N., May, E., Moores, J., Shearer, J. and Williams, S. (1988) The literate home-corner, in P. Smith, (ed.) *Parents and Teachers Together*, London: Macmillan Education.

Minns, H. (1990) *Read It To Me Now! Learning at Home and School*, London: Virago.

Neuman, S. and Roskos, K. (1992) Literacy objects as cultural tools: effects on children's literacy behaviours in play, *Reading Research Quarterly*, Vol. 27, no. 3, pp. 202–35.

QCA (1998) *Baseline Assessment Scales*, London: HMSO.

Roskos, K. and Vukelich, C. (1991) Promoting literacy in play, *Day Care and Early Education*, Fall.

SCAA (1996) *Nursery Education: Desirable Outcomes for Children's Learning on Entering Compulsory Education*, London: School Curriculum and Assessment Authority.

Acknowledgement

I would like to thank Beverley Booth and Sue Endicott, both such gifted teachers, whose children's work appears in this chapter.

8

Drama

Jacki Rowley

For many years, a great deal of drama in primary and early years education has been largely concerned with performance rather than focusing on the dramatic process. In particular, primary schools have concentrated very much on the annual nativity, sadly neglecting drama work throughout the year. This neglect of drama is due in part to many teachers' lack of confidence in tackling what is deemed as a specialist area. Yet a brief examination of the possibilities of drama can challenge the notion which equates drama education solely with performance and reveal more diverse possibilities than first imagined. This chapter examines a number of ways in which drama can be approached in the early years curriculum. It provides a range of practical ideas for engaging children in drama work and explores ways in which the environment can support children's involvement in the dramatic process. The chapter considers the drama continuum and asks questions which are key to work in the early years. For example, when does role play stop and drama begin? People tend to think of drama work as the adoption of different personas and acting in role. However, drama can be seen as a continuum of activities from unstructured play, improvisation and imaginative role play to structured, scripted productions. If we are to develop children's skills in drama work effectively, we need to be able to use a range of techniques confidently. The chapter presents some of these techniques and provides examples of their successful use in nurseries and reception classes. To begin with, however, the reasons for incorporating drama work into the early years curriculum need to be explored.

Why use drama?

What place does drama have in developing early linguistic skills? There has been much work to suggest that it has a central role to play (Bolton, 1979; Fleming, 1995). In the process of talking in role, or negotiating a plot, or interacting with others in role play or drama, children are extending their speaking and listening skills as well as learning the art of working with others in a shared venture. And as Clipson-Boyles (1998) states:

> Drama puts language into action in ways with which children can identify, respond and learn. It brings language alive by providing meaningful contexts. These include roles, purposes, and audiences, all of which give the language authenticity in the eyes of the children.
>
> (Clipson-Boyles, 1998, p. 4)

Drama can provide opportunities for children to take on roles which require particular ways of talking, or the use of specific vocabulary. Children can be encouraged to reflect on the need for formal or informal talk in a variety of situations, important in their developing knowledge of Standard English. Above all, drama provides opportunities for interactive talk and it is through the negotiation of shared meanings that language acquires its poignancy and significance (Bahktin, 1981). Language development is facilitated through talk with others (Vygostky, 1978; Bruner, 1983; Cazden, 1983) and drama is a powerful means of encouraging this dialogue. Drama can also help the reading process and later in the chapter, the relationship between drama and picture books is examined. However, drama does not just contribute to children's development in language and literacy, although that is the focus of this chapter. It can also enable children to:

- develop confidence and self-esteem
- work out rules and understand the reasons behind them
- expand their imagination
- think more creatively and make connections between different aspects of their experience
- develop non-verbal communication skills
- challenge stereotypes
- enhance learning in all areas of the curriculum
- have fun!

Drama can be seen as a continuum of experiences and skills. In the early years, play and role play are the primary means of children exploring the adoption of different roles and provides them with a range of opportunities for exploring novel situations. Unstructured role play can lead to structured role play, which in turn may lead to activities which feature specific drama techniques as a means of engaging children in the dramatic process. This work may then lead on to children writing and producing scripted plays, some of which may be performed to an audience. Children may also work on plays which are already published or could improvise work based on these plays. Therefore it can be seen that drama work can involve a wide range of processes and experiences. In the early years, the seeds of drama are sown in play and the next section moves on to consider the relationship between play, role play and drama.

Play

It is widely accepted that play is a crucial element in young children's social, emotional, linguistic and cognitive development (Moyles, 1994). Play with objects and toys has a particular role in children's development. Young babies love to play with objects and toys in their constant exploration of the world. When children are aged two or three, they often use a variety of props to engage in dramatic play. This can involve them taking on different roles in solo play, varying their tone of voice for each role. This stage is an important precursor to children's later socio-dramatic role play in which they take on a role and interact with others in the unfolding drama. It is therefore essential for early years settings to encourage these early stages of imaginative play and this can be done by providing a range of stimuli for children to engage with.

In the very early stages, Goldschmied and Jackson (1994) advocate the use of 'Treasure Baskets'. These are boxes or baskets in which an adult places a range of items that will be of interest to young babies. None of these are bought toys. Instead, the basket is filled with safe kitchen implements, sponges, tin lids, feathers, balls – whatever the adult feels may interest the baby. Babies can spend hours playing with these objects, discovering their properties by touching, squeezing and tasting. When children are older, they use objects to engage in imaginative play. What these objects are is irrelevant as they are often transformed in the process of the play into whatever children want them to be, but particular objects can stimulate children's imagination. Many nurseries and reception classes therefore ensure there is sufficient provision of small toy play through the use of doll's houses, farm sets, garages and so on. Sand and water trays are often adorned with particular small toys which encourage imaginative play such as boats and animals. Large cement mixing trays from DIY stores are a very useful addition to the stock! These wide, shallow trays can be filled with sand, leaves, rocks, twigs, shells or whatever materials the adult wants to provide in order to create a setting. Once these objects or materials are sprinkled along the bottom of these trays, small figures such as animals or human figures can be used to create particular scenarios such as jungles, street scenes, playgrounds and so on, thus providing a rich stimulus for imaginative play.

Role play

Structured role play areas can be used to stimulate children's dramatic play with others. It is in these areas that children act out their own experiences, share those of others, deal with their fears and explore things that they would like to happen to them in real life. They may engage in early imitative play in which they make an easy, natural transition from their actual situation into that of another person or role. This can involve dressing up in someone else's clothes or copying a familiar action, often in an attempt to recognise their own roles. Role play areas in nurseries and classrooms have traditionally featured 'home-corners', and indeed there is a central place for allowing children to act out issues and roles related to the home. But within early years settings we now see an increasingly varied use of these spaces, ranging from areas which reflect children's everyday reality (shops, clinics) to areas which are rooted in reality, but possibly unfamiliar to the children (travel agents, Victorian classrooms, desert islands). Role play areas can also be developed to encourage children to take on a range of fantasy roles such as monsters, fairy tale characters and talking animals in magic forests. Particularly appealing are role play areas which are based on books the children are familiar with. The island of the Wild Things can encourage a range of extensions to Sendak's story that, no doubt, he would never have dreamed of!

Role play, whether unstructured or guided, serves many purposes for children and its possibilities for adults are now being recognised in therapy and business contexts. Adults may feel that the structured role play area is best left in the ownership of the child. We may feel that adult intervention will stifle creativity and reduce scope, drawing it back into the realm of the teacher or early years worker, focusing on her interests and judgements. Certainly there is the potential for adults to stifle the spontaneity of children's play. However, if carefully judged, adult intervention can extend children's enjoyment of, and participation in, the play.

Initially, adults need to spend time observing children's play in order to ensure that they are sensitive to its nature and so intervene in appropriate ways. As Wood and Attfield (1996) state:

> educators need to observe socio-dramatic play to develop their understanding of what the children are playing with and playing at. This will sensitize them to ongoing themes, rules, con-

ventions, groupings, play partners, children's preferences and their use of space and resources. It will also enable them to reflect critically on what kinds of interventions are desirable. These may range from becoming a successful player alongside the children, to helping structure their own themes, to providing different contexts and resources or a combination of all three.

(Wood and Attfield, 1996, p. 109)

Thus, if we want to enter the world of children's play and role play, we need to introduce ourselves gradually and appropriately with the children's consent and be careful contributors in role.

Adult involvement in play can raise its status in the nursery or classroom (Hendy, 1996). We need to be careful that we do not give children the message that adults only take part in literacy, numeracy, science, design and technology or art activities, thus suggesting that this is where the learning takes place and these are the only activities that are important. By entering the world of play in role we are giving the message that play is valued. If this is the case, assessing and developing children's play is as vital as teaching a child to read. Kitson (1994) examines the role of the adult in extending children's play:

Through the socio-dramatic play, educators are able to create a situation and generate motivation which will encourage the children to behave and function at a cognitive level beyond their norm . . . Educators within the socio-dramatic play situation can stimulate, motivate and facilitate the play, encouraging the children to work at a deeper level than they would if left to their own devices.

(Kitson, 1994, p. 98)

Adult involvement in play can also help to develop children's familiarity with a particular environment and its nature. For example, if a travel agent's shop/office is set up, children may not have encountered such a situation before and so may not be aware of the purpose, function and 'rules'. Some of this can be introduced as the area is developed and set up. Visits to a real-life travel agent's establishment can develop understanding. Back in the nursery or classroom, adults can enter the play and take the opportunity to introduce particular aspects to children, such as what the brochures are for and what the notices say. They can model the activities of a travel agent and engage the children in scenarios that introduce key aspects of the situation.

Adults can also take the opportunity to enter play and challenge particular aspects of it. We may be aware that a small child is constantly allocated the role of 'baby', or a reluctant child never has the opportunity to take a prominent part. Our interaction with these children can be crucial in changing perceptions and shifting the balance of power. Adult intervention can also provide an opportunity for the children to reflect and think of other alternatives in particular scenarios. For example, one group of children were playing in an office. They were certain that the boss was male and the typist female. This was despite the fact that their headteacher at the time was a woman and the clerk a man! An adult entered the play and questioned the children as to their choices. She pointed out that, in fact, these stereotypical roles were not reflected in their particular reality. In addition, the teacher later engaged the children, out of the play situation, in a discussion as to what had happened. These strategies enabled the children to reflect and analyse themselves and, indeed, they led to future occasions in which the children assessed and challenged their own roles, reorganising themselves when necessary.

If children are used to adults entering the world of play in this way, they will be better prepared for large group drama work in which an adult structures a drama situation from a central role within the drama. This technique is often referred to as 'Teacher-in-role'. Before embarking on drama work featuring this technique, we can explain the similarities to children and can even use as a starting point a story or situation that has been acted out in the structured role play area.

One group of children had the Three Bears' cottage as their structured role play area. The story was familiar to them. The role play area contained three masks, three fake furs and a blonde wig. Place mats containing the owners' names were placed on the table, along with three sizes of cutlery, crockery and chairs, thus enhancing mathematical learning. Fiction and non-fiction books on the shelf in the 'house' were all about bears. After a few weeks, the theme was used for a drama session. The masks and wigs were used in the session in order to link the experiences for the children. The teacher was in role as Goldilock's mother. Other children were animals in the wood, giving advice or speaking to Goldilocks as she went into the wood. They marked their animal status by giving themselves ears, a tail, or moving on feet and hands. The teacher structured the drama work, introducing new aspects ('Look, what is that over there? Let's go and find out . . .') and posing challenges for the children.

Drama work does not have to take place in a large open area such as a hall, although of course that kind of space can be useful for some activities. Some successful drama work in the early years has been undertaken by using the whole of the nursery environment as a setting. One nursery had planned work around the theme of 'holidays'.

During one particularly successful series of drama sessions, the workers had set up areas in the nursery that contained sunbeds, palm trees constructed from card and paper, sun umbrellas, paddling pools and sand. Another area contained an 'outdoor' café, with long drinks and cocktails (non-alcoholic!). The writing area had been transformed into a post office, with postcards and a money-changing counter. A shop had been provided which sold sunglasses, suncream and sun hats, amongst other things. Another area contained an 'aeroplane', with seats and pilot area. To get to the aeroplane, the children had to go through the airport and have their passports stamped at the check-in desk. Parents and other family members had been briefed about the work and some of them eagerly took part in the ensuing drama work. Adults were in role as tourist agents, hotel managers, cocktail shakers, irritated holiday-makers and worried parents who had lost their children. The drama work enabled children to imagine that they were on holiday and take part in a range of structured and unstructured drama events as the sessions progressed. Adults did not always direct the drama work; they sometimes followed the children's lead and let the narrative progress on their terms. Sometimes a large group of children were involved in scenarios, at other times small groups went off in their own direction. When children did lose interest, there were a range of activities outside the main area for them to 'escape' to! Some children took periodic rests before returning to engage once again in the drama work. This type of project needs much careful preparation, organisation and additional adult support. Nevertheless, the benefits of such intensive drama work over a number of consecutive sessions are many and varied and all involved found the experience exhilarating. 'Teacher-in-role' can therefore be used to good effect in developing children's engagement in drama. There are also a number of other techniques which can be effective in early years work. The following section outlines a few key examples and describes how they may be used.

Still image

Still image is an extremely useful technique that can be used from an early age. With very young children, it is useful to begin with a set of carefully chosen photographs which show people involved in familiar activities such as cooking. The first step would then be for children to recreate a part of this photograph by choosing a role and putting themselves in that stance, frozen. Eventually, the group should work towards recreating the photograph, becoming aware of where each person is standing and their relationship to each other. This frozen picture is a still image.

Still image work with very young children is generally a long process and needs to be built up in small stages. For example, if we want the children to begin to think about the facial expressions of people in the photograph, work will need to be done on emotions. Children could be introduced to words such as sad, happy, angry and proud. Exercises such as 'Pass The Mask' form a good introduction. In this activity, children sit in a circle and an adult points to a number of invisible 'masks' on the floor before picking each up, putting it on and asking which mask it is. The mask is then peeled off and passed around the circle. These expressions can then be added to the still image work.

Once the children have become confident in recreating photographs they can begin to work on illustrations of key events in popular stories. Very young children are accustomed to action rhymes or joining in the actions when reading books such as Carol Lawson's *Teddy Bear, Teddy Bear*. One nursery class enjoyed becoming the 'little baby' from the Ahlbergs' *Peepo!*, copying his position with teddy, eating in his high chair, splashing in his bath or waving in the mirror. In each case, their stance was taken directly from the illustrations. Likewise, a group of four-year-olds worked with the playground illustration from a familiar book by Shirley Hughes, *Lucy and Tom go to School*. They looked in turn at the illustration in order to choose a role before placing themselves in that position, frozen. Some chose an individual role such as bouncing a ball, whilst others saw the possibilities of joining another child in the act of 'play-fighting' or chatting.

Still image work such as this can form an ideal way into a story. An adult may use the image to ask questions such as, 'What is happening at this moment? What has just happened/might happen next? How does this character feel?' Forming three or more images leads on to talking about story structure, introducing concepts of beginning, middle and end and sequencing the images in the correct order to retell the story. Eventually, still image work with older children is about creating original images rather than reproducing them. These may be moments in a story or they may be on a variety of other topics such as locations, celebrations, conflicts, or imaginary worlds.

Thought tracking

Thought tracking is a way of revealing the thoughts and feelings of a character, often taken from a still image. For example, a group of children can recreate their favourite part of a story (their own image or an illustration). When the children are frozen into their picture, the adult asks the characters what they are thinking. With younger children, the response will often be an emotion ('I'm happy', 'angry') but can become more sophisticated after discussions on well-known books ('I'm sad I took the toy'). Thought tracking then becomes a way of looking at character and story; at motivation, consequences and alternatives. As with still image work, thought tracking can be difficult for young children to understand at first and usually needs careful introduction. For example, familiarising children with Sarah Hayes's *This is The Bear* is a good introduction to speech and thought bubbles. This gives children a pictorial image of the exercise they are engaged in. If the children are asked when reading the book, 'What might it say in this bubble?' they can more easily make the transition to a still image: 'If this person had a thought bubble here, what would it say?'

For the group recreating the playground scene, thought tracking became a useful medium in which to reveal fears and doubts about entering the school playground as opposed to the security of the nursery play area. The sophistication of response varied as some children revealed their physical state ('I'm playing'), others a basic emotion ('I'm scared'), whilst some who had joined with another child revealed thoughts such as 'I like my friend' or 'I don't like fighting'. The exercise concluded with a discussion about entering school and in particular the playground, enabling the group to be advised and reassured.

Hot seating

Hot seating is another method of examining character; either a character from a book, an invented one or an historical or famous person. When introducing this technique, it is usually easier for the teacher to take the role of the character to be questioned. It may also prove useful to use one prop or piece of simple costume to indicate the transition that the adult has made from reality to fantasy and back again. This often needs to be marked clearly for younger children. The group is invited to question the character in order to discover more about their emotions and motivation, for example. At an early stage, children are often interested in other issues, asking questions such as, 'Where do you live?' or 'Do you watch Teletubbies?'

Eventually, children will take on roles themselves. One of the easiest ways to bridge the gap in understanding is to observe children in structured play areas and work from a role that they have created themselves, such as a parent or a shopkeeper. Talk to them about what they are saying or doing and try to maintain and extend that role. One child was hot seated in role as a child visiting a café. Her twin looked increasingly puzzled as she answered questions about where she lived and how many brothers and sisters she had. He opened his mouth to protest, when suddenly the dawn of realisation spread across his face and he announced, 'Oh! I see!' Once this has happened, children love this activity. It extends their role play and own story-telling, as well as their interest in the characters they will meet in stories.

Costuming

The introduction of a simple piece of costume is a powerful stimulus. A child putting on a hat or a wig can transform themselves immediately into another character, perhaps mimicking a known adult or television character. A shy child can assume another identity and become surprisingly vocal.

When using costuming as a drama technique, a piece or pieces of clothing (or possibly an artefact) can be used as clues in a guessing game stimulated by the question, 'Who does this belong to?' The children may volunteer information, or the adult can ask the children questions about the character's home, age, friends and family, physical description and occupation. Scenarios and stories can grow up around this character, or a child or adult can put on the piece of clothing to become that character and be hot seated. The clothing may be chosen to develop a particular aspect of learning.

Hot seating and costuming frequently reveal the power of the stereotypes that children have picked up from books and television. For example, one group was presented with a pink silk dress. They decided that it belonged to a beautiful princess but, despite the fact that this was an inner city, multi-ethnic school, questions about her appearance resulted in suggestions that she had long blond curls and blue eyes. Another group were given a white coat which they thought belonged to a mad scientist or a doctor. Eventually it was agreed that it belonged to a doctor who was immediately described as having a beard and a wife. Asked whether the doctor could have been a woman the children were conclusive in their cry of, 'No!' Costuming is a powerful way of challenging these perceptions from an early age. This has an impact on the children's own stories, and also allows them to recognise and question characters and situations in modern and traditional tales. Once children are practised in creating characters, a pile of dressing-up clothes in the structured play area or outside become even more exciting. Children become skilful at creating a character and adopting their persona, frequently after discussion with others.

Finally, costuming may be used for children to understand the significance of certain pieces of clothing, such as the Tam (or crown) worn by Rastafarian children or the kara (bangle), one of the five symbols of the Sikh religion. Children and adults are often questioned and sometimes mocked about clothing and it is necessary that all children should understand and respect such traditions. Introducing them through an activity such as this can enable children to build up a character, empathise with that character and talk about his beliefs. The teacher would need to be fully informed about the religion concerned and play a lead role in this form of hot seating for it to work effectively.

These four techniques form a good basis for drama work and can be easily integrated into the early years setting. Although puppetry is not itself a drama technique, it is an invaluable part of drama work and is included in this final section in order to provide a range of ideas for use in the nursery or classroom.

Puppets

Puppetry is an extremely old form of entertainment found in many cultures across the world. Some teachers have focused upon puppets as a craft activity, with the emphasis on making rather than playing with them and using them in performances. Older children may wish to make elaborate puppets and younger children may admire commercially made models. But the origins of puppet work with young children for drama purposes lie elsewhere. Very young children often endow inanimate objects with human qualities – one saucepan may talk to another or a stick may walk. This is also seen with toys; not only with dolls or toy animals, but also with toys such as cars or bricks. Children may use one finger to talk to another. In this symbolic play, children are using their imaginations to experiment with observed situations and interactions.

For these purposes, the actual form or appearance of puppets we choose to work with is unimportant. On the one hand, a stock of commercially produced puppets will last, allowing children to experience form and texture and inspiring particular stories. However, puppets created by children are their own. They are not restricted to a particular role and may take on many roles in a short period of time. If a leaf or stick can inspire a child, think what may evolve from a paper-plate face, a stuffed paper bag on a stick or faces painted onto fingers!

The merits of using puppets with young children are great and varied. Frequently, children who are reluctant to speak in front of others, even in a small group, will gain tremendous confidence through using a puppet as it presents a barrier between self and others. One child using two or more puppets together may be experiencing viewpoint and beginning to understand how people feel in certain situations. Therapeutically, a child may be working through her own experiences. As in so much drama work, we are providing a safe environment for children to explore those experiences and emotions they have which are disturbing or frightening. Children working as a group to create stories are developing skills in speaking and listening, co-operation and decision-making. Using puppets allows stories to evolve, free from the constraints imposed by the need to write or record. Children may play and compose independently, or an adult may work with a group to guide and structure the story. Either way, children can express their own experiences and ideas and will reveal what they know and understand about character and story structure. Children's stories can be recorded using a tape recorder, together with photographs or children's own drawings of particular scenes made into a book. This book can accompany the tape or direct quotes can be taken from the recording to make a simple text for the adult and child to read together. Stories created by children using puppets involve dialogue and as such they provide early experiences of plays and can be a first, unintimidating form of performance.

Drama and picture books

Drama needs the world of fiction for its vast resources: its situations, characters, problems, moods and themes. Reading needs the world of drama for its techniques and conventions which facilitate children's engagement in, and response to, texts.

(Grainger, 1998, p. 29)

In the early years, drama which is related to a particular picture book can be a valuable means of both developing children's dramatic skills and engaging them more fully with the characters and plot of a story. Using drama can help children to engage with book characters more fully, sympathise with their actions, understand their decisions and comprehend them more fully. It can encourage children to return to a book and ask for it to be read to them again and again, developing a thirst for stories that will be a spur to their reading development. Working with picture books in this way can also benefit teachers and early years workers. As adults, many of us feel much more comfortable working with books than we do tackling drama work. Using books as a springboard for drama can provide teachers with greater

Title of book: *Where's My Teddy?*	Author: Jez Alborough
Learning objective	**Activity and organisation**
• To develop the ability to take on different roles. • To develop speaking and listening skills – communicating with each other, taking part in shared activities, negotiating, etc.	Set up role play area as a wood. On each side of the wood, set out two houses, one with a large bed and large teddy (the bear's house) and one with a smaller bed and small teddy (the child's house). In the wood, set out a picnic basket, etc. Encourage children to develop play in the area. Enter occasionally to set particular scenarios, e.g. organise a teddy bears' picnic in the woods.
• To develop the ability to demonstrate emotions through body language and movements.	Children imagine that they have lost a favourite teddy. They are wandering around the woods, trying to find it. How do they feel? Can they show that they feel anxious/worried/sad? They find their teddy under a bush. How do they feel? Can they show everyone that they are very happy by the way that they move and look?
• To develop the ability to express feelings and thoughts through body movements and actions. • To develop the ability to empathise with other people's thoughts and emotions.	Children work in pairs. One is bear, one the child. One has large teddy, one small. Set the 'bears' (who have the small teddy by mistake) off, tramping around the wood, large, heavy footsteps, etc. Then ask the children to walk around the wood. They don't notice the bears at first. They start to look for their teddies in the wood. Develop the tension, e.g. You are looking everywhere ... under bushes, in holes in trees (getting stuck inside, etc.) and you can't find your teddy. (Keep other children stomping around.) You are getting very upset. Suddenly, you see a big bear carrying your teddy. (Encourage children to 'pair up' with a bear.) You are both scared of each other. How might you look? What might you do? You want to make friends. How do you do it? Now you have made friends, you can get your bear back.
• To develop the ability to express feelings and thoughts through body movements and actions.	You are Eddy's friends, going to the woods to have a picnic with him. You have to carry your food and drink in a bag/basket. It is very heavy. As you walk in the woods, you get tired and sleepy, the bag is so heavy.

Figure 8.1.   Drama from picture books

• To develop imagination. • To extend speaking and listening skills	Sit down to rest. Suddenly, you see something move. What is it? Get children to contribute ideas to develop the drama. Introduce tension now and again, e.g. there is a storm coming on. Quick, find somewhere to shelter from the rain! You've found a cave, but explore it first. What is in there? You can see something bundled up in the corner ... what is it? As teacher-in-role, enter the cave as Eddy's mum. You can't find Eddy anywhere. You are very upset. Can the children help you to find Eddy and his teddy?
• To extend speaking and listening skills. • To develop children's questioning skills. • To develop understanding of character.	The children hot seat the teacher, who is in role as the bear's mother. The bear has come back to the cottage very frightened after his encounter with Eddy. What happened? What is the bear like to live with?

Figure 8.1. Cont.

confidence when engaging in drama activities (Marsh, 1996). In addition, working with a book through drama can familiarise children with the language used in a story so that in their retelling of it, they can slip easily into 'book language'. Drama can thus be integral to the development of early reading skills. Many of the activities outlined in this chapter can be adapted and used with popular children's books. Figure 8.1 is an example of a teacher's planning for role play and drama work in relation to a popular book in the early years, Jez Alborough's *Where's My Teddy?* The book tells the story of Eddy, a boy who has lost his favourite small teddy. Upset, he searches the wood for it. He finds a teddy which looks like his, but is in fact much larger. As he picks it up, he hears menacing footsteps getting nearer and nearer. Suddenly, Eddy faces a giant bear who is clutching Eddy's small teddy. The bear is also shocked because Eddy is holding his large teddy which he has also lost. Both frightened, they grab their own teddies and run back to the safety of their own beds.

Conclusion

Having outlined these strategies, how can they be planned for and used to best advantage in an early years setting? Taking the word 'drama' back to its original Greek, we find the translation 'deed' or 'action'. As with much that is excellent in early years education, drama is about active learning and discovery. Its relationship to play is strong, and much early drama is to be found in the structured play area, whether guided by an adult or otherwise. Elsewhere, drama can be planned for, inside or outside, by providing dressing-up clothes, puppets or play people or animals. A planned, structured drama lesson of about twenty minutes can take place in a hall, large room or outdoor area. Sometimes this adds impact and excitement to the session. At other times it could be intimidating for young children, who may prefer to work in the security of a smaller, familiar space. If this is the case, using the hall, large room or outdoor area to play games in for the first few sessions will help the children adapt to and become more comfortable with the location. And, as outlined earlier, the whole of the nursery, early years setting or classroom can be taken over for the purposes of building up a dramatic narrative.

However, it is not necessary to use a large space for drama work. Much can be done sitting on a small square of carpet in a corner of the nursery or classroom. There may be opportunities to incorporate a drama technique for five to ten minutes during a group story session. For example, the front cover of Quentin Blake's *Mr Magnolia's Boot* can be used as a stimulus to build up the character of Mr Magnolia and to discuss why the adult was holding up the boot before the story is read to children. Many picture books lend themselves to this kind of work. Strategies may also be used spontaneously. Children taking a sudden interest in a character could have the opportunity to ask that person questions through hot seating, with either an adult or child in role.

So it can be seen that drama can take place anywhere, and it can be taught by anyone. There is no need for specialist training, nor does one have to be a particular kind of person to engage children's interest in drama. Drama work can be part of a structured unit of work in which the children's skills are systematically developed, but it can also occur spontaneously as we follow the children's interests and desires. If a child is demonstrating evidence of the enclosing and enveloping schema, drama work which enables children to explore caves and tunnels (with investigations into their rock formations, cave drawings and creatures that inhabit it) may prove to be very appealing! Above all, the adult's role is to recognise, respond sensitively to and structure what is there in abundance in young children – a natural propensity to play, to pretend, to imitate and to use the imagination to create vivid, whirling worlds of feelings, thoughts and actions.

Suggestions for further reading

Clipson-Boyles, S. (1998) *Drama in Primary English Teaching*, London: David Fulton.

Heald, C. (1993) *Role Play and Drama*, Leamington Spa: Scholastic.
Readman, G. and Lamont, G. (1994) *Drama: A Handbook for Primary Teachers*, London: BBC.

References

Bahktin, M. (1981) *The Dialogic Imagination: Four Essays*, edited by Michael Holquist, London: University of Texas Press.

Bolton, G. M. (1979) *Towards a Theory of Drama in Education*, London: Longman.

Bruner, J. S. (1983) *Child's Talk: Learning to Use Language*, Oxford University Press.

Cazden, C. (1983) Adult assistance to language development: scaffolds, models and direct instruction, in R. P. Parker and F. A. Davis (eds.) *Developing Literacy*, Delaware: International Reading Association.

Clipson-Boyles, S. (1998) *Drama in Primary English Teaching*, London: David Fulton.

Fleming, M. (1995) *Starting Drama Teaching*, London: David Fulton.

Goldschmied, E. and Jackson, S. (1994) *People Under Three: Young Children in Day Care*, London: Routledge.

Grainger, T. (1998) Drama and reading: illuminating their interaction, *English in Education*, Vol. 32, no. 1, pp. 29–36.

Hendy, L. (1996) Drama in the form of interactive story making in the early years classroom, in D. Whitebread (ed.) *Teaching and Learning in the Early Years*, London: Routledge.

Kitson, N. (1994) Fantasy play: a case for adult intervention, in J. Moyles *The Excellence of Play*, Buckingham: Open University Press.

Marsh, J. (1996) The play in the picture book, *Language and Learning*, Oct./Nov., pp. 13–16.

Mills, C. and Mills, D. (1998) *Dispatches: The Early Years*, London: Channel 4 Television.

Moyles, J. (1994) *The Excellence of Play*, Buckingham: Open University Press.

Vygotsky, L. S. (1978) *Mind in Society: The Development of Higher Psychological Processes*, Cambridge, Mass.: Harvard University Press.

Wood, E. and Attfield, J. (1996) *Play, Learning and the Early Childhood Curriculum*, London: Paul Chapman.

Children's books referred to in the text

Ahlberg, J. and Ahlberg, A. (1981) *Peepo!* Puffin Books.
Blake, Q. (1980) *Mr Magnolia's Boot*, Jonathan Cape.
Hughes, S. (1973) *Lucy and Tom go to School*, Picture Corgi.
Hayes, S. (1986) *This is the Bear*, Walker Books.
Lawson, C. (1993) *Teddy Bear, Teddy Bear*, David Bennet Books.
Sendak, M. (1963) *Where the Wild Things Are*, Picture Lions.

9

Computer Literacy

Moira Monteith

_____

Literacy changes

In the past, most computers in schools were used primarily by mathematicians and scientists and presumably by equally technically minded people in business and industry, yet we do not talk about computer numeracy. Literacies are increasing – we now talk of being 'visually literate', and you will read about other literacies in this book. So what do we mean by the term 'computer literate'? There is no external standard that says whether we are or not. One definition is that it refers to how far we can 'find our way round' a computer and what we learn by doing so. If we are too frightened to accomplish much, then we are not 'very computer literate'.

Paulo Freire wrote of the liberating and transformational nature of literacy. I believe that what he said can be applied to computer literacy:

> Reading the word is not preceded merely by reading the world, but by a certain form of writing it or rewriting it, that is, by transforming it by means of conscious practical work. For me, this dynamic movement is central to the literacy process.
>
> (Freire, 1987, p. 35)

The skills involved cannot be learned in isolation simply by using a computer. They need to be used in the context of learning in general, in the world in which we find ourselves. Young children are usually keen to use computers. They can use them effectively to help with their own literacy development and also to design, draw, imitate and control aspects of the world they are currently observing and experiencing.

Nowadays, children come early to the electronic page which, unlike the pages in a book, does not remain the same from one reading to the next. The cursor flashes and content can change with each edition. WWW pages change all the time, from the address at the bottom, as a page is being downloaded from a server elsewhere, to having hot-spots on which children can click to move to other WWW pages. With hypertext links (links from one page to another, or one piece of text to another), the text may still work overall with the usual protocols – for instance, with Roman script moving from left to right and top to bottom – but the links often appear to work sideways. Certainly, the sequence of pages can be interrupted and altered according to the reader's decision.

Elsewhere, in other chapters, emphasis is placed on books as fundamental to the encouragement of reading. No one would disagree with this. Book corners in classrooms, parents and children reading together and well-designed books themselves are all enriching. However, some children do not come from homes which rate books very highly. It is possible that new technologies combined with 'edutainment' will reach everyone. ('Edutainment' is a word coined for a mix of education and entertainment, such as you find in some TV programmes and computer software, including some games.) If edutainment is successful, mass literacy may indeed become attainable.

Meaning is often multiple and various in the world around us. The meanings children derive from a text as sequential as *Rosie's Walk* are complex and varied and even more so from a screen page, such as those in the Sesame Street CD Rom. We need to learn with children that computer literacy breaks boundaries and expands our present view of literacy. The empowering nature of Information and Communications Technology (ICT) should surely be included in any helpful definition of computer literacy.

How we can learn with our children

Our children are growing up in a world where ICT has intruded in a major way so that we cannot tell individually how much our environment is managed for us. We all know that there has been an exponential leap in terms of recent communications developments. However, young children in the next decade will see even further change at a faster rate. They will adapt to that as part of their environment and we must learn more consciously to adapt with them. Computer technology, unlike previous technologies such as photography, gives rise frequently and consistently to situations where adults ask for and take advice from young children and certainly from teenagers. This must surely change the nature of the 'learning contract' in schools. In the nursery years we must be careful not to hamper young children with too much of our 'learned caution'. Sometimes we must learn to learn alongside them.

One of the excellent features of working with computers is the ease with which we can improve items and get rid of mistakes and bugs in the system. It is, therefore, an excellent model for learning. Very young children can understand that there are stages of learning by working on pictures and texts or improving their games scores. We can talk with them quite specifically about the development of their work and learning.

Rules and regulations: access and use

Not every child will have easy access to a computer at home so we need to ensure a level of use in nursery and school that is equable. Ask children to share their time with this important resource and encourage them to collaborate with teaching and support staff to ensure that everyone is involved over a certain period of time, perhaps a week. Keep an open and obvious audit of use somewhere; for example, a list of children's names with a tick each time they have used the computer. Children are very observant when it comes to 'fair play' as we know, and are a great aid in helping each other.

Most families with computers at home make rules about their use (Downes and Reddacliff, 1997). They tend to regulate the time children spend on games or 'playing' at the computer and develop a list of priorities. If parents or elder siblings need to 'work' at the computer, then they usually have a greater claim on its use. Some families have rules about individual use; for example, how long children can use a computer in isolation in a bedroom. Early years settings and schools need to develop their own ground rules and discuss them with family liaison groups.

Similarly, it is helpful to compare how different people are using their computers and what software packages they find useful or interesting. Young children often use computers with adults or older siblings, both in playing games and working with other software, painting, writing letters and email messages, making booklets and multimedia sequences. They are learning about collaborative learning, using the skills of apprenticeship and taking part in a mentoring relationship at an early age. Talking about such uses helps all of us, parents as well as staff, in early years settings and schools. This way, we can try to ensure that all children have broadly similar opportunities and that computer use at home can have positive spillover effects in nurseries and school. As Professor Stephen Heppell noted, often the majority of a school's computers are at home (Heppell, 1996).

Even in areas of comparative financial impoverishment, it is surprising how many computers there are at home, even excluding games machines. David Saunders, a headteacher, recently undertook a survey of computer use in his school (1998). Their OFSTED report stated that the school: 'serves a poor socio-economic community', but he found that 20.9 per cent of children in the nursery class had access to a non-games machine. The nursery also included pupils from two other schools so only 9.7 per cent of his children actually had a computer, but that is still one family in ten. National figures suggest 'there is wide variation in the incidence of home ownership of computers. About one-third of English homes now have access to computers. This proportion is increasing rapidly, and often the facilities available at home are more advanced than those in schools' (Goldstein, 1997, p. 2).

Space for learning

It is important to have the computer within a working environment, rather than put with others of its kind in a draughty corridor or a locked room. Placing one or more computers in an early years setting or classroom helps us to consider more concretely what we are doing with the learning space. Have we got enough room near the computer for other writing and play materials? Is there enough space for several children to sit together? On the other hand, computers do not react well to sand and water being thrown over them or sticky drinks spilt down them.

Unfortunately, health and safety requirements are sometimes ignored. Trolleys are usually designed to be trolleys but are often used as desks. They are only bearable because (a) currently there are not enough computers to go round and it is easier to move them on a trolley (b) children usually sit at them for not much longer than half an hour at most. I have seen many children in difficult working positions; small children with their heads thrown back trying to look at a screen on a computer above them on a trolley; children in a cubby hole with the computer, sometimes with no room to put anything else at all; children with their arms stretched out to reach the keyboard and so on. No office staff would or should put up with such conditions of use. We need to consider children's height and the position of the computer in relation to that. The versatility of portables is particularly beneficial. Children can take them to the book corner, to the writing area, on their tables or on outings and they seem to like their smaller size.

Playing

ICT sometimes reveals certain hang-ups we as adults have about our learning and the level of formality we associate with it. Most adults when learning a new software package will 'play' with it for some time, finding out by discovery, trial and error, by reading some of the manual, using the 'help' section and asking other people. Such time may be considered 'play' as the end is not related to a specific outcome, at least not for the time being. They are not processing, as yet, the final product.

Much software for young children is controlled in the sense that children complete an action by dressing a teddy or matching cars or some such activity. Play in the sense of just using the materials is not possible. However, with more open-ended software such as word processing or paint packages, children can 'play' with very effective results, which clearly helps their learning. Do have computers with relevant software available for young children to use or 'play' with sporadically, when they feel like it. They realise very early on the connections between screen and keyboard, sound and vision. They can use different colours in the palette if they are 'painting' and press letters on the keyboard when 'writing'.

The versatility of computers means they can be placed in different areas such as an 'office' or a 'shop' or a 'house'. Children can print out simple bills or menus or whatever is appropriate for the place where the computer is. In this way they can learn while 'playing' not only how to manipulate keys and mouse and tracker ball, but also how computers are used in a variety of businesses and out-of-school environments.

Games

Games, as we all know, are much more organised forms of play. It is possible that too much time spent with computer games leads children to respond in limited ways to subsequent learning situations. Speed, for example, is essential in many games in order to score. Subsequently speed may be detrimental to developing judgement and discussion skills. Jonathan Grove (Grove and Williams, 1998), found that some 9-year-olds brought with them approaches they had learned from games which hindered their exploration of a model of an ancient Greek Villa created from the Virtual Reality software, Superscape. Instead of looking at what was in the villa, they clicked on all parts of the screen as they thought there would be links to games items, keys, puzzles or escapes. Rupert Wegerif (1997) found that games players, instead of discussing choices when using problem-solving software, tended to click quickly almost without talking. Children shared time in the sense of turn and turn about at the keyboard but did not share information, ideas or opinions.

Certainly most children I have interviewed in reception classes and in Year 1 at school said that they played games with their parents, friends or cousins. There is no doubt that games are widely enjoyed and some people, including Seymour Papert (1993), believe that older children are highly motivated by designing games themselves. However, we need to show children at an early age the diversity of use to which we put computers. Knowledge of such diversity is an integral part of computer literacy. If children play games to such an extent that they consider a games environment to be 'the' computer environment, then they are somewhat hindered in later learning. Computer games are part of every child's (or virtually every child's) environment now and we must help them see that such games are only a part of the diverse world of ICT. As Paulo Freire wrote in a very different context: 'Students remind the teachers of the essential learning task: that learning and teaching are meant to bring about self-knowledge with knowledge of one's culture' (Freire, 1987, p. 23). Our children's cultural environment keeps changing and we can help them learn that their own 'world' can encompass more than they have experienced or imagined so far.

However, it is certainly true that early games playing has produced one fortuitous yet agreeable outcome – children understand high numbers much more quickly than they once did. 'Hundreds' and 'thousands' used to be terms which just meant larger and larger numbers to most young children. Games manufacturers tend to put game scores in high numbers. Now very young children can tell the difference between their scores and those of other players. There is no easy comparison between learning the concept of huge numbers and a literacy construct that we can say was understood as a result of playing computer games. Nevertheless, learning the use of large numbers is a very interesting development in terms of children's capacity to learn when there is motivation to do so. That being so, there may be some pay-off for literacy in playing computer games, but on the whole, it seems more likely that more traditional games, with their dependence on rhyme and repetition, may prove much more useful. Either way, we should not ignore the existence of computer games or consider them as something 'alien' to learning. At the very least, let us use them as a focus for conversation, discuss winning and losing strategies and gain some awareness of the child's knowledge of games culture.

Working

Working and playing, we continue to learn. Clearly, we can do different things with different packages and develop a range of learning experiences, both using computers and away from them.

What can young children do with a word processor?

Observers in a research project with young children in the USA (Olson and Johnston, 1989) recorded exactly what they saw the children doing when they were using computers. Such observations help us understand children's development, rather than have preconceptions about what they should or should not be doing. For instance, children frequently make letter strings; that is, they key in various letters for different lengths of time, for example: zzzzzzzzzzzzzzhtopm, wwwwwq. Sometimes the letter strings may take up half a page. Children often consider that they are 'typing' or 'working in an office' when they do this. They take visible pleasure in the power they have when they press on a particular key and it repeats the letter time and time again. This activity may appear to be 'play' interfering with 'work', but more likely, it is a stage for finding out what the machine can do. They may continue to generate letter strings at times, long after they can type out words, sentences and even stories. There seems no need to try to prevent them doing this (as I know some teachers have done). They grow out of the habit.

Young children also use the delete key with positive glee, often deleting words an adult watcher would wish them to keep. They will often ask (and can be prompted) as to how to make capital letters and sometimes how to put in 'little dots' (as some young children call full stops). You may have to show them where the cursor is two or three times as they need to use it as a point of change. Young children can manipulate a mouse quite well after a few trial runs, even well enough to draw outlines on the screen, should they wish to do so.

Once they know certain words, they will include these amongst the letter strings. For instance, this occurs with their name. Accompanying the 'letter string' and use of delete key activities is the 'hunt and peck' search for letters on the keyboard. When we encourage children to use two hands to hunt and peck, they seem more confident and in charge, rather than continuing with one hand and one finger. In addition, our fingertips are learning zones, so 'learning through your fingers' is no idle phrase.

The fact that the letters on most ordinary keyboards are capitals does not seem to matter as much as adults think. Often, children do find letters more easily at first when they are in lower case but they learn very quickly that there are both big and small forms. Keyboards with larger keys and larger letters can be helpful but are not essential. Word processors that are really toys are not practicable as they are often limited and limiting in scope. Children can move ahead much faster than we often anticipate and do not need hampering by equipment they have outgrown. Instead, it is far better to start with an apparently more challenging keyboard where children can explore further strategies later.

Children can begin activities which are helpful stages on the way to literacy. They can express meaning by writing short statements, connect the symbols on the screen with their own actions, learn to key in words from left to right and top of the screen downwards. One teacher found that a simple word processor was preferable for most young children, compared with one which had an accompanying picture for each statement the child wrote. She considered this to be so because the children took a great deal of time over the picture and consequently spent less time on typing in the letters (Walker, 1997). Her worry was due, perhaps, to lack of equipment and if there had been sufficient computers for children to keep coming back to their own text, the time factor would not be so important. However, it is useful to remember that you might want to encourage only writing sometimes and not necessarily writing to accompany a picture.

Young children often do not remember exactly every word they had decided to write when they are picking out their letters with care. It is possible to act as a recorder for them; to ask what they wish to write and, as they finish a word, to remind them of the next one. Many of the strategies you use when developing children's writing you can use with word processing. So, for instance, adults or older children can act as scribes for stories and accounts longer than a few words. These texts can be 'published' as longer versions in many forms, using simple programs such as Hyperstudio to produce animated versions.

Children go through stages of word processing just as they do writing and there are strong correlations, of course. After observing 24 children over two years, I decided there were 6 obvious stages (Monteith, 1996) which will usually overlap from nursery to first years of schooling. These stages were based on the evolving stages in the 'Concepts about Print Test' as proposed by Marie Clay (Clay, 1979). They are helpful in apprising where an individual child has reached with simple word processing. You can then encourage children to target further skills. Children move through the same stages, but at different rates.

1. *Children can distinguish a number of letters, usually consonants, in the sentences they wish to write and find them on the keyboard. The number increases steadily over a period of weeks.*

2. *Children know the majority of the letters of the alphabet but there is a group they cannot recognise or they do not distinguish one from another. For instance, they mix 'p' and 'b' and similar pairings and also have trouble finding a 'last few' letters.*

3. *Children can guess the first letter of a word and then find it on the keyboard.*

4. *Children can recognise virtually all the letters on the keyboard. They can suggest the first letter of most words they wish to use and often, if asked, the last letter.*

5. *Children can write a number of short words. They start with their name but by this stage they are often writing short prepositions such as 'on' as well as 'the', which they have learnt to spell by frequent use.*

6. *Children include vowels in their 'guessed' spellings though at first they use vowels interchangeably, 'a' for 'o', for example.*

Alongside these stages children learn to use the delete key, make spaces between words (though this can be forgotten in the heat of creation), use the shift key to make capital letters (though not necessarily knowing where to put them) and some can use the cursor to go back into text and find and change letters. Word processing is positively helpful in encouraging children's knowledge of the computer and their own developing literacy.

Problem-solving software

The majority of software packages used with young children falls into this category, ranging from simple 'matching' programs to quite sophisticated packages with numerous options. Children of three years of age can co-ordinate their actions sufficiently well to open software packages on screen, click the correct key(s) when they recognise a particular symbol or perhaps their own name and follow through the package, pressing keys as appropriate.

Many programs appear to imitate activities that children can do elsewhere, such as matching pairs of objects. I used to consider the use of such programs a misuse of computer time, on the grounds that children could do the same activities elsewhere by other means. This still may be true if there are very few computers available but if we have enough for all classrooms (every class needs a minimum of 8, in my opinion) then there is no reason why some children should not be using them for activities such as matching. I have changed my mind about this use of computers since Helen Finlayson and Deirdre Cook have demonstrated so clearly (1998) that children spend longer on task doing the 'same' task when using a computer compared to the same activity at a table or workbench. Since they also quote research indicating that longer time on task coincides with further learning, it seems reasonable to accept such programs in electronic versions.

Programs can focus on specific outcomes, such as learning phonics. Such programs are particularly helpful when their use crosses the boundaries between nursery, Reception and primary schools. Policy on cross-use of software can be a very positive support to children's learning. Problem-solving software is as its generic name indicates: it encourages diverse skills. It is therefore difficult to state whether a given software package does or does not promote learning efficiently, or even if it promotes the kind of learning the advertisers claim. You can look for reviews in the journals and newspapers or you can become part of a group which shares evaluations around its members. Several nurseries, schools and parent groups could, for instance, form their own group for such purposes. You can set up an evaluation yourself, by observing carefully ten or so different children working with the software and assessing how beneficial a particular program is. It is worthwhile remembering, however, that some software which is not particularly engaging in itself can promote discussion about learning or choices or both and, secondly, can act as a starting place for work away from the computer, or with other programs on the computer. Since software changes so rapidly and more is offered each succeeding year, local groups of reviewers are invaluable. Evaluating software yourself is important and empowering, as it gives insight as to what is being achieved and also helps reveal the purposes for which you may wish to purchase software in the future.

Talking books

Nowhere do we need good reviewing more than in relation to talking books which are becoming very popular with both schools and parents. Chris Taylor undertook a research project on the use of talking books in schools and concluded that:

> These packages form a very useful additional tool in the armoury available to help the teaching of reading. The children are able to read them independently and do not spend their time just listening to the stories.
>
> (Taylor, 1996, p. 2)

Many schools use talking books and related software alongside other resources. Hazel James uses a program 'which consolidates stories the children are reading with their teachers and at home . . . children are able to access the stories initially for themselves' (James, 1998, p. 7).

However, some US research has indicated that total reliance on talking books in learning how to read can inhibit successful reading. I suspect that no one will be surprised to hear this. Successful reading practice is built on oral communication and a varied wealth of printed material including some on screen. Reliance on any one particular method must be considered doubtful, particularly after the findings of the Qualifications and Curriculum Authority on the Reading Recovery Programme (1998). I suggest the questions listed in Figure 9.1 as a starting point for your own reviews of talking books. You will need to tailor these to your own policies and requirements.

Photography

Even a very short time ago, digital cameras were way out of the price range for most schools and nurseries. However, they are decreasing

Where there are numbers: 4 = excellent, 3 = good, 2 = fair, 1 = poor				
How well is the story or account told?	4	3	2	1
Does the visual presentation aid the story/account?	4	3	2	1
How appropriate are the audio effects?	4	3	2	1
How effective is the interactive element?	4	3	2	1
How well is the overall package designed?	4	3	2	1
How user friendly is it to operate?	4	3	2	1
What text level work can be planned from it?				
What sentence level work can be planned from it?				
What word level work can be planned from it?				
What will the child achieve by using this?				
Recommendations for use				
Recommendations for accompanying work				
Negative aspects, if any				

Figure 9.1. Criteria for assessing talking books

in price extremely rapidly and, moreover, they give great value for money. Children of four and five years of age can take photographs themselves quite easily. If their first attempts are blurred and fuzzy, they can see the effects themselves if the picture is shown (and enlarged) on a computer screen. Their techniques rapidly improve. In addition, adults can take photos of events in the nursery or on walks or of children's homes and family and these can be stored on a hard disk and called up whenever appropriate. Add-ons to computers, such as zip drives, mean that files which normally take up a great deal of memory and are too large to hold on a floppy disk can be kept and even sent to other people. Photographic quality paper allows prints of virtually the same quality as a photographic print, even when using a reasonably cheap printer.

Photographs can be a stimulus for discussion at a one-to-one, small or large group session. Adults and older children can organise digitised pictures in multiple contexts and, with digital cameras, use them in other electronic formats such as WWW pages and multimedia clips. Teaching and support staff can review the progress of children in their care by examining photos, displaying them and discussing them in small presentations. They can be visual reminders of children's development.

Stephen Marcus (1998) writes:

> Visual information literacy includes the ability to 'read' (i.e. interpret, decode, translate) and design (i.e. create and communicate with) images. In addition, it implies an active rather than a passive orientation. We must decide what objects constitute meaningful features in our environment. We must decide what is worth looking for and looking at. The overall goal is to be able to see oneself in the world more clearly, more accurately and more completely.
>
> (Marcus, 1998, p. 59)

Young children can show us what *their* world is about through the use of photographs.

Use of the Internet

Two uses are clear: (a) for gaining information about research and training in early years learning and (b) for publishing. The second will grow in demand. Currently, people who are not used to the thought of publication wonder why anyone else in the world would wish to look at what, for example, their nursery group is doing. Most of us will not be doing anything so very extraordinary after all.

However, in reality, we will be publishing mainly to a specific audience. Some nursery groups may wish to communicate with other groups in other parts of the country or abroad, but it is more likely that they will put up examples of their own and children's work for the benefit of parents, other relatives and people who might be sending their children to the nursery later. Web pages are becoming easier to create all the time and digital cameras and scanners will allow photos and scans to be placed easily on those pages.

A current example (which may well not exist by the time you are reading this) concerns the 'Jolly Postman' series (written by the Ahlbergs). If you make a search on the Internet by requesting information on the 'Jolly Postman', you will find not only publishers' information about the series but also examples from some schools of their work; for example, a 'post cow' – stories about a cow delivering post, written and illustrated by young children. All you need to do is scan the children's work using a scanner and you have the material to add to your web site.

We will be able to exchange details about children's development in the early years much more readily, perhaps for research purposes or for showing grandparents who live at some distance. Similarly, all staff will be able soon to access web-sites such as the Association for Literacy, the National Grid for Learning and international sites such as one for research into Asian children's development. One of the targets announced by the government in their consultation paper, *Connecting the Learning Society*, that over 75 per cent of teachers and 50% of pupils should have email addresses, will encourage more and more users by 2002.

Speaking and listening

The notion of young children controlling electronic toys may seem a far cry from working on their literacy skills. Nevertheless, Carol Fine and Mary Lou Thornbury have shown in their work (1998) that young children benefit in broad terms from such activities.

> Our experience in using control in the early years is that children talk and listen, revise and review, and evaluate and refine the use of their language in order to be understood and to achieve their joint goals.

> The children in the nursery were using a robust robot called 'Pip'. Their theme was the family life of Mr and Mrs Wolf. For a few days, different groups explored a route to the shops or a route to pick up Baby Wolf from school. They covered the full taxonomy

of skills identified by Val Warren (1992): spatial awareness including the language of position and direction, recognition of numerals including zero, the stages of measurement, recall of the 'grammar' or sequence of commands and development of logical thinking.

(Fine and Thornbury, 1998, p. 10)

It is very important that we use every opportunity to encourage children to speak meaningfully and effectively to each other and to adults.

Recent evidence suggests the failure of British early years education to teach effective spoken language ... A 1995 survey of ten classes of four-year-olds showed that out of 300 two-minute observations collected over three months, only 10 showed spoken interaction between children or between children and adults ... An early years literature search has revealed little or no awareness of the problem.

(Mills and Mills, 1998, p. 10)

Active work with practical and stimulating tasks as outlined by Fine and Thornbury (1998) give many children opportunities for meaningful conversations they might otherwise miss. Pupils gain in terms of language development as well as social co-operation in learning. Similarly:

The free and frequent use of telephone handsets in our Nursery, Reception and Year 1 Classes ensures that our Under-6s have ample opportunity to practise the skills of speaking and listening whilst developing a familiarity with the tools of Communications Technology.

(Gibson, Brand and Watson, 1998, p. 6)

Concept keyboards

From an area of innovation to one much more traditional, even one which can employ our 'legacy' hardware. Teachers frequently used concept keyboards with BBC computers but they are now designed for use across platforms (Resource, 1998). Overlay or concept keyboards are basically flat boards containing a matrix of touch sensitive cells or switches, on top of which a paper overlay can be placed. Pupils, by using these keyboards, can participate in learning activities which require higher level skills than they have yet acquired. Concept keyboards are also useful for children who find a standard keyboard difficult to use.

Pupils press on the relevant images to print out what is required. For instance, they may need certain words or phrases for a story they are writing or illustrating. Overlays can help with sentence construction and with particular words, especially when young children are frustrated with their lack of speed using the 'hunt and peck' approach to typing. However, the word 'concept' to me highlights their potential significance. Overlays allow users to access concepts which they know about but find difficulty in writing or drawing. This is clearly obvious in the outside world, a feature which is helpful for us as teachers to point out to children. I used to wonder how bar staff in a pub could add up two gins and tonic, two pints of bitter, half of mild, a coke and five packets of crisps so quickly until I saw the form of overlay many pubs use. They are actually linking image and cost together. An overlay is an excellent way for children to link word and symbol together.

Summary

- Use of ICT is empowering and this aspect must be included in any helpful definition of computer literacy.
- Computer literacy breaks bounds and expands our view of literacy.
- Discuss learning in general and learning with ICT in particular as often as possible.
- Find out where the computers are, both in school and at home.
- Decide on some rules about their use.
- Make sure that the computers are physically accessible and safe to use.
- An awareness that computer games are only one aspect of ICT must be part of a young child's computer literacy.
- Children can show us quite quickly which stage they have reached through word processing a sentence or two.
- We need local reviewing groups for software and its usage.
- Media mix is all-important: no one should rely solely on one technology.
- Remember that other activities, such as control, can promote literacy also.

Postscript

Since the Teacher Training Agency has stated that the National Curriculum for Initial Teacher Training (DfEE Circular 4/98) will be the basis for the training of teachers in post, it seems sensible to include here the section from this TTA document which refers to the use of ICT in the early years.

Trainees on courses providing for pupils aged 3–8 and 3–11 must be taught the importance of introducing pupils in nursery and reception classes to the use of ICT and to recognise the contribution that ICT can make to this age group, including how to:

a. encourage pupils to become familiar with ICT and positive users of it;

b. ensure that all pupils have opportunities to use ICT, and that their experience takes account of any home use or other previous experience of ICT;

c. identify and teach the skills necessary for handling input devices effectively, *e.g. switches, mouse, keyboard*;

d. use ICT to support the development of language and literacy, through the use of programs which develop reading and writing, *e.g. to reinforce letter/sound correspondence*, and encourage pupils to engage with stories, songs and rhymes presented on the screen, as well as through the use of high quality educational broadcasts;

e. use ICT to support the development of numeracy through the use of computer programs and robots which develop and reinforce the use of mathematical language, and the recognition and exploration of numbers, simple mental operations and patterns;

f. use ICT to support pupils' creative development through the use of computer programs which encourage them to explore and experiment with pattern, shape, pictures, sound and colour;

g. encourage pupils working collaboratively with ICT to share responsibilities for making decisions and reaching conclusions, *e.g. as they progress through a simple computer adventure game.*

(DfEE, 1998, pp. 22–23)

Suggestions for further reading:

MAPE (1998) *MAPE Focus on Literacy Pack*, Northampton: MAPE[1] Publications.

Monteith, M. (ed.) (1998) *IT for Learning Enhancement*, Exeter: Intellect.

Shreeve, A. (ed.) (1997) *IT in English Series*, Coventry: NCET.

References

Clay, M. (1979) *The Early Detection of Reading Difficulties*, Heinemann: London.

Downes, T. (1995) *Learning in an Electronic World*, Newton, NSW: Primary English Teaching Association.

Downes, T. and Reddacliff, C. (1997) *Stage 3 Preliminary Report of Children's Use of Electronic Technologies in the Home*, University of Western Sydney:

Macarthur, Campbelltown, NSW 2560.

Fine, C. and Thornbury, M. (1998) *MAPE Focus on Literacy Pack*, Northampton: MAPE Publications.

Finlayson, H. and Cook, D. (1998) The value of passive software in young children's collaborative work, in M. Monteith (ed.) *IT for Learning Enhancement*, Exeter: Intellect.

Freire, P. (1987) *Reading the Word and the World*, London: Routledge and Kegan Paul.

Gibson, J. Brand, L. and Watson, C. (1998) *Literacy and IT, MAPE Focus on Literacy Pack*, Northampton: MAPE Publications.

Goldstein, G. (1997) *IT in English Schools: A Commentary on Inspection Findings 1995–6*, Coventry: NCET.

Grove, J. and Williams, N. (1998) Explorations in virtual History, in M. Monteith (ed.) *IT for Learning Enhancement*, Exeter: Intellect.

Heppel, S. (1996) Paper given at ITTE Conference, Cambridge.

James, H. (1998) *Literacy and IT, MAPE Focus on Literacy Pack*, Northampton: MAPE Publications.

Marcus, S. (1998) Picture information literacy, in M. Monteith (ed.) *IT for Learning Enhancement*, Exeter: Intellect.

Mills, C. and Mills, D. (1998) *Dispatches: The Early Years*, London: Channel 4 Television.

Monteith, M. (1996) Combining literacies: the use of 'individual time' for word processing with young children, in B. Neate (ed.) *Literacy Saves Lives*, Hertfordshire: UKRA.

Olson, K. and Johnston, J. (1989) *The Use of the Computer as a Writing Tool in a Kindergarten and First Grade Classroom (CIEL)*, Ann Arbor Institute for Social Research, School of Education, Michigan University, USA.

Papert, S. (1993) *The Children's Machine*, London: Harvester Wheatsheaf.

QCA (1998) *Report on Reading Recovery Programme*, London: HMSO.

Resource (1998) www.resourcekt.co.uk.

Saunders, D. (1998) Research carried out as part of MSc in Education Management, Sheffield Hallam University.

Taylor, C. (1996) *Teaching Reading with Talking Story Books*, New Orleans: ICTE Conference.

Walker, L. (1997) Emergent writing and IT at KS1, *Microscope – Early Years Special*, Northampton: MAPE Publications.

Warren, V. (1992) We called our roamer 'John', *Strategies*, Vol. 2, no. 3.

Wegerif, R. (1997) Factors affecting the quality of children's talk at computers, in R. Wegerif and P. Scrimshaw (eds.) *Computers and Talk in the Primary Classroom*, Clevedon: Multilingual Matters.

Note

1. MAPE is an association for the use of ICT in primary education and can be contacted via the Technology Centre, Newman College, Bartley Green, Birmingham B32 3NT.

10

Teletubby Tales: Popular Culture and Media Education

Jackie Marsh

This chapter explores the opportunities offered by the incorporation of work on popular culture into the literacy curriculum. The first part of the chapter provides an overview of studies done in recent years that demonstrate the possibilities and problems associated with work on popular culture in the curriculum. Activities which have been successfully conducted in nurseries and classrooms are then considered and suggestions made for approaches which celebrate children's culture in the classroom. Popular culture for many children in industrialised societies is inextricably linked to the media. Work on the media is now accepted as a valid area of study for older children in many secondary schools. This chapter argues that such work should be started with children who attend nurseries and early years settings in order to develop their analytical skills in relation to the media.

What is popular culture?

We usually think of popular culture as relating to our leisure and home interests, interests that we share with a number of other people. Many of us think of the term as applying to cultural interests that are not considered 'high' culture (for example, opera or classical music). However, Mukerji and Schudson (1991) stress that popular culture is multi-faceted:

> Popular culture refers to the beliefs and practices, and the objects through which they are organized, that are widely shared among a population. This includes folk beliefs, practices and the objects rooted in local traditions, and mass beliefs, practices and objects generated in political and commercial centers. It includes elite

153

cultural forms that have been popularized as well as popular
forms that have been elevated to the museum tradition.

(Mukerji and Schudson, 1991, p. 3)

This captures some of the complexities inherent in the term as popular cultural forms are constantly emerging, changing and fading in
significance. Mukerji and Schudson recognise that we are not dealing
with one form of popular culture but many; each cultural group has
its own particular popular beliefs, practices and objects. It is also not
always easy to distinguish between what is perceived as 'high' and
'low' culture in any one community. It is clear, therefore, that we cannot clearly define what children's popular culture is. It will vary from
community to community, from child to child. However, there are particular forms of children's popular culture which are common to
many children from a wide range of communities. These popular cultural interests are generally related to mass-produced media.

Children's contemporary popular culture in Western industrialised
societies is largely based around toys and television. In fact, the two
are often intertwined as the toy manufacturers work with the media
producers to capture children's interests and their families' money.
Kinder (1991) and Kline (1993) have carefully documented this interplay of media, consumer goods and popular culture. Kline shows how
the combination of the different aspects of consumerism produce a
powerful force which ensures that a new concept/superhero is soon
part of children's lives. Disney brings out a new cartoon or a television company devises a new series and very soon fast food chains
offer related toys. A host of related products are then seen on the
shelves of supermarkets, clothes shops and department stores.
Television adverts whet children's appetites for such goods and the
child and her parents are trapped in a consumerist cycle of supply
and demand. However, whilst it is true that there is a great deal of
manipulation which occurs in the toy and media business, McDonnell
(1994) points out in her exploration of the popularity of the *Teenage
Mutant Ninja Turtles* that, 'marketing techniques can only go so far
towards creating these kinds of phenomena' (p. 138). Children are
ultimately the ones who decide the fate of new products.

Kline (1993) also suggests that children's popular culture today is
more violent and corrupt than that of the past. This is a common conception. However, it is clear that children's play in the days before
television permeated their lives was not free from violence and
aggression. French (1987) carried out a survey of childhood pastimes,
using a small cross-section of people, and found that there was a long
tradition of potentially violent games such as 'cowboys and Indians',

'cops and robbers' and war games. The concept of childhood promoted by certain Western industrialised cultures as one of an era of purity and innocence, prevalent in the work of Kline, appears to affect how many people perceive children's popular culture (Hilton, 1996). McDonnell (1994) points out that adults have always resisted the messages contained in children's popular culture, each generation worrying that its content will degrade the innocent youth of the time:

> It may appear to contemporary crusaders that violence in the popular media is a threat of an entirely different order than these quaint artefacts of the past. But in their day the *Rovers Boys*, silent movies and *True Crime* comics were believed to be every bit as threatening to the existing social order as Ninja Turtles and Terminator movies are today.
>
> (Mc Donnell, 1994, p. 112)

Thus we can see that the alarm surrounding the violence, sexism and racism and xenophobia in much of today's popular culture for children is not new. This is not to deny its legitimacy but instead is a plea for reactions that take a more measured look at how we might begin to get children to grapple with these issues.

Popular culture in the nursery and classroom

Given that children are surrounded by a host of television icons, videos, toys and related products at home and in society at large, why do we need to incorporate work on these texts into the nursery or classroom? Many people would argue that early years settings should provide a refuge from such commercialised interests and should introduce children to tasks and texts which they assume are of inherently better quality. However, many children come to playgroup, nursery or school and find that their culture or lifestyle is not reflected in the books, toys and pictures on offer. This dissonance between home and school literacy practices and the effect this has on working class children's educational experience has been discussed elsewhere (Brice-Heath, 1983; Luke, 1993; Gee, 1996; Lankshear *et al.*, 1997). The situation has improved in recent years as educators strive to ensure that the resources they use reflect the multi-cultural society in which we live. This will inevitably help children to feel more at home in a nursery or school setting. However, the rest of the curriculum generally remains determined by the interests and aims of the workers and teachers who construct it. Children are guided towards a particular version of literature, or particular types of play. Role play areas encourage literacy related to adult-oriented versions of literacy uses in the real world – cafés, shops and post offices. This is not to suggest that these experiences are not valuable and indeed in Chapter 7, Nigel Hall outlines just how important these experiences are in children's literacy development. Nevertheless, at times these are experiences guided by adult agendas rather than children's own interests.

If we did incorporate activities related to children's own cultural interests into the curriculum, what effect will that have on their motivation and interest? Exciting work by Pompe (1992, 1996) and Dyson (1994, 1996) has demonstrated that introducing work into the classroom based on children's popular and media interests can promote an enthusiastic and active engagement with the curriculum. The next section of the chapter moves on to consider ways in which children's popular cultural interests can be harnessed in order to promote literacy.

Popular culture alphabet

Ann Ketch (1991) advocates the creation of a dictionary which uses sweet wrappers in order to develop children's interest in, and recognition of, letters of the alphabet. This idea can be easily extended to feature images from children's popular culture. This involves the creation of a ring binder containing plastic wallets. In each plastic wallet, a blank page is placed with a letter of the alphabet written upon it. On each page, adults and children can paste artefacts from children's popular culture which begin with that letter. So, for example, the 'B' page can contain pictures of Barbie and Beauty and the Beast, 'G' illustrated with images of the Ghostbusters and Gladiators, and so on. One nursery worker made a 'popular culture' alphabet in a scrapbook which he then took into the nursery:

> I was amazed by the kids' reactions. They absolutely loved it, pored over it for hours, excitedly talking and pointing to things they recognised. They began to bring in things to add to the dictionary and before long I had enough to fill 3 books! Always had a problem with some letters, though. Couldn't find much that began with 'Q', for example! 'I' has been made much easier since the Ice Warriors became popular on TV and, of course, we have Xena for 'X'!

This sort of project could be extended to involve the family in promoting children's literacy development. Parents could be given particular letters and asked to collect things with their children that began with that letter. Each child could make her own alphabet book. This would ensure that the contents of the alphabet really did reflect the cultural interests of the children. We cannot assume that all children will share the same passion for Barbie or the Teletubbies!

When working on environmental print, children can be reminded of the print that surrounds them on texts and items relating to popular culture. Catalogues from shops can be a powerful way to engage children in speaking and listening activities related to their own experiences and worlds. For some children, poring over these pictures which are related to popular culture can be a far more effective way of stimulating discussion than sharing other kinds of texts which contain more alien worlds. One nursery teacher describes how he found such work a valuable way into a child's world:

> I was working in a Southwark nursery school supporting bilingual under-5s. Tunde, a Nigerian child (the youngest in his family) was not terribly confident, didn't relate to the nursery staff and didn't engage with the usual literacy activities offered. The nursery had a pile of old catalogues for children to do cutting and sticking. One day Tunde found a catalogue and every day after that he would find me, we would get out the 'patalogues' and he turned the pages, pointing out and talking about the toys he wanted. The ritual and the one-to-one were obviously important to his emotional security, but also important was the familiarity of the catalogues and the objects in them and their link to his own experiences. We could have had pieces of fabric and calabashes and they might have been meaningful, but it was the catalogues that worked for him and that were his culturally significant objects.

Work on letters and print can go alongside such discussion, with children being asked to find images which begin with certain letters, or find objects in the catalogue that contain a logo they recognise.

Role play areas

Role play areas are a key site for introducing themes which are related to children's popular culture. A project in which a 'Batman and Batwoman HQ' was set up in the role play area of a class of six- and seven-year-olds has been described elsewhere (Marsh, Payne and Anderson, 1997). The HQ contained a range of opportunities for engaging in literacy activities, as well as costumes and artefacts which encouraged imaginative play based on the 'Batman' theme. The level of interest in the HQ was extremely high and it attracted children who would otherwise not have entered a role play area. Because the area was stocked with literacy resources, the children also became involved in many more literacy activities than had been anticipated. Given the concern that has been expressed concerning boys' involvement in the literacy curriculum, it was notable that boys who had been identified by their teachers as previously uninterested in the literacy curriculum became obsessed with reading and writing in the 'Bat Cave'! The girls were no less interested, and the project demonstrated the excitement and motivation that work on popular culture can generate. Superhero discourses are an obvious choice for role play areas, but equally attractive are areas based on popular television or comic figures.

Some early years educators feel that trying to divert superhero play into channels which appear to be based on adult priorities is not entirely fair. The argument is that superhero play belongs to the world of children and adult intervention somehow spoils the pleasure derived. Rather than trick, by devious means, unsuspecting children into literacy activities, we should be joining in the superhero play on their terms. There is certainly no reason to dissuade an early years worker from joining in superhero play and engaging in its fast moving action and celebration of gross motor skills and physical stamina. We sometimes join children in the structured role play area; why not run and fly with them in the outdoor area? However, these approaches are not mutually exclusive. There are times when we should leave superhero play well alone and let the children work out their own agendas; there are other times when our involvement in the play will further particular aspects of our work with children, whether that is the development of our relationships with them or the extension of their speaking and listening skills. And there are also occasions on which we should be hijacking the children's interests and using them to frame literacy activities attractively. As Pompe states, 'Standard learning experiences can be tacked on to any committed exploration, so why not choose pleasurable and emotionally satisfying ones?' (Pompe, 1996, p. 124).

Popular culture-related activities

There are many other ways in which popular culture can be used to stimulate literacy activities in the early years setting. In the next example, work on the 'Teletubbies' was introduced into a number of nurseries. Britain has seen the recent success of the children's programme 'Teletubbies'. These are four cuddly creatures who have television screens on their tummies, on which are played short films relating to children's interests. They live in a bunker in which, amongst other things, they eat 'tubby toast' and 'tubby custard'.

In an effort to introduce nursery children to a range of non-narrative texts, work was planned on recipes. It seemed that a good way of interesting the children in the activity was to relate it to their interests. It was therefore decided to make 'tubby custard' with them. The following account of the activity, taken from my diary of the project, clearly demonstrates the motivating effect of such work:

> I set up the activity and was very soon inundated with children who were wanting to take part. I wanted to ensure that every child in the nursery had a chance to participate over the afternoon. Efforts to limit the children working with me to four at a time repeatedly failed and indeed each separate 'cooking' session was watched by a large, vociferous audience! A nursery nurse working in the same room remarked that the children were very excited and it was clear that the activity had had an electrifying effect on the nursery.
>
> I used the activity to introduce a number of concepts. We looked at recipe books and discussed the function and structure of recipes. I modelled reading the instructions on the recipe in order to make the custard, and each child had his/her own copy of the recipe. I pointed to particular words and letters on the recipe card and talked about them. During the custard making, I repeatedly went back to the recipe to read the next instructions. Discussions about the children's viewing habits with regard to the Teletubbies were threaded in with some focused introduction of key terms related to the scientific aspects of the activity, e.g. 'dissolve' and 'temperature'. After the activity, children were asked if they would like to write their own recipes for tubby toast or tubby custard. Many children who were usually reluctant to spend time writing rushed up to the writing table to do so. In one nursery, when informed that the recipe had been downloaded from the Teletubby website,[1] children were keen to visit the site themselves in order to see what else was there and so extended their ICT skills.

Children who were not usually motivated to write independently rushed over to the writing area after making the custard to write their own Teletubby recipes (see Figure 10.1).

This was a simple activity which tapped into children's home interests and therefore enthused and encouraged them to take part in a number of language and literacy activities. There are many more examples of work which could be introduced, based on the Teletubby theme. Here are just a few. How could these easily be adapted to other popular cultural icons?

Figure 10.1 Tubby custard

- Write a letter to the children from the Teletubbies which demands a response (see Figure 10.2)
- Ask the children to write a story which can be read to the Teletubbies at bedtime.
- Children could write lyrics for a new Teletubbies song.
- Children could produce their own Teletubby comics.

Dear Children,
We sometimes get a bit lonely here in Tellytubby land. Could you write to us and let us know all about you? We want to know what you look like, who your friends are, what you like to eat, what you like doing in nursery and anything else you can think of!
Please write back soon,
Lots of love,
Tinky Winky, Dipsy, La La and Po xxxxxx

Figure 10.2. A letter from the Teletubbies

- Ask children to draw a map of Tellytubby Land and label it.
- Children could produce an advert for the Teletubbies programme.
- Tell the children that Noo-Noo has broken down (Noo-Noo is the Teletubbies' hoover). Could they write a set of instructions to fix it?
- Children could use a multi-media package to produce their own Teletubby web page. (Staff need to be careful that they do not infringe copyright by using Teletubby images on the site.)

There are many other ideas which can be adapted to meet a variety of children's tastes. A garage could be set up to repair Batmobiles which necessitated the production of notes, estimates and bills, or a project introduced which facilitates the design and building of a house and garage for Barbie. The latter activity could encourage girls who would not normally use construction toys to join in.

Of course, there are important issues to consider relating to the sexism and violence in much of children's popular culture. Many of us would not want to engage children in such work without challenging some of the stereotyped messages that appear in these texts. There are a number of ways of doing this. Work on toys can be done which prompts children to consider why some toys are assumed to be for girls and some for boys. They can be prompted to design toys that will appeal to both. Children can be asked to consider alternatives to violence. In the work on the Batman and Batwoman HQ described above, children were asked to think about ways in which the villain, the Joker, could be caught without using violence. This is not to say that simply engaging young children in these kinds of discussions will displace well-cemented stereotypical views. Some children are very good at ascertaining what a teacher's motives are through her line of questioning and can give the answer they think will be most acceptable! Nonetheless, through the completion of such work children could have some of their views challenged and be presented with viable alternatives that they may not have considered previously. If we avoid using children's popular culture in the classroom because of our worries about the messages it contains, it will not get rid of the problem. Children will continue to be emotionally enagaged with popular culture outside nursery and school. We need to achieve a balance between recognising children's pleasure in the this culture and the media whilst at the same time providing them with the tools to deconstruct its ideology. Media education offers the opportunity for children to develop these skills so that they can critically analyse the messages they are given by the media. The final section of the chapter moves on to consider the

nature of media education and to analyse what it has to offer the early
years curriculum.

Media education

The relationship between popular culture and media education is well
defined. Many of children's popular cultural interests originate in the
media; for example, in television programmes, videos and comics.
Apart from images from the media stimulating children's work in literacy, the media can be studied in its own right. Media studies as a
curriculum subject has achieved some recognition in the secondary
syllabus and is now offered by many exam boards. The early years
curriculum has yet to realise the potential that media education has
for not only engaging children in work related to the media, but also
increasing their understanding of the world. Given the large number
of possibilities there are for work on media education, where is the
practitioner to start? First, we need to be clear of the theoretical basis
on which media studies needs to be based. Learmonth and Sayer
(1996), in a discussion of what constitutes good practice in media education, assert that:

> Among the most important characteristics of effective teaching
> and learning in media education are . . . a clear conceptual frame-
> work shared by all colleagues involved in teaching media edu-
> cation . . .
>
> (Learmonth and Sayer, 1996, p. 10)

The structure outlined by the BFI (Bazalgette, 1989) is a useful place
to begin to develop this conceptual framework. There are six areas
identified which need to be considered in any work on the media:
media agencies, categories, technologies, languages, audiences and
representation (see Figure 10.3).

Obviously, what we expect of three- and four-year-olds will be very
different from what pupils undertaking a GCSE in Media Studies will
explore using this matrix as a basis. However, there are a number of
ways in which we can begin to develop young children's understanding of the media, using these categories as a framework. We will
look at each of these categories in turn and explore how they can be
addressed in the early years.

Media agencies

Work on media agencies involves looking at who produces media
texts. Ultimately, children should work towards being able to criti-

Media agencies	Who is communicating, and why?	Who produces a text; roles in the production process; media institutions; economics and ideology; intentions and results.
Media categories	What type of text is it?	Different media (television, radio, etc.); forms (documentary, advertising, etc.); genres (science fiction, soap operas, etc.); other ways of categorising texts; how categorisation leads to understanding.
Media technologies	How is it produced?	What kind of technologies are available, to whom, and how to use them; the differences they make to the production processes as well as the final product.
Media languages	How do we know what it means?	How the media produces meanings; codes and conventions; narrative structures.
Media audiences	Who receives it, and what sense do they make of it?	How audiences are identified, constructed, addressed and reached; how audiences find, choose, consume and respond to texts.
Media representations	How does it present its subject?	The relation between media texts and actual places, people, events and ideas; stereotyping and its consequences.

Figure 10.3.   Media education framework (Bazalgette, 1989)

cally analyse how the form and nature of a media text is influenced by the person or agency who produced it. In the early stages, however, it will be necessary to help children identify that media texts are produced by someone and that this 'someone' differs according to the text. So, for example, they will need to understand that newspapers are produced by newspaper agencies and television programmes are made by film producers for television companies. If an early years setting, nursery or school is situated near to a newspaper office or television studio, then a trip can be arranged so that the children can have first-hand experience of a particular agency. If not, then children can be informed about a particular producer of media texts and enter into correspondence with them in order to extend their understanding of the production process. One nursery, for example, wrote letters to a local television company asking them to make more programmes for babies. The company replied asking the children for ideas and this led to much discussion about the types of television programmes babies would like.

Media categories

Work on media categories requires children to reflect on genres and how those genres can be identified. Teachers can underestimate children's abilities to identify features of genres. Children's skills in identifying different types of television programmes, for example, can be very sophisticated. The following discussion ensued when a group of three- and four-year-old children were shown a video which contained an advert, a cartoon, a soap opera and a clip from the news:

(Watching a clip from the Ten O'Clock News)
JM: What sort of programme is this?
David: The news.
JM: How can you tell it's the news?
David: Cos me dad watches it.
Safeena: Cos it shows you naughty things.
Daniel: It shows you about burglars!
(Screen moves to an advert)
JM: Is this still the news?
Michael: No, it's a advert. He changes into a bear.
JM: How do you know it is an advert?
(No answer)
JM: How can I tell if it's an advert and not the news?
Esther: They show you ice cream.
Michael: Cos he changes into a bear.
(Clip of Coronation Street appears)
JM: What's this?
Sajad: Good Neighbours.
JM: How do you know?
Sajad: Me mum watches it.
(Cartoon comes on screen)
JM: What is this?
Hasan: Hunchback.
JM: What sort of programme is it?
(No answer)

JM: Is it an advert?
Safeena: No, it's a cartoon.
JM: How do you know?
Safeena: Cos me brother's got it and I've seen it.
JM: Is it the same sort of programme as the news?
(Children shake their heads.)
JM: Why not?
(Short silence)
Marcus: Cos it's pictures.
JM: Does the news have pictures?
Marcus: No, people.

This discussion was interesting in a number of ways. Some of the children identified the different types of programmes easily, but were not able to state why other than through prior experience. Sajad mistook *Coronation Street* for *Neighbours*, but this indicated an implicit understanding of the soap opera genre. However, Safeena identified the news 'because it shows you naughty things'. She recognised that the news featured stories about unfortunate events in the world. Marcus's assertion that cartoons had 'pictures' reflected his understanding that cartoons had drawings rather than photographs of real people. Esther stating that the advert showed ice cream may have been an indication that she understood the difference between adverts and the news to be that adverts showed us products. Esther and Safeena were amongst the older group in nursery. Younger children tended to state that they could identify programmes because they had seen them before, or a member of their family had watched them. Thus the development appeared to be from an implicit recognition of genres to an ability to identify particular codes and conventions related to these genres. Children can engage in structured work that helps them to recognise and understand these codes and conventions. This involves work on media languages.

Media languages

Work on media languages involves looking at how texts put across their messages and the signs and symbols they use in doing so. For example, how can we tell that a programme is a chat show? We usually recognise it because two or three people are sitting on cosy chairs and one person is being asked questions about himself. We quickly begin to recognise codes and conventions that different media texts use. Children also become adept at 'reading' different texts, recognising what particular things signify and what the producer's intention was. One group of children were asked to look at the opening sequence of *Batman Forever*:

JM: How do you know that this is the baddie? (Looking at a shot of 'the Face' in *Batman Forever*.)
Elijah: Cos of the scary music.
Rosewana: Cos his face is in the dark.

These children were obviously familiar with the conventions of film in which the arrival of 'baddies' is accompanied by sinister sounding music and the set lighting is dark and shadowy. As this example illustrates, children are much better at deconstructing video and film texts than many adults realise (Hodge and Tripp, 1986; Buckingham, 1993). So often, the world of nursery and school draws on knowledge about areas that are new experiences for children. Work on media texts allows children to demonstrate the knowledge that they have, knowledge that they are confident in because it draws on their experience from home. It is important to give children the chance to share this knowledge, ensuring that we engage them in discussions in which their experience is valued. And as Bromley (1996) notes:

as Vygotsky (1986) argues, talk is essential to concept formation. This talk takes place in a social context, before the concepts are internalised by the individual. Thus, children who are able to discuss their reading with each other will master ideas that will form the basis for their future thinking and construction of meaning. This is true whether the children are 'reading' a book, a comic or a video.

(Bromley, 1996, p. 79)

Work on the language of comics can involve the children in a consideration of features such as cartoon drawings, speech bubbles, special effects and onomatopaeia. In one nursery which contained a majority of bilingual children, work on comics excited the children and stimulated much conversation about books they had at home or things they had seen on television. The children discussed whether the comics used photographs of real things and people or drawings. They then went on to produce their own comics, some of them following conventions such as placing a sequence of drawings in boxes. In the example in Figure 10.4, Naseim drew the Teletubbies and related the text as he drew: 'Tinky Winky here. Dipsy here. La la say no go here (drawing speech bubble). Po (indistinguishable). Teletubbies.' Naseim was obviously learning the particular features of language that comics use.

Media technologies

A consideration of the way in which some media are constructed can enable children to explore key concepts and ideas. One group of chil-

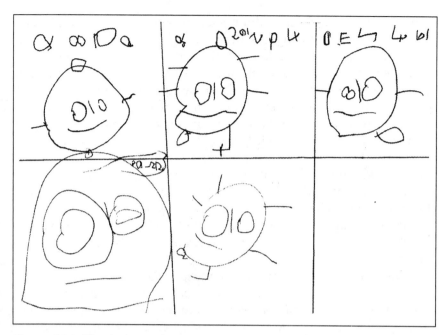

Figure 10.4. Naseim's comic

dren in a nursery were asked if they knew how cartoons were made. They had been watching the cartoon version of *The Lion King*. Imran said: 'They drawed the book and then they put the paper into the machine'. This was a very interesting comment as it indicated that Imran was making a connection between the text version of the story and the video. He had also understood that the visual element of the cartoon was based on drawings, drawings which were also featured in the version of the book he had seen.

Having first-hand experience of using equipment can further children's understanding of aspects of the media. As Bazalgette points out:

> very young children may not be clear about the relationship between, say, a medium and a close up: they may think that a bird seen in close-up is not the same as the one seen in the previous shot, but a different, bigger bird. It may not be possible to clarify this through discussion and slow replay, but play and experimentation with cameras, frames and lenses are far more likely to open up their understanding of the different kinds of shot that are possible.
>
> (Bazalgette, 1992, p. 212)

Children can be introduced to key terms they will meet in media education when using relevant equipment such as cameras and video cameras, e.g. long shot, medium shot, close up, zoom in/out. Many children are already familiar with cameras because of the use of them in some family events. Although they may not have touched them and know how to work them, they are often aware that you point them at something directly in order to capture the image. In one nursery, a teacher involved the children in a project in which they were asked to make a film about nursery life for new children coming in. The teacher began by drawing a storyboard of the film. A storyboard is a series of boxes in which a television/film story can be mapped out frame by frame through writing or drawing, or a combination of both. The children discussed what they would like on the film and the teacher modelled the use of the storyboard. The video was then filmed according to this plan, although of course the day-to-day reality of nursery life meant that plans often had to be adapted at the last minute!

If the thought of working with a video camera is worrying, a photographic camera provides a range of possibilities. A first step is to give children cardboard frames to look through. They can use these to frame the shot that they want. A group of children in a nursery in Sheffield were asked to take some photographs of the nursery to put into a book and show children who had not yet been to the nursery. They were each given a cardboard frame and asked to find four images of the nursery which they could take shots of. They eagerly began the task, although it took some children some time to learn which eye to close when framing a shot with the cardboard rectangle. They rushed around the nursery framing a variety of shots, some rather more unconventional than others! They were then asked to draw the four shots they wanted to take. The children took it in turns to take the photographs, learning how to use the viewfinder (with automatic focus) and trigger button. Using a polaroid camera can give the children instant results and allows them to compare their desired image with the one that turns up on the photograph. Samara's (aged 4) plans and photographs are shown in Figures 10.5 and 10.6.

This work led to the extension of children's speaking and listening skills as they discussed the shots that they wanted and compared them with the results that they got.

Media audiences

Work on media audiences involves asking children to reflect on who a particular text is produced for. The first work on media audiences should involve children in reflecting about their own media choices. Discussions with children need to focus upon what television pro-

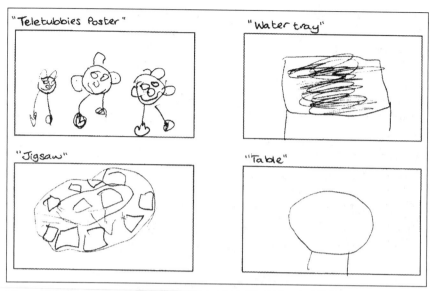

Figure 10.5.   Plans for Sarmara's photographs.

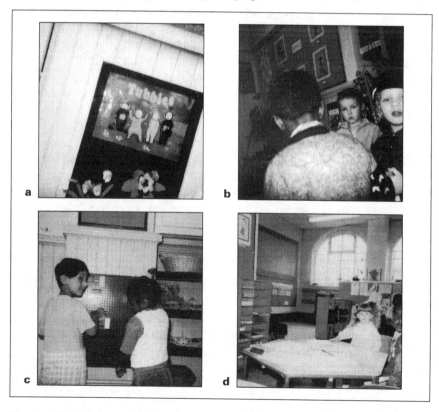

Figure 10.6.   Samara's photographs.

grammes, films and videos they like and why they like them. In later stages of media work this can lead to a sophisticated analysis of how an audience has been identified and targeted, but in the earlier stages it will involve developing children's understanding that different texts are produced for different audiences. What is made for adults may not always appeal to children, and vice versa. Other activities could include showing the children some children's comics and magazines which are aimed at adults. The children can then be asked:

• Who is this written for?
• Would children or grown-ups want to read it?
• What makes you say that?
• What would make you want to read it?
• What sorts of TV programmes/films/magazines do children like?
• What sorts of TV programmes/films/magazines do adults like?

Media representations

This is one of the most difficult areas of media studies to introduce into the early years curriculum. This is because it explores the ways in which media texts represent reality and how it can present particular images in a particular ways in order to produce a certain effect on the audience. It can involve work on media stereotypes and bias, although it does not exclusively relate to these concepts.

In the early stages of media work, it is interesting to explore with children what they perceive as being real or not real. Bazalgette asserts:

> It has become commonplace to assert that 'children can't tell the difference between television and reality', but anyone who actually investigates children's understanding of television quickly discovers that, far from accepting television as reality, children constantly make judgements about *how real it is.*
>
> (Bazalgette, 1992, p. 217)

Thus, when asking a group of children if *Neighbours* was real or not, Ben shouted 'No!' When asked why he had said that, he replied, 'Cos all those things couldn't happen in one day!' This demonstrates quite sophisticated reasoning. Van Noort (1992) describes some work she did with four-year-olds in a nursery. She showed them a video of 'Spot', based on the popular character introduced in the books written by Eric Hill.

> When asked whether Spot was a real dog, like a dog they might have at home as a pet, only one child answered yes. This was a

particularly bright child . . . and at first I was surprised by her answer. It led me to consider again the nature of a four-year-old. This child was fond of Spot stories, liked Spot videos, was emotionally involved with Spot, and identified with his adventures. To her he was real, a friend in the same way a teddy can be. I concluded that the fault lay in the question, not the answer.

(Van Noort, 1992 p. 287)

Developing children's ability to analyse the way in which the media represents particular images can lead to early work on stereotypes. Children can be asked to find advertisements for children's toys and then discuss whether those toys are aimed at boys or girls. As children become more aware of the way in which the media represents reality, they could be asked to analyse images and artefacts in relation to sexism and racism.

Using the BFI framework

Working within the conceptual framework provided by Figure 10.3 can be helpful to teachers who are not used to working with the media. It could also prevent a haphazard approach in which the teacher veers from one activity related to the media to another but does not develop the children's skills, knowledge and understanding in any systematic way. However, there may be different approaches that one can take which would enable these skills and concepts to be developed in a comprehensive manner. Mary Hilton (1998) suggests that rather than using the BFI framework as it stands, children can integrate various aspects of it through work on specific genres. She suggests that we need to take new approaches to media education through the provision of experiences which encourage children to explore and use a range of media forms in work on particular genres such as the news, science fiction and TV soaps.

Similarly, children can work across the categories outlined in Figure 10.3 as they explore particular topics and themes. For example, work on 'Myself' could involve the children taking photographs of their family, taping interviews with their friends and family for a radio programme, making leaflets and newsletters about themselves and perhaps even producing a 'This is Your Life!' television programme. This work would necessarily involve an exploration and understanding of media agencies, languages, technologies, audiences, categories and representations. However, the framework developed by the British Film Institute remains an important tool for ensuring that media education is differentiated from the act of utilising the media in the language and literacy curriculum.

This leads us on to an important consideration. The fact that media education is a valid subject in itself is not in dispute. Children need to be able to develop the skills and concepts necessary to critically analyse and produce media texts. However, one of the main arguments of this chapter is that popular and media texts can be a way of informing and enlivening the language and literacy curriculum in the early years. The two approaches are not mutually exclusive. Children should be provided with opportunities to study the media as part of media education; they should also be encouraged to develop language and literacy skills in the context of media texts.

Conclusion

The early years curriculum should offer a range of opportunities for developing children's knowledge and understanding of the world around them. Usually, the knowledge and understanding we guide them towards is based on an adult consideration of what is valuable and appropriate to learn. Of course, this is necessary if we are to ensure that children develop the skills, knowledge and understanding they need in order to play a part in society. However, adult and child worlds are often far apart and it is therefore inevitable that we need to guard against excluding the interests of children from the curriculum. Motivation is key to young children's learning (Bruce, 1998). Work on popular culture and the media can provide that crucial motivation and ensure that young children want to engage with the literacy activities offered to them.

Notes

1. The official Teletubby website can be found at:

   http://www.bbc.co.uk/education/teletubbies/

Acknowledgements

With thanks to Jeremy Brill, a gifted nursery teacher, for sharing his experiences and insights. I would also like to say a big thank you (again!) to the children and staff at Sharrow Nursery Infant School and Pye Bank Nursery Infant School, Sheffield, for continuing to work with me so enthusiastically.

Suggestions for further reading:

Craggs, C. E. (1992) *Media Education in the Primary School*, London: Routledge.
Dyson, A. H. (1997) *Writing Superheroes: Contemporary Childhood, Popular*

Culture, and Classroom Literacy, New York: Teachers College Press.
Hilton, M. (ed.) (1996) *Potent Fictions: Children's Literacy and the Challenge of Popular Culture*, London: Routledge.

References

Bazalgette, C. (ed.) (1989) *Primary Media Education: A Curriculum Framework*, London: British Film Institute.

Bazalgette, C. (1992), Key aspects of media education, in M. Alvarado, and O. Boyd-Barrett (eds.) *Media Education: An Introduction*, London: British Film Institute.

Brice-Heath, S. (1983) *Ways with Words: Language, Life and Work in Communities and Classrooms*, Cambridge University Press.

Bromley, H. (1996) Did you know that there's no such thing as Never Land?: working with video narratives in the early years in M. Hilton, (ed.) *Potent Fictions: Children's Literacy and the Challenge of Popular Culture*, London: Routledge.

Bruce, T. (1997) *Early Childhood Education*, 2nd edition London: Hodder & Stoughton.

Buckingham, D. (1993) *Children Talking Television: The Making of Television Literacy*, London: Falmer.

Dyson, A. (1994) The Ninjas, the X-Men, and the Ladies: playing with power and identity in an urban primary school, *Teachers College Record*, Vol. 96, no. 2, pp. 219–39.

Dyson, A. (1996) Cultural constellations and childhood identities: on Greek gods, cartoon heroes, and the social lives of schoolchildren, *Harvard Educational Review*, Vol. 66, no. 3, pp. 471–95.

French, J. (1987) *A Historical Study of Children's Heroes and Fantasy Play*, (Research Report) Idaho: Boise State University, School of Education, ERIC Document No: ED 310885.

Gee, P. (1996) *Social Linguistics and Literacies: Ideology in Discourses*, 2nd edition, London: Taylor & Francis.

Hilton, M. (ed.) (1996) *Potent Fictions: Children's Literacy and the Challenge of Popular Culture*, London: Routledge.

Hilton, M. (1998) Teaching the Media in *Language Matters*, Spring 1998, pp. 6–9.

Hodge, B. and Tripp, D. (1986) *Children and Television*, Cambridge: Polity Press.

Ketch, A. (1991) The Delicious Alphabet, *English in Education*, Vol. 25, no. 1, pp. 1–4.

Kinder, M. (1991) *Playing with Power in Movies: Television and Video Games from Muppet Babies to Teenage Mutant Ninja Turtles*, Berkeley: University of California Press.

Kline, S. (1993) *Out of the Garden: Toys and Children's Culture in the Age of TV Marketing*, London: Verso.

Lankshear, C. with Gee, J. P., Knobel, M. and Searle, C. (1997) *Changing Literacies*, Buckingham: Open University Press.

Learmonth, J. and Sayer, M. (1996) *A Review of Good Practice in Media Education*, London: British Film Institute.

Luke, A. (1993) *The Social Construction of Literacy in the Primary School*, Melbourne: Macmillan Education Australia.

Marsh, J., Payne, L. and Anderson, S. (1997) Batman and Batwoman in the classroom, *Primary English* Vol. 5, no. 2, pp. 8–11.

McDonnell, K. (1994) *Kid Culture: Children and Adults and Popular Culture*, Ontario: Second Storey Press.

Mukerji, C. and Schudson, M. (1991) *Rethinking Popular Culture: Contemporary Perspectives in Cultural Studies*, Berkeley: University of California Press.

Pompe, C. (1992) 'When the Aliens wanted water': media education – children's critical frontiers, in M. Styles, E. Bearne, and V. Watson, *After Alice: Exploring Children's Literature*, London: Cassell.

Pompe, C. (1996) 'But they're pink!' – 'Who cares!': popular culture in the primary years, in M. Hilton, (ed.) *Potent Fictions: Children's Literacy and the Challenge of Popular Culture*, London: Routledge.

Van Noort, S. (1992) Nursery children talking about television, in M. Alvarado and O. Boyd-Barrett (eds.) *Media Education: An Introduction*, London: British Film Institute.

11

'I Like It When My Mum Comes to School to Work with Me': Family Literacy

Carol Taylor

> Being at the family literacy group is the only time we really connect . . . it's special for her, being with me and her brother.
>
> (Donna)

There has been an increasing interest in family literacy projects over the past ten years as educators, policy-makers and researchers recognise the role that such projects can play in encouraging parents to develop ways of supporting their children's language development. There has also been a realisation that such projects can encourage parents and carers to develop their own literacy skills and take that first step in the 'return to learning'. Additionally, policy-makers have started to acknowledge that early years settings and schools should not work in isolation and cannot raise standards of literacy on their own. Such establishments have to engage the support of parents and also recognise and respect the varied and different literacies that families and communities use.

There is a great deal of work that illustrates the importance of children's early literacy experiences (Goodman, 1980; Ferrerio and Teberosky, 1982; Hannon, 1995). Bynner and Steedman (1995) outline the long-term effects on attainment of pre-school and early years educational experience. It would appear that the value of family literacy is most obvious in the early years setting where parents can become engaged with their child's development from a young age and can develop their own literacy and learning alongside that of the child. Anyone who has visited a family literacy group or who has had the good fortune to spend some time with the participants will have been aware of that buzz of excitement in relation to learning and the obvious sense of pleasure both children and adults get from working together. To walk into a room where twenty adults and children are engaged in literacy activities, whether in groups, in pairs or individually, where children are patiently explaining to adults how to use the computer, where a parent and child are putting the finishing touches to a hand-made book or where a father and son are sat curled up in the corner sharing *Handa's Surprise* is one of those moments when you remember why you are doing the job!

What is family literacy?

Defining the term 'family literacy' is difficult. We can define both words independently, but the term itself means something more. The actual practice commonly involves working with 'parents'[1] and children, both separately and together for a significant period of time, but it is also much more than this. Good practice also includes, for instance:

- recognising and valuing the literacy practices of the home as well as the school, and seeking to build upon these
- developing not only literacy skills, but also areas such as motivation, behaviour, and self-confidence
- encouraging inter-generational learning; that is, enabling family members to support and develop each other's learning
- enabling adults to develop their own skills and abilities and offering them the chance to continue in education or training if they wish to
- encouraging the development of learning and literacy in the community, not just the nursery or school

The best family literacy practice begins from a recognition that parents are a child's first and most important teachers, that parents know their children better than anyone else and that parents want the best for their children. It also begins from the premise that there are many kinds of literacy and many kinds of families and that the literacy that goes on every day in homes around the world does not necessarily reflect the literacy that happens in schools. Most importantly, it is about empowerment: working alongside families to encourage them to have control over their lives and futures. There are family literacy projects, particularly in the USA, but also in the UK, where the focus is on a deficit model. At the heart of this model is the premise that only the 'schooled' model of literacy is relevant and that disadvantaged adults pass on illiteracy (like a disease) to their children. These programmes focus on transmitting mainstream school literacy practices into the home without recognising the validity, or even presence, of home literacy practices. They also can end up blaming parents and families for the so-called 'lack of literacy' of young children. Most committed family literacy practitioners are aware of the tensions between these two opposing views and have had to spend time working towards a pragmatic approach: one which recognises and values home literacy practices, but also recognises that access to 'mainstream' literacy (or schooled literacy) is the essential key to control over one's life. They have had to work towards a position where a recognition that all families educate their children in literacy is placed alongside the acknowledgement that most parents would welcome information on how literacy 'works'. However, the 'deficit model' attracts large-scale funding as agencies, governments and large organisations feel the need to intervene in the 'literacy problem'. The imbalance of power inherent in such programmes remains a key issue for anyone embarking on family literacy.

A brief history of family literacy

Family literacy as a concept has existed for no more than fifteen years and, until about 1993, the literature and research on the subject were sparse. Earlier work concerned with involving parents in their children's reading development tended to concentrate on efforts to enhance the children's attainment. Gradually, we have begun to consider broader family dimensions such as the role of other family members and their own literacy skills.

It is generally thought that the term 'family literacy' was first used by Denny Taylor in her book of the same name published in the USA in 1983. As an ethnographer, she used the term to describe the literacy practices she had observed in homes she had encountered throughout her research. Shirley Brice-Heath's work, published in the same year, looked at three communities in the Piedmont Carolinas in the USA. This ethnographic study provided detailed descriptions of people's uses of literacy in the community and examined the relationship between home literacies and school literacies, arguing that the extent to which children cope with schooling is related closely to a range of cultural factors. By focusing on story reading, Brice-Heath was able to document significant differences in 'the paths of language socialisation'. She demonstrated that all children learn about literacy but that they do not all learn the same literacy. As Goodman (1997) has pointed out:

> There is no single road to becoming literate . . . there are many ways, equally important but different, in which children are immersed in literacy events that positively influence their development. It is unreasonable and, I believe, actually dangerous to

expect all families to follow the same prescriptions for literacy learning.

(Goodman, 1997, p. 56)

This concept has been an important one for many educators as they have striven to ensure that family literacy projects recognise children's home literacy practices and do not attempt to 'compensate' for a perceived literacy deficiency (Taylor, 1997).

In Britain, in 1992, the Department for Education provided ALBSU[2] with a grant to develop a study of family literacy. The aim was to 'explore whether there is an intergenerational effect in literacy and if family literacy programmes make any difference in preventing reading failure' (ALBSU, 1993, p. 2). When the study was completed, ALBSU reported that:

> we were convinced that there was clear intergenerational effect
> ... and that well-conceived family literacy programmes could
> make a real difference in preventing reading failure.

(ALBSU, 1993, p. 2)

The statistics which that research produced have been well-used since then. For example:

> 72% of children from families where parents had reading problems and who were in the lowest income group, were in the lowest reading group; 54% of children from families where parents had reading problems and who had no school qualifications, were in the lowest reading score group.

(ALBSU, 1993, p. 3)

In 1993, ALBSU were awarded three years' funding in order to develop family literacy programmes. The bulk of the funding was spent on four demonstration projects in different parts of the UK, both urban and rural. The development was based on both the research in this country and the work in the USA, where extensive programmes had been running for a number of years. As soon as the development programmes were up and running, it became clear that the initial results were interesting. Children were making 'greater than expected gains' (NFER, 1995, p. xiii).

> Family Literacy has led to a real improvement in reading and writing skills among parents and children alike. Gains have been greater than in adult literacy programmes and in pre- and early school reading programmes.

(ALBSU, 1993, p. 8)

There is now a general recognition that family literacy projects should be supported and developed further. As Barton states:

> It is one of those ideas that we all approve of, even if we are not clear about what we mean by it. The general feeling of 'it's a good thing' is contained in both the word 'family' and the word 'literacy'.

> (Barton, 1994, p. 2)

In the last four years there has been a massive increase in interest in this area of work, supported by a range of research on practical approaches and the development of a theoretical framework to underpin them (Taylor, 1997). The current support for family literacy programmes in Britain, evident in the White Paper (1997), provides the possibility for some innovative and effective literacy work.

Family literacy in practice: what do you actually do?

At its simplest, family literacy requires a teacher/early years specialist to work with a group of children and an adult worker to work with a group of 'connected' adults. I hesitate to use the word 'related', as this precludes carers, friends, childminders and so on. It requires an effective partnership between two distinct fields of education: nurseries and schools, and adult education. It also includes the provision of time and space to bring both groups together, to work together with both tutor and teacher. Within this general framework, however, a number of different models have been developed, or have emerged, as people work towards a responsive model of family literacy.

Many projects have based their family literacy work on the Basic Skills Agency model, which was developed in their early demonstration programmes and has changed very little since then. This was very structured and consisted of a twelve-week programme in which adults were provided with six hours of accredited basic skills tuition and children were involved in six hours of language and literacy work per week. There were then two hours a week in which adults and children worked together on joint literacy activities. As suggested earlier, this model was very effective, meeting its objectives and leading to 'substantial improvements in children's reading, writing and vocabulary' (NFER, 1995). The same NFER report stated that the retention rate of parents was 91 per cent and their rate of accreditation 95 per cent. Projects had to follow the model closely in order to qualify for funding and often had to use prescribed baseline assessments, tests and accreditation routes.

However, the Basic Skills Agency model does not meet the needs of every community, nursery or school and there is a strong argument for a less rigid approach in the design of family literacy projects. The following case study of a family literacy programme is not intended to be used as a model for all family literacy projects but has been included in order to demonstrate the underlying principles of family literacy work.

Brunstone Nursery Infant School: family literacy in action

The case study concerns a school in an economically deprived urban area, located in an old two-storey building in the middle of a housing estate. The estate houses predominantly white families, with a large number of single parent families. The school has a nursery attached, which is a shining example of good under-fives provision. It has committed and enthusiastic staff and an excellent relationship with the parents. When the school was accepted onto the family literacy project, the head had no hesitation in asking the nursery teacher to become the family literacy teacher. An adult tutor was recruited who was qualified both in basic skills teaching and wanted to be involved with children. It is essential that the adult tutor is well trained, shares the aims of the project, and gets on well with children. (It is worth remembering that some tutors work with adults because they are not too keen on children!)

The adult tutor and nursery teacher hit it off from the start. This is very important and the basis for a good project. Both workers have to remember that this is a partnership between the two services, not a nursery or school project with bolt-on adult provision or a key skills group with children involved. They met on several occasions before deciding how they would approach the parents and what the focus of the project would be. There was funding available for the project to be run for one day a week for an academic year, with the separate groups of parents and children meeting in the morning and both groups coming together in the afternoon. A small amount of funding was set aside for materials, particularly for the adult group's needs, and to cover the possible costs of accreditation for the adults. Creche provision was considered vital to enable people to attend and therefore funding was allocated for this purpose. The teacher decided that she wanted to work with a specific group of children who were entering nursery in the September term and who would benefit from a full year on the project. This would also, she hoped, encourage a set of committed parents who would ultimately become both ambassadors for the school and also important within the nursery itself. There were about fifteen children in the target group. The teacher knew that some of the parents worked or had other commitments that would preclude them from joining the project. She also knew that the ones she most wanted to work with were the ones it would be most difficult to involve. The project began very slowly with the adult tutor spending time in the nursery getting to know the staff, the parents and the children, and the systems in the school. She attended a staff meeting and regularly sat in the staffroom so that the whole school became involved in the project.

After a couple of weeks, the adult worker began to talk to certain adults and asked them if they would like to become involved in a new project concerned with helping their children. Of the fifteen approached, nine agreed to come to a coffee morning and eight turned up. The tutor began to explore with them what they thought of the nursery, what their children were good at, and gradually over the next few weeks a core group was established who met for a couple of hours each week, drank coffee, talked about their children and thoroughly enjoyed themselves. After a short while, the tutor introduced the idea of book making and the adults took to it with great enthusiasm. Over the next term they went on to produce photograph books, picture books, big laminated books and more. About half-way through the term, the tutor gently 'floated' the idea of accreditation and stressed that all this work could be pulled together into a folder in order that the parents could get some certification for it. It is credit to the tutor and teacher that everyone wanted to do it. At the end of six months, nine parents (one had joined half-way through) received a nationally recognised accreditation, developed specifically for family literacy groups, called 'Families and Schools Together'.[3]

What did the children do?

The adult tutor and the teacher met weekly to ensure that the work done by the separate groups had some common threads. As the adult group began to concentrate on books, so the teacher linked the specific literacy support with the children to the theme. Sometimes the children were withdrawn in small groups to work on their literacy skills, with activities directly focused on their needs. Often, the work took place in the nursery setting with the teacher concentrating on oral and dramatic play, on stories and on encouraging interaction with other children. They took books home, made books and shared books.

The joint sessions

Meanwhile, every week the adults and children got together for the joint session. At first, as is often the case, there was some awkwardness in the situation. Adults felt embarrassed in front of the teacher, children did not know who to relate to, parents did not know what to do. However, with twenty adults and children in a room, there was not much room for manoeuvre and very soon, a pattern emerged. In the first term most parents were encouraged to work with their own child, sharing books, making books, using the computer and putting into practice what they had been learning about. In these situations, the teacher often acted as a model, reading stories to children, using positive feedback, giving space to children. They also had trips out to the library, to bookshops in order to buy books, looked at environmental print and so on. Over the weeks, and into the following terms, there was a subtle change. Some parents preferred to work with other people's children, some parents preferred to work with other adults. In fact, in the end, the adults were asking not to work with their children because, 'I want to finish this piece of work'. That their own learning was so important to them was surely an excellent position to have arrived at. The parents had moved from statements such as, 'I'm no good at reading, so he isn't either!' to, twenty-four weeks later, 'When I've got Level 1, can I do Level 2?'

Key elements

From this case study, we can identify a number of key elements of good family literacy practice:

- The adult worker and the teacher must be sympathetic to the project aims and to the ethos of family literacy. Where possible, there should be staff development available for all staff interested in family literacy.
- The workers need to respect one another's specialisms, recognising that adults learn differently from children and vice versa. The project may be jeopardised if differences and problems are not out in the open from the outset, or there is not a determination to resolve problems jointly.
- The teacher and the adult worker must understand that they are not running separated strands of a project. It is their synergy that will be the essential catalyst in generating a successful outcome. Without that synergy, the children's and adults' strands are unrelated and the magical component of intergenerational learning will be absent. Ongoing, weekly planning sessions are essential.

- It has to be borne in mind that the adults may often equate nursery, school and teachers with failure. They may be ill at ease in the school building and will find small chairs and tables demeaning. Above all, they will resent being patronised.
- The project should not superimpose its own aims and objectives over the needs of those taking part. The best adult learning is student-centred, where students can negotiate the content and pace of learning. Sensitivity and flexibility are the key words here.
- Much of the learning depends on developing confidence, so it is essential that success is valued, shared and celebrated.

This case study was one of many diverse family literacy projects supported by the *Read On – Write Away!* literacy initiative situated in Derby City and Derbyshire. This multi-agency initiative embraces two LEAs, three Training and Enterprise Councils (TECs), the Library Service, the Basic Skills Agency and the National Literacy Trust. The initiative aims to improve and to celebrate literacy across the whole age range including, for example, projects such as Books for Babies, family literacy, reading intervention projects, adult literacy and work with young people. One of the main aims of *Read On – Write Away!* is to intertwine these separate strands so that family literacy informs, and is informed by, other strands. Another aim is to bring together projects within any given strand under one umbrella, uniting them with a common purpose and ethos and thus utilising all the good practice and knowledge available. The range of experience and expertise generated by these projects has enabled *Read On – Write Away!* to produce a guide to good practice in family literacy (see Figure 11.1).

Setting up family literacy projects can be a daunting task and the final part of this chapter deals with some of the questions that are frequently asked by teachers and tutors.

Answering the questions

How do you decide which families to work with?

Most projects decide which children they want to target. It could be a certain intake, such as summer-born children, a particular group (for example, one school decided to target its small group of Chinese families), or a group of children with particular literacy difficulties. Some early years settings and schools will decide which families they want to work with. They may have an idea of the literacy needs of some of the families, or of the families they feel may need support. Other nurseries and schools may choose not to target any particular fami-

The Read On - Write Away!
Model of Family Literacy Provision

This document is an outline of the elements which make up a model of good practice in family literacy. It is accepted that there may be other requirements dependent on funding, target groups etc but we put this forward as the basic framework.

Background: this document is the culmination of six months work by a working party made up of teachers, tutors and officers involved in family literacy in Derbyshire and Derby City. Derbyshire LEA has been at the forefront of family literacy development since 1995, with a large number of projects to April 1997. Since then, with the creation of the new unitary authority of Derby City the two LEAs have continued to work together as partners, alongside TECs and national agencies, in Read On - Write Away! the Literacy Initiative.

Over the next four years we will see the development of a minimum 80 family literacy projects across the area. These will be across the age ranges, of differing lengths, and funded by different agencies, but all brought together by their adherence to this model.

1. **Staffing**
   - ➤ *All adult workers adult trained. Minimum requirements: recognised teaching certificate + 9282 + 2 terms' experience in Key Skills groups (when possible, family literacy trained). Experience in school setting desirable but not essential.*
   - ➤ *All school staff to have a recognised teaching certificate and, where possible, family literacy training. Staff should be open to new ideas, be friendly and respect the contribution that parents and other adults can make to the work of schools.*
   - ➤ *With under-fives the most appropriate professional may be the Nursery Officer or nursery assistant.*
2. **Staff development**
   - ➤ *On-going training and specific staff development offered. This will include the teaching of reading, sharing good family literacy practice, knowledge of the 'other' service.*
   - ➤ *This should also include staff development for other staff members not directly involved in the project.*
   - ➤ *Where appropriate school staff should be offered the opportunity to obtain the City and Guilds 9282 accreditation (Initial Teaching Certificate) and any family literacy training which may be available for tutors.*
3. An **agreement** drawn up between the partners. This will include what is expected of both school and the Adult Service and will include lines of responsibility.
4. Time written in for **joint planning** – <u>minimum</u> whole day before programme begins.
5. On-going **liaison** (tutor/teacher) time <u>written in to the agreement</u> of minimum one hour a week.
6. **Co-ordination** - Someone other than the teacher and tutor must have a co-ordinating role and a support mechanism for tutors must be in place before the project starts. This could be a Community Education worker, a member of the Read On - Write Away! team or an SRB Co-ordinator.
7. Projects should always include a baseline assessment, realistic and specific targets and an assessment of progress at specified times and the end of the project. We would expect both qualitative and quantitative analysis of outcomes to check the effectiveness of the work.
8. **Curriculum**
   - ➤ *Suitable separate work with adults – minimum 2 hours a week – in appropriate accommodation with refreshments easily available. This includes appropriate furniture!*
   - ➤ *Suitable separate work with children appropriate to age and any special needs.*
   - ➤ *Regular joint work – with the adults and children together, led by both the tutor and the teacher, jointly planned.*
9. **Progression routes** for adult students – guidance should always be offered. Funding should be made available for this.
10. **Accreditation** – Adults always have the opportunity for accreditation appropriate to their needs.
11. Planning needs to take account of the needs of the students e.g. the provision of translators, language support staff and crèche facilities.
12. Parental/community involvement in a wider forum should be encouraged.

Read On - Write Away!

November 1997

Figure 11.1. *Read On – Write Away!* guidelines

lies, but make an open invitation to all. One school had a family literacy day once a month, with an average of sixty parents involved on each occasion.

How do you recruit the parents?

Every nursery or school develops its own way of doing this, depending on how it has worked with parents in the past. Some establishments feel that they can approach parents directly and ask them if they would like to be involved. Others may choose to send out a blanket invitation – for example, 'Come to a coffee morning and find out about a new project!' Some projects may use the adult tutor, as a new face, to talk to parents about ways of supporting their child's development. Others, with established good relationships with parents, may decide to offer a course such as 'How to work with your child' and mention it to certain parents they would like to see involved.

What do you call the project?

Experienced family literacy tutors will tell you that deciding on the name is the first and most important thing you do. It tells families what the project is about. Some nurseries or schools may use the term 'family literacy project', particularly since the word 'literacy' has recently become a part of everyday language. Some may choose a title which reflects their plans such as 'Families and schools together', or one which suggests a desire to be informal such as 'Drop-In!'

How do you decide what to do with the adults?

What many teachers do not realise is that one of the major differences between working with children and working with adults is that adults negotiate their *own* curriculum. You cannot sit and plan what you want the adults to do, or what you think they might want to do. They will have their own agenda. And if they do not like yours, they will vote with their feet! A good project will be based on a teacher and adult tutor spending time together going over the sorts of things adults could choose to do and some of the things that might be suggested. Quite often this can be very open ended, such as looking at the library, or talking about children. Sometimes it is more specific for example, by asking, 'What do you think about learning to make books?' As the project develops, the adults may begin to determine the agenda themselves.

Some funders insist that the adults are tested on their reading ability. Many projects feel this should be avoided wherever possible.

Attracting non-traditional learners is a major step. Testing them to prove that they have limited skills in literacy seems to have little worth. There does, however, need to be some sort of baseline assessment of all adults in projects. This will be valuable information for evaluation purposes, which is often needed to attract further funding. Projects in the *Read on – Write Away!* initiative often use a short, simple questionnaire which asks adults to write down the names of their children, their address and some facts about their child. From this sparse information, a good adult tutor will be able to make a pretty shrewd assessment of the ability of the parents. It is also important to try and find out what literacy-related activities occur in the home. This usually takes the form of a questionnaire asking about library use, how often parents read with their child, use of the computer and so on. This can be completed as a group activity.

Some nurseries and schools have encountered specific difficulties that relate to their building or the families they work with. For example, if a building is open plan, there may be no discrete space for adults to meet. There may be no room in which a crèche can be organised. Staff have to be willing to adapt and, whilst holding on to basic principles, be flexible in their approach. For example, is there an adult education college nearby which could house the adult group? Could the parents and children then work together in the hall in the afternoon?

Where do you get funding from?

There are a number of sources for funding (see Figure 11.2). Each of these comes with different conditions and expectations attached to them. Some, such as SRB (the Single Regeneration Budget), require very specific and time-consuming administration to meet the conditions of funding. Others, such as the Standards Fund, require an LEA to run programmes in a very specific and structured fashion.

Of course, schools themselves may be able to support their own programmes. Quite often, programmes will get funded as a one-off project and then schools and LEAs are forced to find money to support what are usually highly successful initiatives. If (as it appears is the case) family literacy really works, then the government, LEAs and schools should be finding ways to support it.

When a project has been highly successful, nurseries and schools will obviously want to offer it to another group of parents and children. They should also consider how those who have been involved can continue to be supported in some form or another. There are a variety of ways in which groups can be continued and adults encour-

Single Regeneration Budget (SRB)
European funding
Standards Fund (formerly GEST funding)
Further Education Funding Council (FEFC)
administered through colleges and community
education
LEA funding
Local business support
Basic Skills Agency (does not currently fund family
literacy projects)
Other funding bodies such as Education Extra
Trusts and similar bodies

Figure 11.2. Sources of funding

aged to move on to further learning. Funding may be available from Adult Education or colleges to continue the adult side of the project. Schools can then often release a member of staff for an hour a week to continue working with the children. Colleges may have specific courses which they will offer, such as 'Parents as Educators', for which they will provide a tutor and, occasionally, crèche support. Some nurseries and schools have managed to 'save' money from their original funding to allow them to continue for another term. Some parents have used their newly found self-confidence and literacy skills to lobby their council, or to look for sponsorship. Ideally, all adult groups involved in family literacy should be offered a guidance and progression session from an experienced worker. This enables the group to see the range of opportunities available, from adult literacy to college access courses, from GCSE English to ICT skills. It also enables the adults involved to look at ways in which the group can continue in a different guise if they want to stay together. They may become self-supporting and decide to continue to meet without any input from tutors or teachers. They may decide to embark on specific projects, such as setting up and running a library, or becoming involved in 'Storysacks' projects which involve producing book packs for the nursery or school.

Conclusion

There is a wide variety of projects around the country which come under the term 'family literacy', and one of the problems that we will increasingly face is what is meant by the term. Many of these projects are not about either families or literacy, but may be equally valid and effective and provide us with opportunities to rethink some fundamental aspects of education. Family literacy is about building on what is already happening in families and communities in order to develop societies where different literacies are valued, whilst recognising that 'mainstream' literacy (or schooled literacy) is the route into having a wider set of life choices.

In the best of family literacy practice, there is the chance to develop outside the traditions of formal education and to examine more closely what can be a new development in working with adults and children. When I first started working in this field, I used to explain it to people by using the 'H' model. This used the two sides of the H to demonstrate the kinds of specific skills work that was already going on with adults and children. The cross bar was the innovative part, a means of joining the two strands together and working in a very new way. In good projects, where adult groups are allowed to develop in their own way and where cognisance is taken of the literacy that both children and adults bring with them, some very exciting and effective work can happen. Something does seem to happen which is greater than the sum of the two parts, creating a 'spiral' effect. The models of adult behaviour – reading, studying and writing – have an effect on the children. The adults see what their children can do, how they can help their development and how teachers work with them. Children see their parents in school. Adults and children work together on problems, some of which the children approach more successfully than the adults and vice versa. An excitement about working on things together often spills over into the home and into the lives of other members of the family. It taps into the very basics of being a parent, of not wanting your child to go through what you went through.

Family literacy is an exciting, evolving concept but we should avoid it becoming the flavour of the month, leading to a proliferation of projects which do not have clear aims or carefully thought through strategies. There are no literacy panaceas. Literacy remains a cradle-to-grave entitlement. It has many different strands; everyone should be free to celebrate it. Family literacy is just one aspect of literacy and within this strand we are still learning and constantly developing our practice. We need to consider how to adapt it to meet every early years settings and schools needs and consider how it can complement the National Literacy Strategy. New projects are constantly emerging as we begin to look at developing the whole concept of family literacy. Two things, however, are certain: every individual family literacy project is different from the last, and each is as exciting as the last. Successful family literacy projects remain a thrilling and challenging experience for children and parents, tutors and teachers alike. As we look to these exciting developments, a key question is: 'Where will we be in ten years' time?'

Notes

1. I use the term 'parents' to describe the person who cares for the child, and could, therefore, attend a family literacy group. This could be a childminder, foster carer, older sibling and so on.
2. The Adult Literacy and Basic Skills Unit, which later became the Basic Skills Agency.
3. Accredited by the Open College Network. The Open College Network is the umbrella organisation for regional OCNs, which cover the whole country. They accredit courses that have been locally developed and are often tailored to a client group. They give formal accreditation to students based on the presentation of a portfolio of work. OCN courses can provide a superb route into return to learning for adults who have had bad experiences of formal education. Some OCN courses attract funding from the Further Education Funding Council.

Suggestions for further reading

Nutbrown, C. and Hannon, P. (eds) (1997) *Early Literacy Education with Parents – A Framework for Practice*, Nottingham: The Real Project NES Arnold.

Wolfendale, S. and Topping, K. (1996) *Family Involvement in Literacy – Effective Partnerships in Education*, London: Cassell.

Hannon, P. (1995) *Literacy, Home and School: Research and Practice in Teaching Literacy with Parents*. London: Falmer.

References

ALBSU (1993) *Parents and their Children: the Intergenerational Effect of Poor Basic Skills*, London: ALBSU.
Barton, D. (1994). Exploring family literacy, *RAPAL Bulletin*, no. 24.
Brice-Heath, S. (1983) *Ways with Words: Language, Life and Work in Communities and Classrooms*, Cambridge University Press.
Bynner, J. and Steedman, J. (1995) *Difficulties with Basic Skills: Findings from the 1970 Cohort Study*, London: Basic Skills Agency.
DfEE (1997) *Excellence in Schools*, London: HMSO.
Ferreiro, E. and Teberosky, A. (1982) *Literacy Before Schooling*, Portsmouth, NH: Heinemann.
Goodman, Y. (1980) The roots of literacy, *Claremont Reading Conference Year Book*, Vol. 44, pp. 1–32.
Goodman, Y. (1997) Multiple roads to literacy, in D. Taylor, (ed.) *Many Families, Many Literacies*, Portsmouth, NH: Heinemann.
Hannon, P. (1995) *Literacy, Home and School: Research and Practice in Teaching Literacy with Parents*, London: Falmer.
NFER (1995) *Family Literacy Works*, London: BSA.
Taylor, D. (1983) *Family Literacy: Young Children Learning to Read and Write*, Portsmouth, NH: Heinemann.

Taylor, D. (ed.) (1997) *Many Families, Many Literacies*, Portsmouth, NH: Heinemann.

12

Desirable Planning for Language and Literacy

Mary Brailsford, Diane Hetherington and
Evelyn Abram

Throughout this book we have seen that there are many forms of literacy practices which are subject to all kinds of socio-cultural influences and customs. In addition to this, each child is a unique, special individual with his or her own previous experience, interests and ways of learning. It is therefore clear that planning the early years literacy curriculum needs an approach which is comprehensive and inclusive. It is a complex juggling act which needs constant monitoring and adjustment if it is to meet the needs of children. Primarily, children should be encouraged to become independent learners and be involved in motivating, purposeful tasks (Whitebread, 1997). This chapter outlines how the early years literacy curriculum can be planned to provide opportunities for the children which are meaningful and have a real purpose. It is built on the assumption that child-initiated literacy behaviour is welcomed by the adults and that children's literacy practices are treated seriously and with respect.

The chapter focuses on planning in nurseries. Planning the language and literacy curriculum in the primary school has been dealt with elsewhere (Literacy and Numeracy National Project, 1997; Merchant and Marsh, 1998). However, this chapter does nor preclude planning for four-year-olds in reception classes. They need the same broad approaches to the planning and delivery of the curriculum that is outlined here. As Whitehead stresses:

> literacy learning and teaching in this phase must remain part of a distinctive early years tradition . . . The mismatch between the well-established international definition of the early years (nought, or three, to eight) and the current education legislation

in England and Wales does not necssarily stifle what can be
achieved with, and by, four- to eight-year-olds.

(Whitehead, 1996, p. 72)

This chapter outlines two different approaches to planning. Both feature examples of planning which are based on work with 3–5-year-olds
in nursery classes and schools. In addition, the planning is based on the
structure of the academic year (i.e. three terms). It is recognised that
there will be many types of early years provision which do not work
on this model. However, there are some underlying principles which
will apply in any kind of early years setting. Before we move on to consider the approaches to planning suggested in this chapter, we want to
look at these underlying principles which should underpin the planning of the language and literacy curriculum in the early years.

The space for literacy to emerge

The beginning of planning for literacy must be the learning environment. Our aim must be to organise the learning environment to ensure
that 'the status of literacy is high and its value is reinforced by frequent
occurrance' (Hall, 1987, p. 82). Goodman (1980, p. 31) points out that
'literacy develops naturally in all children in our literate society'. From
the very early stages, children interact with the wealth of texts around
them and try to make sense of them. The literacy environment needs
to take account of the child as an active meaning-maker. It needs to
provide children with a wide range of opportunities to engage with
texts, to develop confidence in themselves as speakers, listeners, readers and writers. It needs to provide opportunities for self-directed tasks
and ensure that there is plenty of stimulus for children. There need to
be clearly designated areas for particular activities, areas which contain
resources which the children come to recognise and gain familiarity
with. One of the key areas is a graphic area. Some nurseries refer to this
as a 'writing area', but we would like to broaden the concept to include
reference to children's early experimentations with mark-making and
drawing. Kress (1997) has outlined how children's early writing and
drawing are inextricably linked. Ann Browne's chapter in this book contains a range of suggestions for resourcing the writing curriculum. The
following list draws together suggestions for the graphic area:

- a table or space to write
- a variety of paper (plain, lined, books, forms, order books etc.)
- an assortment of writing and drawing tools (pencils, pens, felt tips,
  chalk etc.)
- chalk boards and chalks

- items of environmental print such as alphabet posters, group lists, children's name cards, notices
- magnetic letters and board
- noticeboard on which to put children's notices and writing
- whiteboard and water-based pens
- plastic letters
- alphabet books and picture dictionaries. If the children speak English as an additional language, it is important to include dictionaries in their first language. For monolingual children, this can raise awareness of other languages
- key word chart
- other stationery, e.g. paper clips, hole punches etc.
- an adult writing when possible.

It is also important to ensure that there is an attractive, welcoming reading area which encourages children to engage in reading behaviour. This reading area should include:

- picture books
- books of nursery rhymes and poems
- non-fiction books
- books made by children and families
- comics and magazines
- posters showing book illustrations and nursery rhymes
- posters showing positive images of reading
- a cassette player and story tapes with books
- comfortable seating for individuals or small groups to share stories
- character toys which can be used to support the story
- magnet board and figures related to popular stories.

Some nurseries and playgroups also have designated 'speaking and listening' areas in addition to the range of oracy activities which occur across the curriculum. Such an area could contain:

- a 'telephone box' which children could enter and use
- two telephones connected together for two-way conversations
- a small settee where children could sit and chat, with a range of stimuli to provoke talk e.g. unusual object on the coffee table
- a tape-recorder which could be used to leave messages or tell stories
- a 'story-telling' chair, with a special patchwork quilt draped over it – when children sit in the chair, they become a storyteller . . .
- a 'video box' (cardboard box with square cut out) which children could get into and relate their thoughts/ideas on a particular subject (as in the TV programme!)

However, it is important to ensure that language literacy resources are provided in all areas of the nursery or early years setting, not just designated areas. Books related to particular areas of the curriculum could be placed in areas designated for that particular area of learning. For example, books on art and artists could be placed in the art area, books on woodwork and woodcraft in the design and woodwork area, and so on. Writing resources need to be placed in a variety of areas such as the design and technology area, for use when drawing designs.

The outside area should also contain a range of reading and writing activities. If the garage in the outside area needs mechanics who can make notes and write invoices, then the use of clipboards and pens can be encouraged. Clipboards, paper and pens are useful to have readily available both inside and outside the nursery or early years setting and children should be encouraged to use them frequently. Easels which contain black or white boards and on which can be used chalks and markers are very attractive to children. And, of course, literacy resources are often an essential feature of structured role play areas, as Hall points out in Chapter 7. Language and literacy resources need to permeate every corner of the early years environment in order to promote a range of literacy practices.

The role of the adult

Children need to see others engaged in literacy and oracy tasks in order to learn about the purposes and nature of reading, writing, speaking and listening in the world around them. Under-5s workers have a crucial role to play in acting as role models for literate behaviour. It is not enough to provide resources to encourage literacy and oracy development; we must also engage with those resources ourselves. In Chapter 4, Elaine Hallet suggests various ways in which the adult can support children's language and literacy development. In terms of planning the language and literacy curriculum in the early years, account needs to be taken of these roles and opportunities provided for adults to undertake them all at different times. We should not only be initiating literacy events or providing support; we also need to model literacy practices to children. The number of adults available in the under 5s setting will also influence planning. If your nursery has a number of nursery nurses and frequent help from parents, you will obviously be able to plan a range of activities which are not possible to sustain in a small nursery with one or two adults. It is important, however, to value the role of all adults in delivering the language and literacy curriculum. A useful way to view the role of adults is to think of the seven 's's: supplying, supporting, scaffolding, sharing, showing, saying and seeing. Figure 12.1 explains each of these.

Roles of the adult in the nursery	
Supplying	Providing the resources necessary for children to develop their language and literacy skills.
Supporting	Helping children to achieve their aims by intervening sensitively when appropriate.
Scaffolding	Providing a framework for children so that they can achieve with help what they may be able to do on their own · tomorrow.
Sharing	Sharing ideas, thoughts and experiences with children. Sharing books with children. Making literacy a social experience.
Showing	Providing a role model for children. Demonstrating ways of doing things.
Saying	Giving feedback to children on their language and literacy achievements. Helping them to develop the metacognitive skills necessary to analyse and discuss their own development.
Seeing	Observing children's development closely in order to plan effectively for their future development. Assessing their needs sensitively.

Figure 12.1. Roles of the adult in the nursery

Planning the language curriculum

Planning is the cornerstone of effective teaching. QCA (1997) advise that:

> Good planning is essential for ensuring a broad, balanced and purposeful curriculum. As well as identifying *what* children should learn, curriculum plans also need to take account of *how* it is intended the teaching and learning will take place.
>
> (QCA, 1997, p. 5)

Planning the early years language and literacy curriculum needs to take a number of factors into account. The most important of these is that each young child has his or her own individual needs which should be met. Planning must start from what the child needs to learn and experience, not from what adults assume should be taught. Bruce (1998) has stressed that workers in the early years need to be skilled at assessing what each child's individual needs are. When we consider the complexity of young children's learning, it is clear that the early years are key in children's cognitive development. This puts much responsibility on the adult to be sensitive to the stages of children's learning and to ensure that the appropriate scaffolding for future learning is in place. It is also clear that it is not possible, nor desirable, to plan for every single learning experience a child will encounter in an early years setting. The nature of learning is such that any amount of detailed planning cannot precipitate the sudden interests of children, nor the questions they ask about particular things. It cannot account for those moments when something unexpected happens: a visitor, or a turn of the weather, or a particular statement by a child, or an object they bring in which captures the interest of others. Planning can provide merely a skeleton onto which the children, early years workers and other adults will fasten flesh and muscles, shape organs, work in thoughts and feelings and thus bring the language and literacy curriculum to life.

In addition to this, it is clear that the developmental stage of the child is crucial in planning for his learning. There is not space within this chapter to consider planning issues in relation to young babies and toddlers. Needless to say, these children will need individualised plans which emphasise heuristic play, development of sensori-motor skills and the exploration of their enviornment with the help of 'keyed in' adults. As children develop they will still need planning which takes account of their individual needs but, as they enter nurseries in which they are one of a large group, the needs of all these individuals need to be co-ordinated in a cohesive way. Below are outlined two methods of planning. There are many other planning methods which can be used but it may be useful to consider generic issues using these two processes as examples.

Planning the early years language and literacy curriculum

Planning needs to move from *long-term* planning which outlines what activities and experiences the children should engage with over a year, to *medium-term* planning which delineates the curriculum to be covered over a term, to, finally, *short-term* planning which includes weekly and daily plans. It is the synthesis of long-term, medium- and short-term planning which is the key to success.

Long-term planning for language and literacy

In deciding what the overall picture for learning should look like, the starting place is to look at each individual child and decide what her needs are with regard to language and literacy. For each child, a list should be made of individual needs and goals. Then, when structuring the broader picture of what the learning environment should offer over the year, staff can use children's individual records to ensure that the needs of every child are catered for. The curriculum in England must cover the six areas of the *Desirable Outcomes* and long-term planning can ensure that there is a balance across these areas over time.

Curriculum content

The use of themes when planning can lead to a holistic and cohesive experience for children. Obviously, not all of the experiences you want the children to have will be fitted within the theme, but it can provide a strong framework for planning. It is important to ensure that you have a balance of themes across the year so that all areas of the curriculum have an opportunity to be a major focus within the theme. It is also worth remembering that, for those children who enter the nursery at three and leave before the term in which they are five, you need to ensure that they do not experience the same topic during these years.

The example which follows is from a nursery which plans a two-year rolling programme with a range of themes spread over twenty-four months so that the topics are always new and exciting to each child. In addition, within these topics, activities are planned which develop and consolidate appropriate skills. The planning should be flexible enough to incorporate revision and extension where necessary. It is important to review the content of the topics and actitivies at intervals in order to make adjustments which will improve the provision.

Obviously, the language and literacy elements of the *Desirable Outcomes* need to be referred to when planning the curriculum in England. However, we want to broaden the terms of reference out to look at the range of oracy and literacy skills, knowledge and understanding children need to develop in the early years. Children need opportunities, when they are at the appropriate stage, to:

in relation to speaking and listening:

- speak in small/large groups with increasing confidence (in first language as well as English if the child is bilingual)
- talk and exchange ideas with peers and with familiar adults with increasing confidence

- relate their own experiences and observations
- play with words
- sit quietly in a group and listen attentively
- listen to and follow verbal instructions
- ask questions
- listen and respond to nursery rhymes, stories and poems
- make up stories
- engage in talk related to role play
- use talk effectively across the curriculum
- develop and extend confidence in using new and existing vocabulary

in relation to reading:

- become familiar with a range of fiction and non-fiction texts
- enjoy and respond to texts
- browse, behave like a reader
- understand that books can be a source of information
- be selective about books and make choices
- follow direction of print
- handle books appropriately
- respond to print with confidence
- retell favourite stories
- become aware of concepts of print, e.g. words, letters, etc.
- learn the names and most common sounds of letters
- recognise familiar words

in relation to writing:

- use pictures and marks to convey meaning
- develop a positive attitude towards writing and gain confidence in making marks on paper
- use characters and symbols of their first language in their mark-making
- experiment with mark-making in a variety of media
- write for a variety of purposes, using a range of forms and for different purposes
- plan and review writing where appropriate
- develop fine motor control and hand/eye co-ordination
- form the letters of their name
- be confident as a writer.

It is important that you are focused and selective about what you want the children to learn. If you are planning within a particular curriculum framework, such as the *Desirable Outcomes* which are statutory in England, check that your planning ensures sufficient coverage. In additon, make sure there are opportunities for the children to revisit and consolidate knowledge, understanding and skills. We will now outline two different methods of planning the nursery language and literacy curriculum. As stated earlier, these are suggested only as models. Each nursery and under-5s setting has particular needs and specific contexts in which they work. There are many different ways of planning the curriculum and there is not one method which is more effective than others. These factors mean that it is not desirable to be prescriptive about planning formats. Nevertheless, it may be helpful to follow a planning process through in order to think through some key principles.

Themes and topics

One method of planning is to plot the themes/topics by allocating them across the terms, clearly indicating the time you have available. Some topics and themes will be particularly suited to specific times of the year, especially seasonal activities and celebrations. Figure 12.2 is an example of a two-year cycle of themes. Each theme lasts for a term in this system, but of course twelve half-termly topics could be devised to cover the same time period. The themes shown below have a heavy emphasis on particular areas of learning, but each theme has been selected to ensure that all elements of the *Desirable Outcomes* can be covered within each one. The areas relating to the *Desirable Outcomes* are italicised.

Autumn term	Spring term	Summer term
Year 1		
Nursery rhymes and traditional stories *(Language and Literacy)*	Shopping *(Mathematics/Physical Development)*	Ourselves *(Knowledge and Understanding of the World – Science/Personal and Social)*
Year 2		
Past and present *(Knowledge and Understanding of the World – History)*	Journeys *(Knowledge and Understanding of the World – Geography/ Technology)*	Artists and musicians *(Aesthetic and Creative)*

Figure 12.2. Two-year cycle of themes

Once the themes for each term or half-term are identified, aims and objectives for each area of the curriculum can be outlined. We will use the themes for year one of the cycle as an example. In Figure 12.3 experiences which the staff want the children to have in reading, writing, speaking and listening are delineated.

Once long-term planning is in place, the medium-term plan can be devised (see Figure 12.4). The format for this will differ from setting to setting. This will outline what experiences will be offered over a half-term or term.

	Nursery rhymes and traditional stories	Shopping	Ourselves
Speaking and listening	See later section on medium-term planning	• Taking part in role play with confidence in a variety of shop settings • Going on visits to shops to buy items needed • Asking for items appropriately • Talking to 'customers' appropriately • Talking about own shopping experiences	• Talking about past and present events, in their lives – special events, etc. • Talking about friends and family • Naming/labelling different body parts • Talking about/ describing features, e.g. hair and eye colour • Work on sounds, e.g. listening walks • Speaking and listening in related role play, e.g. health clinic, opticians
Reading		• Environmental print – logos and packaging • Labels • Advertisements • Price lists • Related texts, e.g. *The Shopping Basket*	• Recognising their own name in different contexts • Related texts, e.g. non-fiction texts on senses and the body
Writing		• Shopping lists • Labels • Advertisements • Price lists	• Labels for parts of the body • Writing about themselves and their family • Own names, e.g. on simple graphs of hair and eye colour • Making cards for special occasions, e.g. birthdays

Figure 12.3.   Aims and objectives within each theme

	Past and present	Journeys	Artists and musicians
Speaking and listening	• Describe and talk about past and present events in the children's lives – use these as the basis for making up stories. An adult could scribe these conversations and make them into a book for the children to illustrate for all to look at and read in the class story corner • Role play situations could include old style washing play complete with posser, wash tub and wash board, contrasting with home corner automatic washing machines (if you have one!) • Discuss new and old toys	• Taking part in role play with confidence, e.g. Travel Agents/ Airports? Aeroplanes? Stations/Trains, etc. Introducing appropriate vocabulary for each situation • Visits to and rides on local transport, e.g. bus, train, tram. Talking about the experience – what they can see, hear, smell, touch, etc. • Describing their journey to the setting, mentioning local landmarks • Talking about a journey they have been on	• Using the language of colour, shape, texture and sound • Role play situations may include recording studio with microphones, tape recorders or even a karaoke machine! • Visits to local art galleries, theatre tours • Invite parent musicians or older brothers and sisters in to play different instruments for the children to listen to • Interview local artists and musicians
Reading	• Relevant non-fiction books • Relevant fiction • Old and new shop signs	• Environmental print – signs, notices • Timetable • Holiday brochures • Postcards • Relevant stories	• Staff to annotate related children's work • Non-fiction texts on musicians and artists • 'Art alphabet'
Writing	• Writing about events in own past (staff as scribe at times)	• Letters • Postcards	• Writing music using manuscript paper • Making posters to invite parents to the class's art gallery • Writing letters to favourite pop stars

Figure 12.3.   Cont

Once the medium-term planning is outlined, the staff can then use this to decide what activities and experiences they are going to plan each week (short-term planning).

The specific learning objective for each of the areas of learning should be decided upon, based on the children's previous experiences or developmental needs. We suggest that these learning objectives should remain the same for the week, or longer if necessary. The activ-

Nursery rhymes and traditional stories		
Speaking and listening	**Reading**	**Writing**
Explores rhyming words	Enjoys books	Uses symbols, words and letters to communicate meaning
My Cat Likes to Hide in Boxes	Read range of nursery rhyme books and traditional tales	Invitations to a party at the
Shoe Cottage		Three Bears' cottage
	Handles them with care	
	Children reading as a group, teacher modelling use of books	Shopping list for making cakes for
Listens to nursery rhymes and rhyming puns		the Baker's shop
	Understands how they are organised	Recipes for currant buns
Nursery rhyme and poetry anthologies	Making books – individual stories, class book of rhymes	
	Children as writers/illustrators, adult as scribe	Shows an awareness of some of the different purposes of writing
Makes up own stories		
Small imaginative play	Knows words and pictures carry meaning	
Puppets/props	Closes shop with sign	Writing a letter to the wolf
	Talks about text in focused way	Labelling own painting
Takes part in role play with confidence	Begins to associate sounds with patterns in rhymes	Writing on a greeting card
Three Bears' house	Games related to rhymes, e.g.	Sign for Baker's shop
Billy Goats Gruff	Humpty Dumpty	
The old woman who lived in a shoe	Rhyming wall	
		Knows words and pictures carry meaning
Baker's shop (Five currant buns . . .)	Recognises familiar words	
	Big book – underlining words	Writes a notice for the nursery/setting
	Activities to match rhyming words	
	Activities to match letters from words	Tells adult what own writing is meant to say
	Identifying names on group registers and lists	

Figure 12.4. Medium-term planning – themes

ities, however, might change daily or every two or three days or stay the same over the week. This gives the children the opportunity to visit and revisit activities in order to extend or consolidate their learning. Within each activity, there should be opportunities to differentiate teaching to meet individual children's needs. Figure 12.5 is an example of weekly planning.

	Desirable Outcome/ Specific learning focus	Monday	Tuesday	Wednesday	Thursday	Friday
Speaking and listening	To have a concept of rhyme/ begin to associate sounds with patterns in rhymes	**Rhyming Wall** Encourage the children to think of all the words that rhyme with 'wall'. Write each word onto a paper brick which is stuck onto the wall. Select other key words to build up a wall, e.g. 'men' *Resources*: Rectangular brick shapes cut from paper; black felt pen; large piece of paper/ card/backing paper; glue stick. *Organisation*: Small groups, adult scribe *Assessment*: Individual children's concept of rhyme		**Rhyming Eggs** Encourage children to think of the words that rhyme from 'Humpty Dumpty'. Write each word onto a paper egg. Cut each egg in half. Can the children put matching pairs together again? *Resources*: Paper cut in egg shapes, scissors, pens *Organisation*: Small groups, adult scribe *Assessment*: Individual children's concept of rhyme **Humpty Dumpty rewritten** Ask children to substitute new rhymes, e.g. Humpty Dumpty sat on a ... car Humpty Dumpty had a great ... star, etc. Scribe responses to make nonsense rhyme *Resources*: Easel, paper, felt pen *Organisation*: Small groups, adult scribe *Assessment:* Individual children's concept of rhyme	
Reading	To know that in English, print is read from left to right and from top to bottom To know that stories/ rhymes have a sequence	**Humpty Dumpty** Use an enlarged copy of the rhyme, read it together. Adult points to words as children say them. Children are given their own sheet to illustrate. Let children sing the rhyme, using their sheet to point to the words as they go to demonstrate directionality. *Resources*: Enlarged text. Photocopy of rhyme for each child. Pencils, felt tips. *Organisation*: Small groups. *Assessment*: Have children undertsood the directionality of print? **All jumbled up** Adult says lines in different order. Can children correct him/her? *Resources*: Rhyme *Organisation*: Small groups. *Assessment*: Can children re-sequence rhyme?		**Humpty Dumpty** Adult/child to sing/say rhyme together as above whilst adult points to each word. Children encouraged to find each word tile in order. Stick onto the top of the base board with Blu-tac working top to bottom, left to right. *Resources*: Enlarged text, individual pieces of card with words on, Blu-tac. *Organisation*: Small groups. *Assessment*: Have children understood the directionality of print? **Sequencing Humpty Dumpty** Sequencing pictures from 'Humpty Dumpty'. Order as they say the rhyme. Use glue to stick the pictures in sequence on paper. *Resources*: Four pictures from rhyme on A4 sheet *Organisation*: Small groups *Assessment*: Can children sequence picture in order?	

Figure 12.5. Weekly planning

	Desirable Outcome/ Specific learning focus	Monday	Tuesday	Wednesday	Thursday	Friday
Writing	Write with confidence for a variety of purposes and audiences To be aware of some of the different purposes of writing		**Writing rhymes** In writing area, put zig-zag books shaped like an egg. Encourage children to create their own version of the Humpty-Dumpty rhyme to share with others at group time. *Resources*: Zig-Zag egg books, pencils, felt tips. Organisation: Individual children. Adult scribe if appropriate. *Assessment*: Assess stage of child's writing development.	**Writing letters** Shared writing activity. Adult scribes letter to Humpty Dumpty which tells him about the 'safe'places he could sit, e.g. on grass, etc. Adult points out key features of letters as she/he writes it. Children then encouraged to write their own letters to Humpty Dumpty. *Resources*: Whiteboard, marker pen. A4 blank sheets *Organisation*: Small groups, adult scribe *Assessment*: Are children aware of the nature/ purpose of letters? Assess stage of child's writing development.	

Figure 12.5. Cont.

Continuing, linked and blocked units of work

We now want to move on to consider a different form of planning. There are certain activities and experiences which it is important to ensure are always occurring in the nursery or early years setting in order to develop children's oracy and literacy skills. These cannot always be fitted neatly into a topic and therefore need to be planned separately. It may therefore be necessary to create 'ongoing' planning in addition to topic planning in order to ensure full coverage of the language and literacy curriculum. In addition to the ongoing work, it is also often necessary to plan learning around a particular topic or theme. Young children's learning is holistic in that they do not learn in 'subjects' as such (Bruce, 1998) and topic work is one means of making this experience as seamless as possible. Therefore, in addition to ongoing work, it is also necessary to plan a topic or theme. Finally, it may be the case that an early years setting wants to focus in depth on a particular aspect of learning over a specific period of time, or devise a role play area which will stimulate a range of activities. In this case, they may want to devise a specific blocked unit of work which will outline learning objectives and activities in relation to that particular area. Figure 12.6 emphasises the interrelationship between these forms of planning.

Figure 12.7 is an extract from one nursery's **ongoing** unit of work which is set out on a format that contains learning objectives, suggested activities, resources and organisation. Daily planning ensures that learning objectives are matched to different levels of ability. Staff

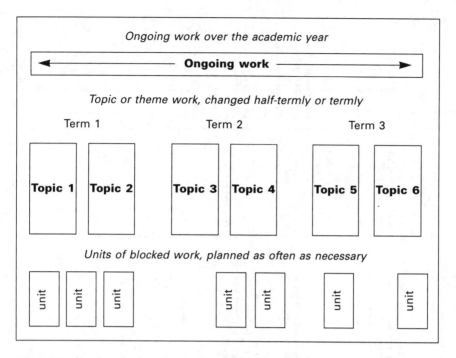

Figure 12.6. Ongoing, topic and blocked planning

assess the children against the learning objectives and this is recorded in the children's individual records.

Figure 12.8 provides an example of the nursery's **topic** planning, which is changed half-termly. As in the previous example of topic planning, specific activities and experiences are planned in relation to language and literacy within each topic, as well as other areas of the *Desirable Outcomes*. These activities can be part of the ongoing work but are adapted to the topic. For example, children being made aware of the different purposes of writing is a feature of the ongoing work. When undertaking the topic of 'Shopping', the topic planning may include activities which draw the children's attention to the purpose of print in shops; for example, labels, open and closed signs, shopping lists.

In addition to this, the nursery also plans specific **units of work** which are related to particular areas or special events. For example, planning the role play area is carried out as a separate unit of work. This work is carried out at the same time as the ongoing and topic work is occurring. There is sometimes a need to focus planning in depth on a particular area in order to exploit all the potential learning which can be gained. An example is the unit in Figure 12.9, based on a café which was set up in a role play area. Planning the specific

Sharrow Nursery: ongoing reading scheme of work

Learning objective	Activity	Resources	Organisation
Children learn to enjoy books, handle them carefully, understanding how they are organised.	Provide a range of good quality books, fiction and non-fiction, in a comfortable, homely book area. Include dual-text books wherever possible. Adults model use. Encourage children to browse.	A range of good quality picture, fiction non-fiction books.	←
Children learn concepts of print.	Staff share books with children, showing children how to hold, turn pages, talk about front/back, title, ask questions, e.g. What is this book about? • Talk about texts, words, letters, spaces, etc. • Staff read stories at group times and discuss them. • Staff read books with enthusiasm.	Books with dual text. Comfortable book areas – one at each end of the nursery.	Individual/pairs/groups browsing. Adult reading with child. Small groups in book corners, with adult. Group times.
Children learn that books can be a source of information.	Staff explain to children how books can be a source of information Model use. Use books on display and alongside activities for reference.	Reference and information books.	
Children learn that Roman script is read from left to right and from top to bottom. Children are aware that other scripts may be read differently. To recognise and know that there are other scripts as well as English and to value them.	Staff, when sharing dual-text book with children, discuss both texts and name them, i.e. Urdu, Bengali, Cantonese, English, etc. Discuss with children how Roman script is read from left to right and from top to bottom and how other scripts are read differently.	Dual-text books.	
Children learn to be selective about books and make choices, e.g. choose favourite books.	Children choose books for staff to read to them. Staff discuss children's choices with them. 'Book of the Week' table.		
• To be able to differentiate between print and pictures. • Understand that print carries meaning. • Recognise the connection between speech and writing/print. • Understand that writing/print is a means of communicating.	Discussions over a period of time, e.g.: • as adult reads, point to print, say this is what the writing says, etc. • discuss pictures and point out distinction between pictures and print • ask children to talk about what is happening in the pictures • ask the children to point to the writing • when scribing for children, talk about what you are doing; read it back to them.		→
Understand what a word is.	• Discuss words when reading. • Counting words in sentences. • Find words for the same object/concept in different languages.		

Sharrow Nursery: topic scheme of work – families

Learning objective	Activity	Resources	Organisation
Children develop the ability to join in a conversation, listening attentively and answering questions.	Discussion: How many people in your family? Discussions about past and present events in lives. Giving children the opportunity to talk about their own experiences. Discuss different kinds of families, e.g. foster, adopted, extended, etc.	Photographs of families, pictures and books about different families.	Small and large group discussions.
Speak for a range of purposes. Children develop confidence and fluency orally. Develop vocabulary and imaginative language.	Role play: kitchen and sitting room – describing, informing, instructing, predicting, maintaining conversations, etc. Adult enter role play to ask questions, discuss, etc. Introduce particular scenarios to stimulate talk, e.g. relatives coming from Pakistan to visit.	Home corner furniture.	Small groups. Adult support at times.
Develop enjoyment of stories. Extend children's ability to discuss stories and reflect on meanings/characters/plots.	Read to children a range of books about families, e.g. 'When I was a Giant', 'My Grandfather', etc. Discuss the picture/ stories with the children.	Relevant books.	Small/large groups.
Developing ability to recognise and write own name. Developing phoneme-grapheme	Children read and write their own names, with adult support if necessary. Talk about the letters in their names. Move on to work on names of people in their family.	Paper, pencils.	Individuals, with adult support.
Develop confidence in themselves as writers. Become aware that print carries meaning. Become aware of the range of forms, purposes and audiences for writing.	Range of writing activities related to families, e.g.: letters/postcards to relatives cards for family members list of members of family family trees.	Paper, postcards, card, pencils, pens.	Individuals, with adult support. Individual choice, writing area.
Developing writing skills: hard/eye co-ordination, ability to form letters with control over shape, size, orientation, distinguish between upper and lower case.	Drawing members of their family and writing their names. Adult to act as scribe when necessary. Making books about 'My Family'.	Paper, books, pens, pencils, photographs.	Individuals, with adult support.
Developing awareness of the range of forms/ purposes/audiences for writing. Developing use of imaginative language in writing. Developing phoneme-grapheme correspondence.	Shared writing, adult act as scribe. Write a poem about families. Start each line with: Families are . . . Families are . . . Discuss letters/words as you write.	Whiteboard, marker pen.	Small/large group Adult as scribe.

Figure 12.8. Extract from topic scheme of work

Sharrow Nursery: unit of work – café

Learning objective	Activity	Resources	Organisation
Develop confidence and fluency when using language. Extend and develop vocabulary	Visit to supermarket café. On visit, get children to talk about setting, context, signs, menus, etc. Experience buying a drink, something to eat, paying for it, etc. Compare with routines of home.	Visit to café.	Small and large group discussions.
Children develop the ability to join in a conversation, listening attentively and answering questions. Provide opportunities for children to talk about past and present experiences.	Discussion: After visit to café – what do we remember about it? How did we know what food and drinks they had? What did you enjoy most about the visit?		Small and large group discussions.
Speak for a range of purposes. Children develop confidence and fluency orally. Develop vocabulary and imaginative language.	In the café – discuss all aspects as it is set up, relate to own experiences. In role play, children to take on different roles – cook, waiter, customer. Encourage children to ask each other what they want to eat and drink, etc. Adult to enter role play area and stimulate conversation, ask questions, etc. Introduce scenario to encourage talk, e.g. customer complains that the food has made him/her ill. Letter from health department.	Small tablets with cloths, flowers and chairs, kitchen equipment, phone. Menus, appointments books, order forms, pens, pencils, open/closed signs. labels and posters Writing resources – paper, pens, pencils.	Small groups. Adult input.
Understand that print carries meaning. Write for a range of purposes and audiences, using a variety of forms.	When setting up – write labels, notices, signs, menus. When using – orders, bills, lists, receipts.	Paper, card, books.	Individuals, with adult support
Develop enjoyment of stories. Extend children's ability to discuss stories and reflect on meanings/characters/plots	Read to children a range of books set in cafés, e.g. Mrs Wobble the Waitress. Discuss the pictures/stories with the children.	Relevant books.	Small and large groups.
Develop confidence in themselves as writers. Develop awareness that print carries meaning. Become aware of the range of forms, purposes and audiences for writing. Developing phoneme–grapheme correspondence.	Range of writing activities related to the café: letters to council, leaflets (to advertise café), adverts, receipts for café, newspapers and magazines for children to read in café, stories based in the café, slogans for café, etc.	Writing materials, e.g. pens, pencils, lined and unlined paper, cards, envelopes, books.	Individuals, with adult support. Individual choice in writing area. Small/large group. Adult as scribe.

unit of work enabled the staff to focus on specific areas of learning which this role play area could promote. In this case it was language and literacy, linked with technology. A different kind of role play area, for example a supermarket, may have led to more focused work on mathematics.

Other specifc 'blocked' units of work which could be planned in this way include:

- festivals
- book week
- poetry week
- puppet theatre
- storytelling week
- drama work
- work based on a particular book.

This multi-layered planning is all drawn together on the outline planner for the half-term. This roughly sketches what is to be taught week by week, although it should be stressed that this is not set in stone. Planning should be flexible and it could be the case that activities which were planned to last one week are extended to two weeks. However, outline planning enables an early years setting to ensure that there is continuity and progression across the half-term. The ongoing plan enables staff to decide which aspects of the ongoing, topic or specific block of work is occurring each week.

Finally, the weekly plan needs to be drawn from the medium-term plans. This needs to be done on a weekly basis and is often done at the end of one week in preparation for the next. On the weekly plan, the staff decide which books, songs and topics for discussion are the focus for the week and these are highlighted. In addition to all of this, the staff need to respond to individual children's needs. This is then included on weekly planning. So, for example, if the staff feel that some children need specific work on writing their name, they will be targeted and this activity will be featured in the planning.

In addition, a column headed 'Staff to focus on following children' is added to the weekly planning as a daily reminder. The nursery staff use this column to write the names of the group of children who are the observational focus for the week. This group of children changes weekly so that all children are the focus twice a term. Then during the week, *all* the nursery staff observe and work alongside this group of children, although not exclusively so. At the end of the week, they then sit down to discuss and share their observations on these children in order to inform future planning for them (for further ideas on group contributions to children's profiles, see Chapter 13).

Finally, it is important to ensure that outdoor activities include opportunities to develop language and literacy. These can be planned using the same ongoing, topic or blocked model of planning. Figure 12.10 contains an example of an ongoing planning sheet for outdoor activities.

Planning should be manageable as well as useful. Formats need to be devised which are simple to complete and which can be understood by anyone who comes to work in the nursery. Some nurseries and early years settings display their planning for parents to see but if you do that you will need to ensure that your planning formats are straightforward and do not require knowledge of specialist terminology. It is also worth repeating that there will be many, many learning opportunities in the nursery and early years setting which are not outlined on the planning sheets. Adults need to respond to these, follow them through at the time and not worry that they are not written down anywhere!

Working as a team

It is important that all the nursery staff plan together as a team in order to ensure that all have ownership of the curriculum. Weekly planning meetings in which all adults who work in the nursery take part can ensure that plans are reviewed to meet individual children's needs. In these meetings, individual children's key workers can inform the rest of the group what the needs of specific children are in order to ensure that these are met across the week. Key workers need to ensure that individual children's development is tracked carefully and their needs communicated to others in order to inform future planning. This should happen on a daily basis if necessary. It is the successful juggling of overall provision for the development of skills, knowledge and understanding in language and literacy with the attention to the specific stage of development of individual children that is the hallmark of successful planning in the early years. This makes the link between planning and assessment particularly important, as Fran Paffard makes clear in Chapter 13.

Conclusion

This chapter has considered a range of different strategies for planning the early years curriculum. There are many more which have not been examined here and which many nurseries use successfully. Perhaps the most useful way to conclude would be to draw together what we consider to be the skills, knowledge and understanding required by early

Sharrow Nursery: outdoor activities linked to topic 'Families'   Area: language and literacy

	Speaking and listening	Reading	Writing
Learning objectives over half-term	Develop confidence and fluency when using language. Extend and develop vocabulary. Children develop the ability to join in a conversation. Provide opportunities for children to talk about past and present experiences. Speak for a range of purposes. Children develop confidence and fluency orally. Develop vocabulary and imaginative language.	Develop enjoyment of stories. Extend children's ability to discuss stories and reflect on meanings/characters/plots. Know that print carries meaning. Developing phoneme–grapheme correspondence. Develop concepts of print. Use books to find information.	Understand that print carries meaning. Write for a range of purposes and audiences, using a variety of forms. Develop confidence in themselves as writers. Develop awareness that print carries meaning. Become aware of the range of forms, purposes and audiences for writing.
Week 1 *The house*	House play – with house frame, crockery, tables and chairs. Discussion about families and routines at home, different roles.	Newspapers, magazines and comics in house. Recipe books.	Opportunities for writing – letters and postcards to relatives, telephone messages, shopping lists.
Week 2 *The house*		Books about families on book stand, large bean bags, chairs.	
Week 3 *A journey with the family*	Role play: bus. Taking turns to be the driver. Where is the bus going? How many people on the bus?	Reading destination names. Petrol pump – reading the signs/numbers. Reading newspapers on the bus. Looking at books about buses	Writing signs for the bus. Writing timetables.
Week 4 *Shopping with/for the family*	Role play: shop. Take on various roles, e.g. customer, assistant, manager. Taking faulty goods back.	Reading labels, signs, packaging. Looking at books about shops.	Writing labels, signs. Shopping lists.
Week 5 *Going on holiday with the family*	Set up sand pit as seaside area – shells, bucket and spade, deckchairs, etc. Paddling pool – supervised at **all** times it is out. Travel agents – use house frame, tables, etc. Aeroplane – seats in line, etc. Use these as stimuli for conversations with children	Holiday books. Looking at travel brochures. Reading names on tickets, passports, etc.	Writing letters/postcards home. Filling in holiday forms. Writing passports, tickets, etc.

Figure 12.10.   Planning for language and literacy in the outdoor area

years workers if they are to plan an effective language and literacy curriculum. If these principles inform planning, then whatever method is used, or whatever the context, the children will be provided with a myriad of opportunities to develop as confident, competent and enthusiastic readers, writers, speakers and listeners.

Planning the early years language and literacy curriculum requires early years workers to:

- have a sound knowledge of how children learn and reflect carefully on the teaching and learning process
- be familiar with the skills, knowledge and understanding needed for children to develop language and literacy skills
- know what range of experiences and activities will develop these skills, knowledge and understanding
- have a knowledge of the developmental needs of the individual children they work with
- know how to support children at each stage of their development
- ensure that they build upon children's previous experiences and learning
- be clear about the role of adults in children's language and literacy development
- know how to structure and utilise the learning environment to facilitate children's learning
- be familiar with statutory requirements for the curriculum, e.g. *Desirable Outcomes*
- ensure that they plan for language and literacy within a broad and balanced curriculum
- ensure that planning demonstrates continuity and progression and allows for differentiation
- devise planning formats which are clear, easy to use and outline key aspects, e.g. learning objectives, assessment, organisation, resources
- be flexible and able to adapt plans to meet specific needs and circumstances
- be aware that there will be many opportunities to develop children's language and literacy skills which are not specifically planned for and which arise spontaneously
- share ideas and plans with others, communicate well as a member of a team
- know how to make learning enjoyable!

Suggestions for further reading

Edgington, M. (1998) *The Nursery Teacher in Action: Teaching 3-, 4- and 5-Year-Olds,* 2nd edition, London: Paul Chapman.

Whitebread, D. (1996) *Teaching and Learning in the Early Years,* London: Routledge.

References

Bruce, T. (1997) *Early Childhood Education,* 2nd edition, London: Hodder & Stoughton.

Goodman, Y. (1980) The roots of literacy, *Claremont Reading Conference Yearbook,* Vol. 44, pp. 1–32.

Hall, N. (1987) *The Emergence of Literacy,* London: Hodder & Stoughton.

Kress, G. (1997) *Before Writing,* London: Routledge.

Merchant, G. and Marsh, J. (1998) *Co-ordinating Primary language and Literacy: The Subject Leader's Handbook,* London: Paul Chapman.

QCA (1997) *Looking at Children's Learning,* London: HMSO.

QCA (1998) *Desirable Outcomes for Children's Learning On Entering Compulsory Education,* London: HMSO.

Whitebread, D. (1997) *Teaching and Learning in the Early Years,* London: Routledge.

Whitehead, M. (1996) *The Development of Language and Literacy,* London: Hodder & Stoughton.

13

Level 3 and the Ringling Tingling Man: Assessing Language and Literacy

Fran Paffard

Hana was a British-born four-year-old from a Moroccan family. Her first language was Arabic. Silent for the first few weeks in the nursery, she quickly blossomed into an animated communicator in English. Hana loved to talk and in particular loved the tape recorder, set up in a corner of the class with blank tapes for children to record their own thoughts and stories. She spent long periods of time hunched breathily over it, composing her latest story. Invariably, they would begin with her own personal story convention, 'Once upon a little tiny time'. There would then be a pause and she would continue in a coaxing voice, 'Are you sitting in a comfortably? Then I will tell you this really good story,' and off she would go again. The Ringling Tingling Man was one of her later creations and, as with many of her stories, his tale was never completed. It was enough for Hana to have created him and unleashed him into the world. 'The Ringling Tingling Man was good and nice to children and he never smack them even when they are very very naughty . . .' Thinking about Hana now, I find myself wondering how her literacy skills would be judged against the current forms of assessment that are commonly used in early years education. She left nursery a confident teller of tales, but encouragement to write produced howls of, 'I can't doooo it'. She had only recently begun to draw representational pictures and was far too eager to talk to be regarded as a good listener. Orally inventive and an idiosyncratic composer of story forms, Hana was as yet unimpressed by the transcription and decoding of print. She wrote her name in a form recognisable to us but it was scattered over all four corners of the paper and did not respect the difference between 'upper and lower case letters' (QCA, 1998). Above all, remembering Hana brings home to me the pernicious fiction of the 'normal child' against whom all our children are to be measured.

This chapter explores the place of assessment in young children's developing literacy. The values and purposes embedded in different forms of assessment will be reviewed. The chapter begins with a glimpse of the development of an individual child, Hana, since unless we keep the child at the centre of our thinking, we shall soon be led astray. With her and every other unique child in mind, the chapter then moves on to look at a range of effective practices in assessing young children's literacy.

Underlying principles

As Drummond (1993) points out, 'the key issues in assessment are moral and philosophical, not organisational and pedagogical' (Drummond, 1993, p. 12). Assessment in the early years must be firmly based on the principles of early years education, asserting the very positive nature of assessment as it focuses on what the child can do. If we view children as active constructors of their world, then we need a literacy curriculum that gives them the initiative in developing literacy and an active role in assessing their own progress. If we believe that children learn best through play and through interaction, then we need to be providing a wide range of opportunities for literacy in these contexts and to be observing and assessing their progress as an integral part of the day. If we believe that their learning is not compartmentalised, then we should be alert to their literacy development occurring as part of a holistic learning process and be aware that each child's route into learning is unique. We need to respect the rights of children to explore and learn in the here and now and not regard either their literacy, or our assessments, as merely preparation for later.

Why we assess is the key to what we assess and how we do it. Edgington (1998) offers six main purposes for assessing and recording children's learning:

1. to find out about children as individuals
2. to monitor the progress (or lack of it) of individual children
3. to inform curriculum planning
4. to enable staff to evaluate the provision they make
5. to provide a focus for communication with others
6. to make the job more enjoyable.

(Edgington, 1998, pp. 121–2)

More recently, we may perhaps need to add a seventh point: to make teachers, nurseries and schools accountable. Whilst all of these purposes are valid and closely inter-relate, the main focus of this chapter is on understanding and assessing the progress of individual children.

What we teach and what we assess are inextricably linked, and what we assess will inevitably influence the curriculum we offer the child. Kelly (1992) has argued that, 'This interplay between curriculum and assessment is crucial to the quality of both' (Kelly, 1992, p. 16). Effective assessment will not only monitor individual children, but also help to evaluate the curriculum and our own philosophies and practices. There is an implicit assumption in recent government initiatives that literacy is a straightforward achievement. The National Literacy Strategy baldly defines it as a 'communication skill' (DfEE, 1998, p. 82). The generally accepted view is that literacy is about learning to read and write, but the reality is more complex. Literacy takes place within the context of all learning. It is a part of a symbolic system that has at its heart all the richness of oral communication, without which the written word has no meaning. And, as was stated in the introduction to this book, Whitehead (1997) suggests that:

> literacy itself will suffer if not established on a broad and deep foundation of worthwhile experiences of symbolising and representing meanings through non-verbal communication skills, gesture, movement, dance, music, listening, talking, drawing, painting, modelling, building, story-telling, poetry-sharing, scientific and mathematical investigations, rituals and religious celebrations.
>
> (Whitehead, 1997, p. 177)

Literacy in this light is a rich carousel of representation through which children gain entry into a diverse world of forms for communicating meaning, expressing thoughts and feelings, and creating new ways of seeing themselves and their environment. Immediately, it becomes apparent that this complex interpretation of literacy will not be amenable to simple tests of children's progress.

How we view the purposes of literacy will also decree much about the means we use to get there and how we will judge our steps along the way. Do we want children who have only the reading and writing skills that will enable them to function in the workplace? Or do we want children whose lives are transformed by the power of literacy, children who will be talkers, readers and writers for life?

Whilst assessment must aim to be as objective as possible, the complex learning processes of young children make this a formidable task. Assessment is inevitably subjective whether we like it or not. Our notions of childhood and our educational values are culturally determined. A seven-year-old in a British school who cannot read will almost certainly be a cause for concern; the same child in Denmark will only just be starting out on structured reading and writing programmes. As Mills and Mills (1998) recently argued, our present education system is set on teaching all reception age children to write their names and know all the sounds and letters of the alphabet regardless of their interest or ability to do so, when comparisons with Hungary and Denmark show clearly that children acquire these skills with ease a couple of years later.

Our view of literacy needs to be critically examined rather than accepted unquestioningly. As Tobin, Wu and Davidson (1989) so convincingly demonstrate, our cultural values affect our curriculum and our judgements of children:

> In China, the emphasis in language development is on enunciation, diction, memorization, and self-confidence in speaking and performing . . . Language in Japan – at least the kind of language teachers teach children – is viewed less as a tool for self-expression than as a medium for expressing group solidarity and shared purpose. Americans, in contrast, view words as the key to promoting individuality, autonomy, problem-solving, friendship and cognitive development in children. In America, children are taught the rules and conventions of self-expression and free speech.
>
> (Tobin, Wu and Davidson, 1989, pp. 102–3)

The salutary lesson here is to critically analyse the value systems in which we operate. Also important to consider is the polycultural society in which we live and the conflicting views this can give to children's own conceptions of literacy. As Gregory (1997) has so revealingly documented, the different forms and purposes of literacy that bilingual children meet at home and at school can mean that schools often fail to build on the understanding and experiences that children bring from home.

Given the principles and the context we have outlined, let us briefly consider the various forms of assessment and how they fit into the overall picture. *Formative* assessments have long been the stuff of early years work. They are characteristically individual, detailed and descriptive, aiming to capture the spirit of children, focusing on what they can do and how to further their development. Formative assessments are ongoing, concerned with process rather than product.

Summative assessments aim to give a snapshot of the child's attainments at a particular point. These assessments are generally systematic and standardised so that the child's attainments can be compared against some frame of reference. This can be norm-referenced (compared against some agreed average of achievement) or criterion-referenced (compared against a particular set of criteria) as are the

National Curriculum SATs. In reality there is often little difference between the two since the criteria and the expected norms for children are closely related. In both cases, the setting of external measures of achievement, and particularly scores, is unlikely to do justice to the range and diversity of a child's development. A third option, more in harmony with formative assessment, is *ipsative* assessment in which the child's achievements are compared against his own previous achievements. These are particularly helpful when they draw on the evidence provided by formative assessments. Formats such as the Primary Language Record (CLPE, 1988) have used these kinds of assessment with great success.

Finally, *diagnostic* assessment enables teachers to look in depth at a particular aspect of a child's learning and diagnose what the child can and cannot do. It is most often used in cases where a teacher may be concerned about a particular aspect of a child's learning and wants to find out exactly what the child's needs are. However, in a sense all assessment is diagnostic. The main difference with this and other forms of assessment is the depth to which the assessment procedures go in uncovering children's skills, knowledge and understanding. It is a deep and narrow look at a specific area rather than a broad brush-stroke across the child's experiences.

Having dealt briefly with the wider question of why we need to assess children's literacy and what forms of assessment we can use, let us look more closely at the practicalities involved in implementing effective literacy assessment in early years settings.

Who should be involved?

Assessment involves power. It is an awesome responsibility to sit in judgement on another human being and it is one that should be shared. That parents and carers are their children's first teachers is both a truism and a fact that has yet to be truly recognised in practice. Children do not arrive in early years settings as empty vessels, but have a wealth and diversity of experience behind them. Records from playgroup or other settings, admissions forms, settling-in forms, and the first parent and child conferences can all provide valuable information on which to build. Parents can and should be active collaborators in both supporting and assessing children's literacy development, using a flexible range of structures: PACT schemes, home–school books with room for comments, regular conferences, parents reading, writing and talking in class.

Where possible, assessment should also be shared between a key worker with prime responsibility for keeping a child's records and a team who will all feed in their own observations and analysis. The team should be committed to collaborating, remaining flexible and receptive to sharing views and information. The ideal of an objective view of the child is far more likely to be realised by this counterbalancing of different views than by supposedly objective tick lists or tests. This is especially the case when those views represent different training, as with teachers and nursery nurses, and different kinds of relationships with the child, as with parents and staff. This is, however, proposing both a more arduous and more fulfilling task than the brief standardised assessments of checklists and tests. In this light, all the concerned adults are acting as action researchers, viewing and reviewing their understandings in a spirit of passionate enquiry. This demands highly knowledgeable, deeply reflective practitioners who are able to perceive individual threads of learning amongst the densely woven fabric of children's play. They need to be able to hold in their heads the many possible interpretations of a child's actions and be able to tune into the child. They need to intervene (or not), using their intimate knowledge of the child, which will enable them to extend the learning which is occurring.

Self-assessment

Recent research on children's self-esteem (Roberts, 1995; Goleman, 1995) has clarified the extent to which children's own emotions and dispositions affect their learning, and their involvement in the process of evaluating their learning is increasingly being shown to be crucial to their success (Gura, 1996). Stephen (5:4) repeatedly tore up his work saying, 'It's rubbish, it's just scribble.' His older brother Mark had said similar things when he was in the nursery. Stephen was amazed to be shown Mark's own samples of writing from nursery onwards, each struggle valued and preserved. Stephen was encouraged to try again and Mark, reflecting proudly on his progress, became the competent writer who shared his skills with his brother.

We need to 'let children into the secret' (Hutchin, 1996, p. 16) of their own learning and engage them in an ongoing dialogue that takes their interests and their own view of learning seriously. Involving children in self-assessment shares the power with them and, through the encouragement of reflection and meta-cognition, enables them to gain greater understanding of the processes of learning (Eisner, 1996; Gardner, 1993). Just as a bilingual child may have a greater understanding of how language works through his ability to understand more than one language, so too all children can benefit from thinking about thinking and about the things that have helped them to learn. Tina (5:2) told me proudly that she had learned to do her laces. When I asked her how she had learnt she told me: 'Well, you know yesterday I tried and I tried and I just couldn't, and when I went to bed I was thinking about it in my head and when I woke up I knew in my fingers!' Equally, we need to recognise the power of their community of peers. 'I can't do S,' said Justin (4:2), despairingly. 'I can do sharks, but not S.' 'Yeah,' said his friend Ross (4:4), consolingly. 'You just never know which way they're going to go.'

What should be assessed?

In terms of even the simplest interpretation of literacy, the adult needs to understand and recognise children's development of mark-making, iconic and symbolic representations, access to culturally set forms of symbols and calligraphic skills. We need to understand and support children's specific development in phonic, graphophonic, syntactic, semantic and bibliographic knowledge, and to be prepared to find them in unexpected places.

Anna (4:6) hasn't spoken much since her mother died, but every day she constructs her funfair in the blockplay and carefully re-enacts her day out there. Her play reworks and reviews her understanding of a symbolic system in a way which will enable her to transfer skills to her reworking of written language, but it also fulfils her own deep need as adult-led activities would not. Shane (3:7) spends most of his time out of doors circling, wheeling and diving, perfecting on a grand scale those movements which provide the foundation of the circles and curves needed for letter formation. Shakil (4:3) is endlessly caught up in a cycle of violent role play as Duplo cars crash and people die, his whirling scenarios the patchwork pieces of later dramatic compositions. Jade's (4:10) insistence on singing 'stinky winky bum bum' is not only a cheeky piece of insubordination, but also a piece of phonic word play which is more fun and informative than is to be found in all the textbooks and reading schemes. Gulcan (1:2), who repeatedly pulls down the photo book of babies from the shelf and babbles to it as she turns the pages, already knows lots about how books work and sees reading as a worthwhile activity. Each of these children is engaged in a literacy activity worth observing, analysing and acting on within the context of their individual development and need.

Literacy development, as we have seen, cannot be confined to formal instruction in reading and writing but occurs spontaneously within many different contexts. What we choose to see as significant in the development of literacy depends on a deep understanding of the many processes involved. Riley (1998) suggests that the emergence of literacy into conventional forms is an interactive process combining 'meaning-making' and 'code-breaking' strategies, both of which need to be recognised and supported. Latifah (3:4), sweeping her hand through the fingerpaint and saying, 'Look a rainbow, like in Rainbow room,' is both using symbols to represent her world and linking them with other symbolic knowledge. Matthew (4:0), excitedly recounting the fight he witnessed outside the pub, is extending his oral skills and struggling to put his experience into narrative form. Harry (4:3), looking at the 'Halifax' sign and saying, 'That's in my name,' is beginning to focus on environmental print and to recognise individual orthographic features. Saida (4:1), laughing because her friend Billy's name sounds like the Punjabi name for cat, has discovered homonyms. Zoe (4:10), scribbling urgently on scrumpled pieces of paper and stuffing them into envelopes, is 'paying the bills' and demonstrating her knowledge of the purposes of writing. Dominic (4:8), painstakingly copying 'Crayola washable felt pens' onto a piece of paper, is extending his repertoire of mastered words. He knows now that there is a right way to write and is intent on achieving it. If we look only for narrow achievements, the easily observable and the superficial, then we miss the deep learning going on underneath.

The research of Athey (1990), which highlighted the complexities of children's learning through absorption in schematic patterns of behaviour, has given us a new light to shine on children's development of literacy. Not only are the graphic forms of writing first experimented within action and across different media, but more fundamentally we can key into a deep level of interest in the interactions, the stories and the provision we offer them. Damien (4:4), engrossed in exploring a horizontal schema, loved producing lines of writing on the computer and would spend hours writing letters on very long thin pieces of paper. He was interested in the directionality of print on the page and the stories he loved were *The Line-Up Book*, *The Elephant and the Bad Baby* and *The Enormous Turnip*, each with their long, horizontal lines.

Where should children be assessed?

Everything we know about young children's learning tells us that the child reveals her greatest knowledge and skills during child-initiated activities, and in particular during play. It is important to remember the distortions that can occur if we try to assess children in a test environment, and when tests they are given do not make sense to them. As Donaldson's (1978) famous revision of Piaget's work demonstrated, a task that children were unable to do in a vacuum, they performed with ease when it was presented to them in a way that made 'human sense'. Thus the child's abilities should be observed and analysed during the everyday good practice of the early years setting; alone and in groups, outside and inside, remembering that learning takes place during lunchtime, by the coat pegs and in the toilets. Hall and Robinson (1995) have demonstrated how confidently children take on literate behaviour, given a variety of provision as part of imaginative play. Nor should it be forgotten that the setting is only one part of the child's life and that important information and experiences from home will add greatly to our understanding. Jimmy (4.0) proudly wrote, on all his pictures, the Chinese character for water that he had learnt at community school that week.

When should children be assessed?

Essentially, assessment must be a continuing record of the child's progress, constantly reviewing and updating the shared understanding of his learning. Regular, informal discussion with child and parents makes this a part of everyday life. Termly or yearly formal parent conferences allow a deeper, more solid review of progress to take place. Observation itself needs to pick up on spontaneous happenings of note but can also be more organised to track a particular child over time, or to survey the use of a particular area. As it is important to assess children in different contexts, it is also essential to look at children at different times. Children reveal their knowledge in different ways and leaping to conclusions may lead us to seriously underestimate a child. Children who are silent when they arrive or at group time may be vociferous at lunchtime or when playing outside. Knowledge of how children behave in the home can check our assumptions made about them in school. Jordan (4:2), a sociable and energetic constructor at school, was an only child who peopled his home world with imaginary friends and through the telling of extraordinary adventures. Ideally, a balance needs to be struck between maintaining frequent observations (making sure that quiet or self-sufficient children do not slip through the net), allowing time for dense narrative descriptions that can be unpicked at leisure, and noting the particular significant moments (Hutchin, 1996) which mark a change or progression in a child's thinking.

How should we assess?

With all the pressures on the early years professional, it is hardly surprising that many educators feel that they have no time to stop, observe and reflect on the learning going on. Yet without this, everything that we do is of dubious value. Drummond (1993) argues for beginning that familiar cycle of early education practice – plan, do, observe, record, plan – at a different point. If we start with observing, analysing and reflecting on children's learning, the curriculum we offer children is likely to be a far better match to their individual and corporate concerns.

Interactions

Some of the most important assessments we do as early years practitioners never make it onto paper. The initial response to, 'Look what I can do!', 'Come and see our garage,' or, 'It's gone all soggy,' are the most crucial to the child. As Gura (1996) points out, 'evaluative praise' can have the opposite effect to the one intended. Comments such as, 'That's lovely, dear,' or, 'I like the colour,' can lead to over-dependence on the judgements of adults and undermine independent thought and children's trust in themselves. Instead, descriptive or informational comments focusing on attributes of work or the processes involved and discussions with children about their own intentions and meanings will provide children with a context for seriously assessing and celebrating their own work. To display interest to a child without committing yourself to a particular aspect of his learning is one of the surest ways of getting children to reveal their innermost thoughts. One of the most powerful words that can be uttered to a child is a gently interested, 'Mmmm?' We should also be wary of our own responses to children's perceptions of reality: 'My mum teaches me to write, at school I just play.' As professionals, such conceptions of learning are deeply threatening to us but it is the child's understandings that we need to work with, not deny, if we are to support her learning.

Observations

Drummond (1993) frames the process of assessment as having three stages: collecting evidence, making judgements and then deciding on outcomes. Observation provides valuable evidence that must then be carefully analysed and the judgements used to inform future planning and action. Observation can be free or focused. We can provide full narrative descriptions to be analysed later or look for particular aspects of learning; each has its place. Observation doesn't need to be (and often cannot be) removed from the life of the class or setting. Often, the richest observations come whilst participating with children in an activity, frequently at a tangent to the subject in hand. 'See this,' said Murat (3.11), holding up his bread at the lunch table. 'It's a triangle.' He took a bite. 'Now it's an L shape, and now it's a number 1!'

In recent years, early years teams have evolved increasingly efficient ways of recording these valuable, but fleeting, moments. The notebook has been largely superseded by the Post-it note and the address label so that moments such as these can be scribbled down and then transferred at the end of the day or week to more permanent forms of records. Many early years settings have folders or clipboards pinned up in different areas so that any interesting observations can be jotted down and collated later. These fragments may seem small but they are the stuff of learning and can be reflected on and analysed later by the staff team.

One of the most potent strategies for a team (however small) is the end-of-day review. This can be ten to fifteen minutes when staff sit down, collate and share observations, interpret their findings and use them as the basis for planning, both for individual children and for the curriculum. One nursery school noticed a large number of children who were interested in enveloping and enclosing (Athey, 1990) and decided to extend this across their provision. They introduced the picture book *My Cat Likes To Hide in Boxes* as a theme, provided hidey-holes in the garden, placed wrapping-up materials in the workshop and provided different sized cats for different sized boxes. The staff used children's interests to inform their planning and creatively matched these interests to the curriculum. It provided a focus that lasted productively for several weeks.

Sampling

Observations are one form of evidence. However, it is important to collect a range of forms of evidence to build up a holistic picture of children's abilities. Most nurseries and schools now keep folders with regular samples of children's work. These need to be meaningful examples of children's own work, not merely samples of adult-directed tasks. Neither should they be work collected on a single day. There is also a danger here that sampling may focus on the end product and that some children will produce reams of drawings and writing which are easy to store, whilst others will be immersed in huge constructions, wild dramatic play or other forms of representation which are equally valid, but far harder to preserve. Photographs are a powerful tool here and whilst they cannot capture the full experience, they can, with accompanying notes, record an important moment. Recording talk, whether it is taped or a scribbled transcription, is very revealing. The actual words children use demonstrate their oral skills and their thinking and are very powerful indicators of a child's progress. For every sample of children's thinking, the context in which it takes place is important. A piece of paper with two scribbles on will tell us little on its own but the accompanying note adds considerably to our knowledge of a child's growing biliteracy, as in the following example:

2:10:97 Amjid came straight in and wrote this from right to left. He said, 'That's my Koran writing, I do it at my house.' First time I've seen him writing.

Profiles

From this collection of samples, observations, conversations and photographs, significant evidence can be selected to form a profile. This is a cumulative, developmental record charting children's progress over time. Increasingly, early years settings are involving children and families in this process so that children are consulted on which pictures, photos and observations are included, often sticking them in themselves. These treasured books can then be kept accessible for children, staff and parents to read, discuss and reflect on.

Summative records

There are points in a child's educational life when a summary of her achievements needs to be made; for example when the child moves from one setting to another. For the harassed teacher receiving thirty reports at once, formative assessments are too detailed and need to be summarised if they are to be helpful. Summative assessments that rely wholly on one-off tests or tick lists can tell us little of value and are unlikely to reflect the child's capabilities. As discussed earlier, summative assessments that are ipsative and track the individual child's progress are more likely to give a true picture of the individual child and a more helpful starting point for furthering their development. These records should draw on the accumulated evidence and knowledge of all those involved with the child. They should be precise about what children can do, the skills they have and their stage of conceptual development, but should also focus on their interests and their attitudes towards literacy since these will be crucial in their development. Systems such as the PROCESS (Stierer *et al.*, 1993) format that include brief samples of children's work and observations alongside the summative comments give a stronger 'snapshot' of the

Language and Literacy Conference   Child's name Stefan Krystofik   **Age** 4:3   **Week beginning** 12/6/98

Mode	Checklist of achievement	Observations in week of focus	Comments from child	Comments from family	Suggestions for follow-up
Speaking and listening	Listens to others Talks about his/her experiences Listens to others attentively Responds appropriately to others Responds to direct questions Initiates questions Talks with friends Confident in talking in small groups Confident in talking in large groups Takes part in role play with confidence Interested in words Can talk about talking Makes up own stories Joins in group storytelling Speaks confidently in first language Uses first language most of the time, beginning to attempt English words in context Switches between two languages confidently	15.6.98 Stefan reported what he had found in the wildlife garden to his group. He was very excited and described his turning over of the log, and the creatures he found underneath, very well. 17.6.98 Stefan is more confident in role play. He joined in the play in the sweet shop and used appropriate vocabulary, e.g. 'Do you want to buy/it costs/ . . .', etc.	17.6.98 Afterwards, I told him that he was very good at being a shopkeeper. He beamed and said 'Yeah . . . I knowed what to say.'	16.6.98 Stefan's dad said that Stefan never stops talking at home! He thought that Stefan's oral skills were very good.	Continue to ask Stefan to report back on visits, etc. Ask Stefan to tape his recounts. Listen to it played back alongside him and ask him to reflect on it.
	Is aware that print carries meaning Responds to books with pleasure Enjoys taking part in shared reading activities Browses independently Reads a range of fiction and non-fiction Can talk about books – pictures/ characters/plot Retells story in own words Joins in with repeated phrases/rhymes – using prediction skills	12.6.98 Stefan retold *The Bear Hunt* and used lots of expression in the retelling. He now handles books well and knows basics concepts of print, e.g. title, words, letters. 13.6.98 We played 'I spy . . . something that rhymes with . . .'. Stefan loved this and was able to	12.6.98 I asked Stefan what he liked best about reading. He said, 'I like books about bears'. I asked him what he was good at when	16.6.98 Stefan's dad said that Stefan didn't show much interest in books at home but he did like to look at	Collect together bear books. Ask parents' group to make a bear storysack in next round – he could then borrow this.

Reading	Retells story, pointing to words (no one-to-one correspondence) Retells story, pointing to words with one-to-one correspondence Knows basic concepts of print – directionality/front/back/title/word/letter, etc. Has good phonological awareness skills – can 'hear' rhymes, etc. Can clap out syllables in name and other familiar words Recognises name Recognises some familiar words Knows names and sounds of alphabet Can 'sound out' monosyllabic words where appropriate	14.6.98 Stefan read all the signs in the sweet shop (role play) to a 'customer'. He made them all up, but pointed to the signs as he read them.	...the words and I tell 'em to you!' He is developing in confidence all the time.	work on phonological awareness.
Writing	Is aware that print carries meaning Knows some of the purposes of writing Attempts to write using marks, letter-like shapes or pictures Appropriate pencil grasp Can re-read writing Can talk about his/her writing Writes in a variety of forms, e.g. letters, lists, signs Initiates writing activities Writes in order to inform taks Takes part in literacy activities in role play areas Responds to stimuli well Can attempt own name independently Can write own name with correct use of upper/lower case Has one-to-one phoneme–grapheme correspondence 'Sounding out' words as he/she writes	14.6.97 Stefan is still reluctant to spend any time in the graphic area but is showing increasing interest in other children's writing in the review time. However, today he sat in the area and wrote letters to the bear on the shelf. He is making a variety of letter-like marks. 16.6.97 Stefan making the patterns of letter shapes in the outdoor area with the squeezy bottle. He insisted on watering the shrubs at the same time!	15.6.97 Asked Stefan what he thought he was good at in writing. Said 'nothing'. Would not respond during any further conversations – I tried to build his confidence, talking about what I thought he was good at. 16.6.97 Stefan's dad said that Stefan didn't write much at home but that his mum 'made him do his letters' every night. I arranged to do a home visit to explore this further.	Develop confidence in writing – lots of praise and feedback. Set up writing activities in role play related to bears, e.g. invites to Teddy Bears' Picnic. Initiate discussion with parents about approaches to writing at home.

Figure 13.1.   Literacy conference

individual child than the comments alone. This kind of summative assessment can be both a stock-taking and a celebration of the child's unique achievements and will provide invaluable information on which to build. Summative assessments should contain evidence of particular milestones in children's development and provide a specific review of skills, understanding and knowledge. Figure 13.1 is an example of one nursery's 'Language and literacy conference' which provides a snapshot of a child's skills at a particular point in time. Over a week, the key worker engages the child in conversations about his own learning and includes observations from that week's activities. It includes comments from the child's family which are also collected over the same week. The idea is to provide a snapshot of the child's attainment at a particular moment in time. The statements in the 'Checklist of achievement' column are highlighted as appropriate. The written observations provide an example of the types of comments made on the conferences by the nursery workers.

Although this conference is provided as an example of one nursery's form of summative record sheet, this is not to suggest that this format will suit all contexts. Early years settings need to devise record-keeping systems which meet their own particular needs and which enable them to reflect the range of provision offered. The form of record-keeping devised needs to be constantly monitored and reviewed to ensure that it continues to fulfil these needs.

Above all, it is essential that summative records provide a rounded picture of a child's attainment, are manageable for early years staff to compile and provide useful information to other teachers, parents and interested parties. It is crucial that these records enable early years workers to feed the accumulated evidence into future planning for children's learning.

Conclusion

In this chapter, I have suggested that assessment of young children's literacy needs to reflect the principles of early years education and offer a broad interpretation of literacy. It should therefore be positive, celebrating children's achievements and valuing their struggles and mistakes. It should be formative, concerned with process as well as product, with meaning-making as well as code-breaking. It should take place as an integral part of children's daily experiences, be based firmly on careful observation and analysis and should include all the significant people in children's lives. Most importantly, the children themselves should be involved in their own self-assessment. Above all, effective assessment must be helpful to the child. Assessment that does not support the child's development is at best a waste of precious time and at worst can damage the child's self-esteem and thus her capacity to learn. Instead, if assessment can help us tune into the child's experiences, understandings, expectations and enthusiasms, then we can move more effectively to support her development of a powerful range of literacies for life. Developmental assessments require thinking practitioners who will draw from a range of sources to create forms and methods rooted in thoughtful practice, tailored to their needs, and always open to change. I have argued that assessment is a judgement not a measurement and, as Drummond reminds us, 'Assessment is essentially provisional, partial, tentative, exploratory and, inevitably, incomplete' (Drummond, 1993, p. 14). To finish where I began, with Hana, I am reminded of those occasions when she did tell a story to the end, demonstrating a thoughtful level of self-assessment. Again, there would be some husky breathing and then she would say, 'Did you enjoy that my story? . . . Quite good, really. . . .'

Suggestions for further reading

Blenkin, G. M. and Kelly, A. V. (1992) *Assessment in Early Childhood Education*, London: Paul Chapman.
Drummond, M. J. (1993) *Assessing Children's Learning*, London: David Fulton.
Hutchin, V. (1995) *Tracking Significant Achievement: the Early Years*, London: Hodder & Stoughton.

References

Athey, C. (1990) *Extending Thought in Young Children*, London: Paul Chapman.
Blenkin, G. M. and Kelly, A. V. (1992) *Assessment in Early Childhood Education*, London: Paul Chapman.
Centre for Language in Primary Education/ILEA (1988) *The Primary Language Record: Handbook for Teachers*, London: CLPE.
DfEE (1997) *National Framework for Baseline Assessment*, London: HMSO.
DfEE (1998) *The National Literacy Strategy*, London: HMSO.
Donaldson, M. (1978) *Children's Minds*, Glasgow: Fontana.
Drummond, M. J. (1993) *Assessing Children's Learning*, London: David Fulton.
Edgington, M. (1998) *The Nursery Teacher in Action*, 2nd edition, London: Paul Chapman.
Eisner, E. (1996) *Cognition and Curriculum*, London: Longman.
Gardner, H. (1993) *The Unschooled Mind*, London: Fontana.
Goleman, D. (1995) *Emotional Intelligence*, London: Bloomsbury.
Goodman, Y. (1978) Kid watching: an alternative to testing, *National Elementary School Principles*, Vol. 57, no. 4, pp. 41–5.
Gregory, E. (1997) *Making Sense of a New World*, London: Paul Chapman.

Gura, P. (1996) What I want for Cinderella: self-esteem and self-assessment, *Early Education*, Summer, pp. 3–5.

Hall, N. and Robinson, A. (1995) *Exploring Writing and Play in the Early Years*, London: David Fulton.

Hutchin, V. (1996) *Tracking Significant Achievement: The Early Years*, London: Hodder & Stoughton.

Kelly, A. V. (1992) *Concepts of assessment*: an overview in Blenkin, G. and Kelly, A. V. (1992) *Assessment in Early Childhood Education*, London: Paul Chapman.

Mills, C. and Mills, D. (1998) *Dispatches: The Early Years*, London: Channel 4 Television.

Riley, J. (1998) The transition phase between emergent literacy and conventional beginning reading: new research findings, *Early Years*, Vol. 16, no 1, pp. 55–9.

Roberts, R. (1995) *Self-esteem and Successful Early Learning*, London: Hodder & Stoughton.

QCA (1998) *Desirable Outcomes for Children's Learning on Entering Compulsory Education*, London: HMSO.

Stierer, B., Devereux, J., Gifford, S., Laycock, E. and Yerbury, J. (1993) *Profiling, Recording and Observing: A Resource Pack For the Early Years*, London: Routledge.

Tobin, D., Wu, D. and Davidson, D. (1989) *Preschool in Three Cultures*, New Haven: Yale University Press.

Whitehead, M. (1997) *Language and Literacy in the Early Years*, 2nd edition, London: Paul Chapman.

Index